THE COLUMBIA YEARS

Aerosmith '72–'82

THE COLUMBIA YEARS

Aerosmith '72–'82

MARTIN POPOFF

SCHIFFER PUBLISHING

4880 Lower Valley Road • Atglen, PA 19310

Other Schiffer books by Martin Popoff

Seven Decades of Deep Purple: An Unofficial History
978-0-7643-6991-9

DIO: The Unholy Scriptures; The Complete Unofficial Chronicle of Ronnie James Dio's Solo Canon
978-0-7643-6940-7

Hallowed by Their Name: The Unofficial Iron Maiden Bible
978-0-7643-6816-5

Library of Congress Control Number: 2026932915

Designed by Molly Shields
Cover design by Danielle Farmer
Type set in YuletideLog/Cambria

ISBN: 978-0-7643-7216-2
ePub: 978-1-5073-0739-7

Printed in India
10 9 8 7 6 5 4 3 2 1

Published by Schiffer Publishing, Ltd.
4880 Lower Valley Road
Atglen, PA 19310
Phone: (610) 593-1777; Fax: (610) 593-2002
Email: Info@schifferbooks.com
Web: www.schifferbooks.com

FSC
www.fsc.org
MIX
Paper from responsible sources
FSC® C016779

CONTENTS

AEROSMITH

Introduction

Welcome, folks, to our celebration of the most-beloved songs from a bunch of guys critics used to call "America's greatest rock 'n' roll band."

That bumper sticker-ready phraseology is a little different from "the only band that matters," which is what they called the Clash. It's also different from "America's Led Zeppelin" or "America's Deep Purple," which got applied to a clutch of bands each. But there's a direct connection that's being made there to the Rolling Stones being called "the world's greatest rock 'n' roll band," which I actually think those cats wholly deserve.

If you hadn't noticed, what they said about Aerosmith isn't quite as impressive as what the Stones got, but it's still pretty good. And it's actually pretty supportable too. To be sure, in a haze of drug and drink, Aerosmith could suck live (and, at times, get into physical fights and fall off the stage). But when they were on, they were untouchable (this is what gets said about Zeppelin as well, isn't it?). As well, they were a massive and successful act across a number of decades. Even up into the first decade of the 2000s, when the records dried up, they could still put bums in seats, given the cavalcade of timeless hits trotted out nightly. And yeah, late '80s and into the early '90s, they were selling way more records than the Stones could ever dream (on) of.

They were in fact also called "America's Rolling Stones," which also made sense. Steeped in the blues but playing rock 'n' roll, they were also a five-piece of the same instrumentation, and, weirdly, their front man also had big lips. What's more, he could dance like Mick and dress the part too.

Being as old as dirt, I got every Aerosmith album as a new release. And also, being thirteen years old when *Rocks* came out, you can bet that Aerosmith was the band for my generation. I absolutely recall sneering that both the Stones and Led Zeppelin sounded out of gas, trying to sell us records like *Black and Blue* and *Presence*, compared to the heavy, whip-smart way Aerosmith was writing and recording at the time. It really was a case of move over and let Mr. Joe Perry take over.

Speaking of Led Zeppelin, I once did a book called *Led Zeppelin: All the Albums, All the Songs*. And speaking of the Clash, I once did a book on them with that exact subtitle too. The exercise we're about to embark upon here together is very much in the spirit of those books, albeit without demarcating each chapter down further into individual songs. More accurately, it's similar in format to my usual biographical books, but it is closer to the Zep and the Clash in terms of focus upon the albums and the songs and not so much personal goings-on and documentation of tours.

The other difference is that we're going to keep the focus tight and analyze only the songs across the first seven albums, along with side trips to the live album and the first hits compilation. As the title of this tome alludes to, this covers the period when the band was working for Columbia Records, before signing to Geffen in the mid-'80s (let's ignore the fact that they re-signed to Columbia later on!). As well, this is where the magic glows brightest for most fans. But as importantly, seven records' worth of songs resulted in a sensible book in terms of word count and page count; pointedly, a book that covers about as much territory as my books on Led Zeppelin and the Clash.

If I may offer one more nostalgic memory flash. I recall never wanting an album more than I wanted *Rocks*. My partner in music obsession crime back then and there in Trail, British Columbia, Forrest Toop, well, he must have picked up *Rocks* on a family trip to Spokane, Washington. So, I dunno, he had an American copy that I guess was available a week or two or a month before any of our record stores in Trail got it. I just recall spending every waking hour wishing I had my own copy—and even more so when we were playing his, which was all the damn time.

Okay, I have to add that if I'm lying about all this, it's only because there was exactly one other instance when this happened, and I'm sure I'm on record talking about it somewhere, so I'd better mention it. That was when he had Judas Priest's *Killing Machine* on import, and I had to wait to get a Canadian *Hell Bent for Leather*, which, surprise, had an extra song on it.

But no, as I sit here fifty years later, I'm pretty sure that the emotions around *Rocks* were more intense. For a couple of years there, there might have been heavier bands, but no one seemed so skilled and so confident and so on top of the world as Aerosmith. And that powerful sentiment included any opinions we had toward the aforementioned storied institutions, along with our own generation's possibly more famous band, Kiss. Just as *Toys in the Attic*, *Rocks*, and *Draw the Line* made Jimmy Page look doddering and nodding, suddenly we looked at Kiss as drawing with crayons.

Just like they said so in *Circus*, *Creem*, and *Hit Parader*, Aerosmith were absolutely "America's greatest rock 'n' roll band," and that stone-cold fact is what made putting together this book about those records such sweet emotion indeed.

Martin Popoff
martinp@inforamp.net
martinpopoff.com

PROLOGUE

The Early Years

We think of Aerosmith as a Boston band, but their roots are those of rock 'n' roll nomads, albeit within a tight range, taking in everything from New York City and points in New Hampshire through to summer camps and the wild woods.

Steven "Tyler" Tallarico grew up in a musical family in Yonkers, New York, listening to his father play the piano, and even joining his band, who entertained campers at the Trow-Rico summer retreat, with Tyler learning the drums so he could be of use to Pops. But in terms of rock 'n' roll, he started in his early teens on the guitar, while his buddy Ray Tabano played drums. Next came the Maniacs and then the Strangers, along with the Dantes, which also included Ray, with Tyler singing. The Strangers became the Strangeurs, and now Steven was fully front man, knocking out the latest hits by Them, the Rolling Stones, the Pretty Things, and later the Yardbirds, a personal favorite of Tyler's.

Westchester County was their stomping grounds as they opened for such acts as the Byrds and Lovin' Spoonful and even got some recording done. In late 1966, after opening for the Yardbirds, the Strangeurs became the Chain Reaction, issuing a single before Tyler was chucked out of high school on marijuana charges. Then came another pot bust, in Miami in 1968, along with the bust-up of the Chain Reaction, after a pile of memorable gigs and eventually another single.

There's a period when Steven had a band called the Chain and then Fox Chase, where he and the boys set up shop at Trow-Rico, attempting to live there in the winter and freezing their butts off, playing a mix of covers and originals at such places as Dartmouth College in New Hampshire. But by early 1970, Steven's growing streak of perfectionism stunted the progress of that band, as it had done during the Chain Reaction singles sessions a couple of years earlier.

Trying yet again with a new band called William Proud, Tyler caught wind that Jeff Beck was looking for a vocalist. His plan was to gather up some guys and record a demo of the Beatles' "I'm Down," which he would get over to Beck. For the project, Tyler enlisted David "Pudge" Scott, Tom Hamilton, and Joe Perry.

Perry, from an academically inclined family, had grown up in a small-town south of Boston called Hopedale. Like Tyler, he'd spent a bunch of time out in nature, usually Lake Sunapee or the woods around his neighborhood. His first band was called Chimes of Freedom, and he was the singer. All the while, he was woodshedding on guitar and soaking up the same British blues boom influences that had been enthralling Tyler. Shipped off to boarding school in Vermont (his grades had been suffering due to his undiagnosed ADHD), he played with the bands Just Us and the Surfing Aarjacks. Dropping out of school and working at the resort at Lake Sunapee, this is when he meets David Scott and they form Pipe Dream, later Plastic Glass and then (without Scott), the Jam Band, which would include Joey Kramer as well.

Plastic Glass is where Hamilton comes in. Born in Colorado but growing up in the small town of New London, New Hampshire, Tom started on guitar at the age of twelve, and by the time he was in Sam Citrus and the Tangerines, he had switched to bass.

Speaking with Paul Gargano, Tom says, "Orange was a big color back then, because there was a thing called California sunshine, an acid that was orange, a little orange pill. There were bands like the Strawberry Alarm Clock. That's probably why we picked the name Merciless Tangerines, to get into that fresh-fruit kind of thing. All orange—that was funny. We didn't have an act or anything. We just played the songs and had our orange pants and orange shirts on. Actually, the other night, I wore a completely orange outfit onstage. I called my wife and told her about it, and she said, 'You will never wear that again. Never wear that again unless I see it first.' As far as being up there onstage and performing, obviously I'm nowhere near as flamboyant as Steven or Joe, but I'm loving it up there. I love interacting with the audience. I don't know if people can see it, but usually through a show, there's a lot of eye contact going on. And I really dig that. Actually, I was going to go to drama school before I joined the band, because I love being up in front of a crowd and performing. I was headed to possibly being an actor."

Speaking with Sam Dunn, Tom explained that "the town that I come from, in New Hampshire, is tiny. There's no pizza place, there's no Chinese restaurant, there's no record store, and there was no radio station. Everything that I heard when I was really young, when I was maybe fourteen, fifteen, was the summer kids coming up from Boston and New York bringing all this cool stuff. So, I think I had a hunger to hear our band on the radio, without necessarily having it that clearly in my mind. Radio back then was something where the deejay could pick a song, and you would hear all his strange, weird combinations, because weird was good then."

At this point, Tom meets David "Pudge" Scott and enters our story with Plastic Glass, playing, now with Joe Perry, places like the Barn and the Lake Sunapee Yacht Club. Eventually, Hamilton had the displeasure of telling his parents that he wasn't going to go to drama school. Instead, in the summer of 1970, he told them he was moving to Boston to start a new band with Joe Perry, and this is when the Jam Band happens, headquartered out of an apartment at #22, 1325 Commonwealth, with rehearsal space at the university.

Pudge would actually pop up and pound along on drums, but soon Joey Kramer would be added to the mix. Kramer, like Tyler, was from Yonkers, but he was now in Boston. Having picked up the sticks at thirteen, his first bands, beginning back in 1964, were the likes of the Dynamics, the Medallions, the King Bees, and the Radicals. Joey and

Steven knew each other from back in Yonkers. Joey had even borrowed Steven's drum kit once, and Steven guested with the King Bees, singing the Stones. The two even bumped into each other at Woodstock. In Boston, Kramer enrolled at the esteemed Berklee College of Music, but his tenure was short-lived.

Tom remembers a wonderful confluence. "Well, you had the English bands, Led Zeppelin, The Who, Ten Years After, and Fleetwood Mac, back then, was an amazing blues band. You had from the West Coast the Doors, Janis Joplin, and Jimi Hendrix, I guess—I don't know if I consider him West Coast or English—but it was unbelievable. And here we are, we were in Massachusetts, or New Hampshire, rather, right when all these forces were joining, and it was just an unbelievable time when people appreciated weird music and things being different. Strange and not typical was totally accepted, and it allowed for some really amazing things to take place that are still influencing music now.

"Joe and I had been playing together in bands before Aerosmith, when we were teenagers," continues Hamilton. "We technically weren't great musicians, but we just got the loudest amps we could, turned them up, and played as fast as we could. We still liked to play MC5 songs, so we were very much in that turn-up, crank-it-up, play-loud, play-fast mode. Steven was sort of on a parallel groove with his band. They were very professional, very polished, more towards pop, brilliant harmonies, much more sophisticated instrumentation. Oh my God, they had the perfect hair, the clothes, the amps, drums—it was really amazing. And so, Steven, not to speak for Steven, but he was really enthused by the Rolling Stones, and I think everybody has seen that. We got a lot of shit about it, as a matter fact, in the beginning. But that was true of Joe and I too. We were both Beatles and Stones fans. Beatles, when that whole thing happened, that totally set my life in the direction that it's been on since then. And Joey was way into funk bands—Kool & the Gang, James Brown—and so when we finally met up and got together, those elements ended up as the sound of the band. You had the loud crunching part of Joe and I, and you had the funky beats of Joey and then you had Steven, who could bring a lot of actual theory knowledge to the table, so we had more-interesting complex guitar parts and arrangements."

As Tom alludes to, the guys appreciated Joey's funk groove combined with his propensity to hit hard. "I have the ability to push my weight around and fool around in other aspects of different kinds of music," Joey told me. "I'm very heavily rooted in rhythm and blues. I love James Brown and Tower of Power, and Earth, Wind & Fire; that's the type of thing I like to play, that I really don't have a use for, specifically, inside the context of Aerosmith. But I don't read music. Pretty much what I do is I'm a feel guy; I'm a groove guy."

When Kramer auditioned for the Jam Band, Joe and Tom were noncommittal, because they were pretty sure they wanted their "singing drummer" acquaintance, Steven Tallarico, instead. Steven was glad to join, but he was adamant he didn't want to drum. Ergo here comes Joey Kramer, with Ray Tabano sometimes in, sometimes not, along with Pudge. Now everybody had essentially cut out of school and home early, disappointed their parents, and also cut ties with any sort of regular career path. It was rock 'n' roll or nothing, as hugely knowledgeable fans and now as serious practitioners, under the command of perfectionist Steven Tyler, fed up at this point with passengers and determined to take one last shot at fame and fortune.

Coming up with a new band name, the guys pondered Hooker as well as Spike Jones. But it was Joey who suggested Aerosmith, which arose, somehow, from *Aerial Ballet*, the name of a 1968 album by Harry Nilsson.

The newly minted Aerosmith, whipped into shape by the drill sergeant instruction of Steven, played their first paid show on November 6, 1970, at the Nipmuc Regional High School in Mendon, a small inland town in Massachusetts. The "paid" qualifier is there because the band had in fact previously performed for the student body in their basement rehearsal space at Boston University. By the summer of 1971, constant arguments with Ray, who was working on the side and lacked dedication when it came to getting better on the guitar, necessitated a change.

Joe Perry had seen Brad Whitford playing guitar in a band called Justin Thyme. Whitford was from Boston and had started out in such bands as Symbols of Resistance, Spring Rain, Teapot Dome, Morlocks, and Earth Incorporated. Although he was first inspired by the Dave Clark Five, it was Led Zeppelin and Humble Pie that later determined his path and his approach to guitar playing. Like Kramer, Whitford had attended Berklee but dropped out. It was at this point that Brad found himself playing a Justin Thyme gig at Lake Sunapee that turned out to be an Aerosmith audition of sorts.

"I saw Zeppelin, and that was huge for me," reflects Brad. "I saw them in, I think it was '68, the first time, and yeah, that had a huge influence on Aerosmith, and just a huge influence on myself. When I first saw Jimmy Page, I was just blown away. I think I walked 6 inches off the ground for about a year after I saw them [laughs]. Jimmy had the whole concept of sound figured out. That first record, I thought the sound of it was just revolutionary at the time. And now when I listen back, it still holds up. Just so cool.

"We all have an anchor in the blues," continues Whitford. "We're all fans of many types of music, but certainly the basis of where we came from was this deep appreciation of blues-based hard rock, really. We were huge fans of a lot of what was coming out of England at the time. Like so many of our contemporaries, we were blown away by people like the Stones and the Yardbirds. We so desperately wanted to do our own version of that. We all got off on that. We were never bored with the blues per se, but we had this love and enthusiasm for Deep Purple, Led Zeppelin, the stuff with the real hard edge. But the blues has a real soul to it, and any time we could take that and combine it with the harder stuff, and come up with ideas, sure enough, we did."

After Brad joined, he moved into their apartment while Joey and Steven got another place. His first shows were in Vermont, late August 1971, at a club called the Savage Beast. Garnering a rejection from Epic Records and then playing a showcase in New York, the band soon signed a promotional deal with heavy-hitter Frank Connelly. This eventually led to Frank working a deal with the newly minted Leber Krebs management group—Steve Leber and David Krebs—who made Aerosmith their second signing ever. Leber set up a showcase gig at Max's Kansas City, attended by Ahmet Ertegun of Atlantic Records and Clive Davis from Columbia. Initially wanting to join the ranks of the storied Atlantic label, with all manner of blues and rock greats as part of its roster, on July 15, 1972, the band wound up signing with Columbia.

Recalls David Krebs, "When we signed Aerosmith, Frank Connelly, the original manager in Boston, we brought him to Max's Kansas City. And two labels were invited, Clive Davis and Ahmet. Ahmet said they're a year away. Clive signed them. By the time the year was up, it didn't matter. And from there, a couple years later I was at a CBS Records convention, and they showed this video of Ted Nugent with a new album coming up, and it was just amazing. I said I want to manage him. And that's how we ended up on both Columbia and Epic.

"For Aerosmith to break on Columbia in those years was totally against the grain, because the natural home for that kind of music was Atlantic. They had Zeppelin and several other bands. Columbia was really the home of Barbra Streisand meets Simon & Garfunkel. If you look at the pecking order in terms of the intellectual side of rock—I hope I'm not making something up—you find that Columbia was like Harvard and Atlantic was like Brooklyn College. And since heavy metal and hard rock was really a blue-collar phenomenon, we used to think in the following way: Wow, what a great, cheap sense of psychiatry for somebody working on a factory line all week and coming out and having a couple beers and seeing Aerosmith and Ted Nugent together. That'd be pretty good."

Continues David, "When we signed Aerosmith with Frank Connelly as our partner, and by the way, we decided—and this is Steve Leber's concept, not mine—but we signed them as managers, but we also signed them as their record production company. And I think we got half the publishing, so Aerosmith retained 75 percent of the gross monies from songwriting. But the point I'm making is this. Looking back, if you are the manager of an act that becomes big at a label, there is lots of politics that come down, and, in certain instances, the managers were pushed aside. Like, I think that's part of the story of Bruce Springsteen's original manager. By being the record production company, Aerosmith was signed to us, and we were the signatory to the deal with Columbia, which gave us, in my opinion, looking back, a lot more say."

What Aerosmith got as part of their Columbia deal was the rights back to their masters after twenty years, which was an advantage not usually negotiated or even considered back in the day. With a $45,000 advance also secured as part of the agreement, it was now time to make the first Aerosmith album.

1
Aerosmith

"That was the first time I saw amplifiers taller than the guys playing."

In the ramp-up toward what would become the *Aerosmith* album, recorded and issued less than six months after their fateful signing, the band's sound had gotten harder.

"I remember when we first got together," says Tom, in conversation with Sam Dunn. "We used to have this really cheap stereo system in the apartment where we all lived together, and we listened to the *Machine Head* album constantly. We were just blown away by that record. That and the Jeff Beck record *Rough and Ready*, which really portrayed the combination of funk and rock, like no other record that we had heard before. So those two records stand out so much for me. Joe and I, before then, we played a lot of Jeff Beck songs from the Jeff

Beck record, and a lot of Yardbirds. And the thing we like about the Yardbirds is that they got quiet and then it got really loud, super-energetic, supertight, taking those blues riffs and just amping it up.

"Plus, I was obsessed with Cream and the Who," laughs Tom. "I saw Cream in Boston here, at this club called the Psychedelic Supermarket. And the night they played there, there were only about a hundred people in the place. That was the first time I saw amplifiers taller than the guys playing. I just couldn't believe it; I couldn't get over it. There's Iron Butterfly—don't forget them. I remember having that record, and I'm thinking, 'Oh my God, I'm hearing the voice of Thor, and this is unbelievable.' And then a buddy of mine went to private school, and he came over with the first Led Zeppelin record, and I remember going to his house and saying, 'This Iron Butterfly record is the most wicked thing you're ever going to hear.' He starts laughing; he says, 'Oh no, you gotta put *this* on.' And I couldn't believe my ears. It was such a leap from anything that anybody had ever done."

And now it was time for Aerosmith to take their shot. The band entered Intermedia Studios at 331 Newbury Street in Boston in October 1972, with Adrian Barber producing, Buddy Verga assisting, and then Barber, Caryl Wienstock, and Bob Stoughton sharing engineering duties. The facilities were sixteen-track and had been used by a number of major labels, but for nothing too rockin'. The band had about a half-dozen songs written, and more would have to be cooked up on the fly. At this point it was very much Steven Tyler leading the way, or bearing most the responsibility, but willingly.

Barber, from England, had recorded with the Beatles, Cream, Aretha Franklin, the Allman Brothers, the Rascals, Buffalo Springfield, Bee Gees, and even Velvet Underground, but these were mostly engineering gigs. There wasn't much experience there and really nothing too guitar-charged, which would prove to be a problem.

Explains Tom, "Yeah, if you look at the way that pop music was, or popular music, rock 'n' roll, whatever you want to call it, it was this new kind of music. And in a lot of ways, it was still playing by the rules of what came before, like swing and jazz. And when rock 'n' roll first started, it was rebellious. You didn't have recording engineers that were trained in how to do that, and that goes for a lot of other aspects, you know, technical aspects, it terms of how it was evolving, and how musicians were evolving.

And you have the effect of marijuana and LSD, and the idea of, oh my God, let's create something that is beyond real. I don't want to hear something that sounds like just what it's supposed to be; I want to hear something that sounds beyond what it usually is supposed to be.

"Which, in our early records, a lot of the engineers we worked with, that's what they were trained to do. They were trained to control us. They were trained in how to take the instruments and control them, so that the vocal could be the one big thing that was happening. But then musicians, us included, were in there saying, 'No, I want the drums to be really loud' and 'I want to hear a lot of bass' and 'We want the guitars to be really intense and distorted.' I mean, that was well underway when we started making records, but still, you could feel that it was new. And I remember having arguments in the studios with people we were working with, saying, 'No, don't tighten that snare drum' and 'Who cares if it bleeds into the mic next to it? That's what we want.'"

Generally speaking, the band remembers the *Aerosmith* sessions as a blur, the effect exacerbated by drug use and a degree of insecurity and trepidation. They just did what they were told, basically, when not being paralyzed with fear. Steven is well aware that he wasn't singing in his natural voice. He was trying to sound like an old bluesman, which is pretty much what Ozzy Osbourne did on the first Black Sabbath album and what Roger Daltrey did on his early singles with the Who. Poignantly, Tyler rues that nobody told him not to do it, so it happened.

"The band was very uptight," recalls Steven, in his autobiography. "We were so nervous that when the red recording light came on, we froze. We were scared shitless. I changed my voice into the Muppet, Kermit the Frog, to sound more like a blues singer. Kermit Tyler: I would unscrew the light bulb so no one would know we were recording. One of my favorite things to say before we recorded a song was 'Play it like you would if no one's looking, guys.' They'd be recording, and we'd be so nervous, making mistakes and hesitating, and I'd go, 'Fuck being nervous; just play!'"

"Intermedia Sound was a studio where they did a lot of TV commercials," explained Joey, in the Aerosmith oral-history book *Walk This Way*, done in conjunction with Stephen Davis. "First time I'm ever in a recording studio in my life and I'm scared shitless, really excited to be doing this. And I made hundreds of mistakes. Oh God. And it was so simple. We set up the instruments, put mics in front of them, and played our songs live a couple of times. That was it. That's how we did the first album. If we were good, Adrian would yell, 'Yes, it's got the fire. It's got the bloody fire!' in his priceless English accent that we made fun of. That's how we knew we had a take. Steven and I almost killed each other because I had problems with my timekeeping. I hated playing in a confined area."

"The album was recorded on sixteen tracks with those real big knobs," adds Joe Perry. "Today, everything's computerized and digitized. Back then, we just had this reel of tape. It was my first time in the studio and Steven's first chance to make an album. You can hear how uptight the band was, how little confidence we had. Steven even changed the way his voice sounds. We were uptight, afraid to make mistakes. No one was hounding us. It was pressure from within ourselves, so much pressure that the record came out sounding thin and sterile. We were total novices with no idea what to go for. A lot of the songs already existed because Steven had them from previous bands or had written them while we were together, like 'Mama Kin,' and we worked them into our shtick. I didn't even know, or give a shit, about songwriting, so we just went in there, pushed the knobs, and said, 'Go for it.' Then the red light came on, and we froze up like fucking Eskimos. It was a big drag."

And back to the rootsy nature of the material, like Tom says, this was still early days, and the cited comparatives were storied, older bands anyway. So, it wasn't like anything particularly modern was on anybody's minds. In other words, these were people accustomed to recording traditional music, and Aerosmith had something of the historical about them anyway, links to the British blues boom, as it were. In other words, the grim, late '60s production values matched the desperate, amped-up, white-knuckle blues of the material.

"They were sort of an extension of the Yardbirds meets the Rolling Stones," muses manager David Krebs, again speaking with Dunn. "And they also had more than one star, which was always a sign that you've got longevity potential. Between Tyler and Perry, and I think even Joey Kramer as a drummer, at that time. He always got a standing ovation for a drum solo, which I think is probably weird today. And when you look at the competition that played against them, Aerosmith always shined. I mean, we managed the New York Dolls and Aerosmith at the same time, and there was a package in the early '70s: Mott the Hoople, special guest Dolls. Aerosmith opening, and 5,000 seats. I was at those, obviously, and Aerosmith was able to deliver a 5,000-seater, and the Dolls weren't. The Dolls really were great in 200 seats. I never said this to anybody else, but the Dolls were, once out of ten times, the best band in the world, and the other nine, they were the worst band in the world. And I've never seen that kind of dichotomy again."

What composed the *Aerosmith* album would be heavier than the Yardbirds and Led Zeppelin, and certainly the Stones. But as David says, "Aerosmith doesn't really stand up to be classified as a heavy metal band. They are much more of a hard rock band. And if you look at the bands that have been the biggest draws in terms of stadium shows, well, this may be oversimplifying, but the hard rock bands are the ones who are able to draw 50,000 people. When you get less melodic, the less likely you can do that. And Aerosmith wrote great songs. That was always a good beginning [laughs]."

As for Steven getting compared to Mick Jagger, reinforced by the two pictures of Steven on the *Aerosmith* album, David says, "I saw the resemblance of Tyler, physically, but as a performer, singer, whatever, I don't think Jagger's voice is as good as Tyler's. It was a superficial similarity that people saw. But from a writing point of view, it was easy to call them the American Rolling Stones."

Before the prospective fan got to the music enclosed, he was confronted with the band looking badass on the cover, practically feral, with Tom Hamilton resembling the wildest member of the Alice Cooper band, Glen Buxton. There are variants of the cover, with the text treated differently up top and the photo first displayed as a small inset in a sea of sky and then positioned much larger at the bottom of the frame. On the back, there was another inset shot of the band in collage format. The pictures were taken by Robert Agriopoulos, with the overall design handled by Ed Lee and Hiroshi Morishima.

There's also a lengthy hype essay written by Boston journalist Stu Werbin, who describes the band as "aggressive, troublemaking punks with too much uncontrollable energy to sit in classrooms studying algebra." He continues to lay it on thick, getting the point across that these guys were practically cursed to play rock 'n' roll, a theme that I'll return to later. He closes with "It's not to be listened to, it's to be played. Turn the volume up loud, roll back the carpet if you have one, and learn to dance. It's for the young, and the young in the head, and anybody who can still take it raw."

Past the sleeve and into opening track "Make It," one instantly hears the raw, embodied by the "trapsy" drum production and the natural distortion on the guitars, no effects particularly, but hairy all the same.

"Make It" is an early one, with Steven scrawling out the lyrics on the back of a Kleenex box in the car during the relocation from New Hampshire to Boston to start the new band. He was inspired by the skyline of the big city, and the idea of making it there in contrast to all the backwater spots the band had been playing. The opening lyric was envisioned as the words one might want to be singing as the band opened for someone like the Rolling Stones, and as a result, it proved useful as a show opener in any situation. It is known to have been played live as far back as December 1971, when the band opened for Humble Pie in New York City.

"We were very clear: We wanted to make it," says Hamilton. "We were going to be rich and famous. We used that term 'rich and famous' to kind of make fun of our own ambition too. A guy that used to sing with Joe and I before Steven joined used to say, 'Oh, you guys just want to get rich and famous. That's all you care about.' He was like a blues purist. And so, I think our desire for that was that we saw these British bands. You would go and see Rod Stewart, back then when he was a rocker and he was skinny. You'd see these English bands with velvet pants and tight shirts, and we wanted to be doing that, as much as sort of being successful in other ways. We wanted to go up and do what our idols were doing. And I remember that in the studio too. When we would listen to playbacks—this is true, I think, of everybody—you just want to hear something come out of those speakers that makes you feel like when you listened to the first Zeppelin album or the Who *Live at Leeds* album. That was a big part of it for us."

Joey Kramer said as much as well, that although everybody in the band was completely different from each other, they all had one goal, to be big rock stars, but more so, respected by their peers.

All told, "Make It" strikes a moderately modern stance, moving beyond the British blues boom through its hanging chords at the verses, its riffiness at the chorus, and then a menacing break sequence for the guitar solo, although it's Joey who goes the most nuts. It's also got a sort of prebreak structure that is more melodic, with Steven singing in harmony with a high guitar lick, but again, not particularly steeped in the blues idiom. At the end, there's a gesture toward modulation and a come-around to some of the early parts. A lot happens in under four minutes. But the main point about this song—which, yes, I remember that we even picked up on this as ten-year-olds getting the album as a new release—is that despite the scrappy sound, it leaves blues and boogie rock behind. Or at a minimum, it shows the band in motion, en route to the mid-'70s, much like Kiss would do on the first three albums—it's not exactly Black Sabbath, but for an American band, we'll take it.

Although the next track, "Somebody," was slight, and definitely a boogie rocker. It makes sense that it would sound a bit retro, given that it goes back to 1970, to Steven's Chain Reaction days, and was inspired by the bridge section of the Rolling Stones' version of "Route 66," even if it's hard to see the connection. It's also derived from a riff that a childhood friend of Tyler's, Steve Emspack, used to play, back during the William Proud days. Emspack had put it together on a twelve-string acoustic in mid-1969, before heading off to Woodstock. The song is faithfully credited to S. Tyler and S. Emspack.

"Route 66" was a song that Steven would have the band play over and over again during rehearsals at Boston University to get tight, to find a groove. Beyond its modest construct, there's a hint of the band's future funk riffing in "Somebody," with Joey and Tom locking in rhythmically. Kramer in particular helps the song along with a novel, shuffle-feel, open-and-closing high-hat pattern. The funky riff on this song is particularly dirty of tone. For most of the record, Brad used a 1968 Gibson Les Paul Gold Top, playing through Sound City cabinets, and Joe used a black 1959 Fender Stratocaster, playing through a Marshall stack.

In the solo section, Steven sings falsetto along with the guitar, something Ian Gillan was famous for next to his nemesis Ritchie Blackmore. Again, given its vintage, it's no surprise that "Somebody" is one of two originals played at the first paid Aerosmith gig ever (the other being "Movin' Out"), with "Route 66" also part of the set. This is the aforementioned November 6 show in Mendon, Massachusetts.

"Dream On" began as a piano piece, with Steven composing it on an upright Steinway in the mid-'60s, when, as Steven recalls, he was seventeen or eighteen years old. He also puts the location as the living room of the

Trow-Rico Lodge in Sunapee, with the final lyrics coming together during the recording sessions. Tyler said he was inspired by the hours spent as a toddler under the piano listening to his father play. It's distinguished by the guitar parts, with Brad playing what Steven would play on the piano with his left hand and Joe playing the parts Steven would play with his right hand. The signature keyboard lick is played on harpsichord, accompanied by Mellotron washes behind it, given that the band couldn't afford proper orchestration. It's also in F minor, an odd, melancholic key, turning the song quite creepy sounding, at the beginning, like something the Doors might do. Both the harpsichord and Joe's clean, arpeggiated lead parts give the song a baroque or renaissance music feel. It ends with a gong splash, and a haunting, repetitive octave-jumping keyboard pattern that sounds like a skipping record or a stuck alarm.

Remarked Steven in his autobiography, "I loved Yma Sumac, the Inca princess with the staggering five-octave range. 'Look in the mirror; the past is gone.' That's the Yma Sumac vocal swoop. Singers generally don't go from the bridge to the chorus with a bridge note like that, but it worked melodically for me. It's like the Isley Brothers singing 'It's Your Thing,' where after the solo, the first line of the verse is sung an octave higher, then slides down an octave for the next. I would sing along with Yma Sumac, that ear-piercing banshee shriek beginning in the highest register. She sang these strange, otherworldly songs in movies like *Secret of the Incas* and looked like an over-the-top Hollywood version of an Inca queen. Sam, Dave, and Sumac—an inspirational trinity.

"I used an exaggerated black-speak voice on all the tracks except 'Dream On,'" continues Steven. "I thought it was really cool. The only problem was nobody knew it was me. I didn't like my voice, and it was early on, and I wanted to *put on* a little. To this day, some people still come up to me and ask, 'Who's that singing on the first album?' I was into James Brown and Sly Stone and just wanted to sound more R&B."

"Dream On" is often cited as one of the first examples of a power ballad, given its quiet/loud dynamic and epic, melodramatic chorus, especially near the end, where Steven unleashes some of his signature screams, part high notes, part falsetto, lots of vocal fry. Ironically, at the lyric end, what's portrayed, quite poetically albeit succinctly, is someone old and tired, reflecting back on a hard life lived, or at least half of one, with lots of regrets along the way. Given its ballad status, Joe had always been wary of it, and it didn't get played live often, at least not until it became a hit after a second attempt at pushing it. Perry had an interesting take, at least early on, that a hard rock band shouldn't play ballads, but they could do a slow blues as a sort of replacement.

What happened was that "Dream On" was issued as the only single from the album, on June 27, 1973, six months after the album had shown up in shops. Backed with "Somebody," the song got to #59 on the *Billboard* charts but was a massive regional hit. After the band broke in 1975, Leber and Krebs decided to give it another shot. The song opened at #81, eventually peaking at #6. The single version was a full minute shorter than the nearly progressive rock version that appears on the album.

Side 1 of the original vinyl closes with "One Way Street," although the original plan was to have this song at the end of side 2. The track was written on piano at the band's apartment at 1325 Commonwealth and credited solely to Steven, as was "Dream On." Lyrically, it was inspired by a relationship issue Steven had with a girl.

Explains Tyler, "Of all the songs I wrote on that first album, 'One Way Street' has some of my favorite lyrics. 'You got a thousand boys / You say you need 'em / You take what's good for you and I'll take my freedom.' The original title was 'Tits in a Crib.' That's what I wanted to call it, but that was forty years ago, and things weren't as loose as they are today. I wrote it about this girl I was seeing. I'd talk her into coming over because she was such a trip. She had a baby, and when she came over, she'd bring the kid and his crib, saying, 'I have no babysitter tonight.' The line 'You got a thousand boys / You say you need 'em' came from where we were living at the time, in Needham, Massachusetts. I'll do anything for a rhyme. I can't think of that girl's name now, but God, she was the skinniest, cutest little trollop."

Recalled Brad in *Walk This Way*, "I actually loved recording our first album. I played my old Les Paul and did the solo on 'One Way Street,' still one of my favorite moments. Then the neck of that guitar gave up the ghost and I got another Les Paul, but it never sounded quite the same. We recorded on equipment that now seems to have come from some archaic era. The mixing board looked like it was made out of cardboard, but we just thought it was so exciting, so incredibly cool to be making our first record."

At the music end, "One Way Street" is a jammy but driving shuffle, clocking in at 7:12 but never feeling long. It's inspired by the Rolling Stones' "Midnight Rambler." Steven sings thespian and bluesy, getting in a few of his future-patented cat howls. There's also a bunch of harmonica and barrelhouse piano. Over to guitar, Whitford is particularly proud of his impromptu solo on this one, trading off with Joe as Hamilton and Kramer dig into the jamming section of the song late in the sequence. After this there's a "crowd participation" clapping section that also sounds a bit gospel, followed by more of the hypnotic riff, over which Tyler works on more of the vocal techniques that would soon clock him as one of the best (i.e., rapping, scatting, screeching, falsetto, even some more singing along with the guitars). "One Way Street" was played at the band's Academy of Music showcase in late 1971, and it was also recorded for the early demo that got the band rejected by Epic.

Side 2 of the original vinyl opens with the aggressive and energetic "Mama Kin," which was originally slated to close side 2. Steven felt so confident about the song, he got "Ma' Kin" tattooed on his arm, with both him and Joe joking that his arm was too skinny to fit the full title. Inspired by Blodwyn Pig's "See My Way," again, like the previously cited lift, it's hard to see the resemblance. It's another boogie rocker like "Somebody," but it's detectably more world-beating, especially given Joey's driving drum performance. Steven wrote the song on an acoustic guitar with no strings that Kramer found in the trash on Beacon Street. Fixing the warp in the neck the best he could, he eventually got just four strings on it and wrote the song.

Further distinguishing the song is the sax work of David Woodford, who actually played live with the band as well. He supports the riff and he also solos, but most importantly, he is the first to demonstrate how comfortable Aerosmith's funky music is with saxophone as part of it. As well, there are backing vocals in the prechorus, and both these things speak to the band's favorable comparisons to the Rolling Stones.

Lyrically, "Mama Kin" is colorful and both humorous and poetic, as well as imbued with meaning. For example, the "Bald as an egg at 18, and working for your daddy's a drag" line was a reference to the band's road manager Mark Lehman. "I think Steven's lyrics are really great," says Joey. "There are a lot of ways in which he hasn't really been given credit for the lyricist that he is. Because he ponders and he works so painstakingly. The time and effort he puts into his lyrics, I mean, I know, because I'm there. I've seen him go through sometimes three, four, five sets of lyrics to a song before he's happy with what he's got. I mean, the guy really works hard in that area." Oddly, the lyric reads as if keeping in touch with Mama Kin means staying grounded, but Steven says it's more like keeping in touch with the wild spirit that made you a rocker in the first place.

"It's one of our earliest compositions," Brad told me. "I don't know, it kind of takes us back. It's a roots song. And we were pleased to see that Guns N' Roses were playing it, that they liked it so much. It's just a huge compliment or vote of confidence for that song, you know, these young guys playing it and dishing it out. You see that it really touched somebody. It's one of those songs that shows where we came from, where we got our fire. When we do that onstage, you can see the enthusiasm; it's an important track."

Indeed, Guns N' Roses famously covered "Mama Kin" on their debut EP, which later expanded into the *G N' R Lies* release, which has certified at five-times platinum. Guns N' Roses, of course, were quite sensibly framed as the second coming of Aerosmith, ironically blowing up in the late '80s, just when the original would be blowing up bigger than they ever had.

The original pressings of *Aerosmith* indicate on the back cover that the next song is "Write Me," while the record inside calls it "Write Me a Letter." This goes for the original Canadian issue as well. In any event, the song was a late addition. Steven recalls having a hard time with it over a five- or six-month period when the band had been rehearsing it in the Boston Bruins dressing room. Joey then perked up with what Steven called a "can-can rhythm thing," and the song, previously called "Bite Me," started to come together. It was one of the last tracks mixed for the album, getting completed on December 12, 1972. The Beatles' "Got to Get You into My Life" served as an inspiration for the intro piece, with Tyler wisecracking that it's because Aerosmith hadn't learned how to write hooks yet.

Again, tilting the band away from the blues toward the hard rock bracket is the dark and heavy break section as well as its up-tempo swagger. And then tilting it back is the harmonica, along with the sort of girl group backing vocals. The song opens with a memorable drum lick that sounds like John Bonham taking a run at the "Maybe I'm a Leo" intro whacks on *Machine Head*.

Next is "Movin' Out," written in early 1971 while the guys were smoking pot on the waterbed at 1325 Commonwealth. It's credited to Tyler and Perry, the first of many to come to bear this classic stamp of quality. As Tyler recalls, Joe had the music, and taking draws on the pipe, he says they closed the door, and the lyrics came to him stream of consciousness. The significance of the first collaboration with Joe was not lost on Steven, who proclaimed the song their "firstborn" and their "first Aerosmithed song."

What's impressive about this one is that it's a highly creative, exciting, dramatic, and at times hard-hitting take on the blues, very much in the spirit of Led Zeppelin. So, it's anchored in the British blues boom, or even more so, evocative of a direct connection to the blues of the American South. But then it's taken in a progressive direction, and then right off into modern hard rock inside the intensely rhythmic "Nobody knows where you can find me" section. Way up into 1987's *Permanent Vacation*, we'd get a song called "Hangman's Jury" that bears something of a resemblance to this early classic.

Aerosmith closes with what would be the album's only cover, although John Sebastian's "On the Road Again" was seriously worked up for inclusion—a fine recording of it can be heard on the *Pandora's Box* rarities and hits collection, which also includes an alternate take of "Movin' Out." Recalls Joey with respect to "On the Road Again," "This was one of the first songs that we learned. We played it at clubs and high school dances, and other than that, I have no recollection of the recording of it. Needless to say, where I was at the time."

But "Walkin the Dog," written by Rufus Thomas (early editions show the song as "Walkin' the Dig" on the back cover), fits right into the feisty back-alley blues rock of the rest of the album, sounding like an Aerosmith original and quite a hard rocking one at that, opening flute licks notwithstanding. Perhaps the lurch toward hard rock comes from the fact that Aerosmith's version is already one step removed, having been based on the Rolling Stones' version. This one also comes to the band honestly, having been played at least as far back as that November 6 Mendon gig.

Something about this track, whether it's in Steven Tyler's vocal phrasing, or the delightful chicken-scratch guitar section, or even just the idea itself of including an up-tempo rock 'n' roll cover, reminds me of the New York Dolls, especially up onto that band's second and last album, *Too Much Too Soon*. Let's not forget that the two bands shared management.

"We did a lot of shows with the Dolls as well and did some touring with them," notes Whitford. "I liked their 'I don't give a shit' sort of attitude. It was just so from-the-gut and straight-ahead rock, just for the pure energy of it. I love that. They just rocked it for the pure faith of rocking it. And if they wanted to shock you, they would do that [laughs]. But I thought it was very pure, very real."

Adds Tom, less favorably, "We would go to New York, and everybody was 'Oh my God, the Dolls!' And the Dolls, to me, they couldn't even fucking play. And we would go to New York, and everybody was saying, 'Wow, look at them, what they're doing. Why can't you guys do that?' And I'm thinking like, Jesus Christ, you're telling me all I've got to do is learn three notes and put on women's outfits, and that's all you need to do to make it? I didn't appreciate the whole camp thing. But they were the darlings of the New York press. We did do a couple of tours with them where we were out in the hinterlands, the Midwest, in those areas. That's when people weren't so sophisticated and jaded and getting the joke.

"But in the end, when they came out with 'Personality Crisis,' I started to realize, okay, it's really about the vibe and the attitude and the joke. So I started to appreciate them more. I remember, one day we were playing in Sedalia, Missouri, outdoors, and those guys had to go on in the middle of the afternoon. It was about 95 degrees, just miserably boiling hot. And they were out there in the hot sun, and Arthur Kane had his shirt off, standing there with his gut hanging out and just playing his bass [laughs]."

Much less like the Dolls was a slow ballad in three-four waltz time called "Major Barbara," which had been worked up for the album but left off, specifically replaced by "Walkin' the Dog." This melodically out-there track was another one that was included as part of the Academy of Music showcase. There's a recording of it on the *Pandora's Box* release, but it's not from the Intermedia sessions. Rather, it's from a visit to Power Station, in New York, on May 20, 1971, and frankly the band sounds more professional then than they did six months later.

Upon release, *Aerosmith* stalled at #166 on the *Billboard* charts, definitely not the hit that Clive Davis, David Krebs, Steve Leber, Frank Connelly, and the "aggressive, troublemaking punks" in the band were hoping for. They were particularly dismayed that *Rolling Stone* didn't review it, especially given that the album's liner note essay was written by a contributor to that magazine. *Billboard* and *Cash Box* also didn't review it. What's more, Columbia put the record out on January 5, 1973, the same day they issued Bruce Springsteen's debut album, *Greetings from Asbury Park, N.J.*, which was favored by the label brass and promoted more heavily than *Aerosmith*. Says David, "For every dollar they spent on Aerosmith, they spent $1,000 on Springsteen. He was much more of a natural Columbia act."

A first tour supporting Mahavishnu Orchestra went as badly as expected, although things were beginning to turn around once the boys were put on the road with Mott the Hoople. Up into mid-December '73, the guys appeared on *American Bandstand* performing "Dream On."

Reviewing the band's performance on one of the Mahavishnu support slots, Scott Canouse from the *Berwick Enterprise* remarked that "the warm-up group from Boston, Aerosmith, played some well-arranged rock 'n' roll. The five-man group has been together for about a year, although a few of the members had played together in different bands before. Aerosmith has played warm-up for the Mahavishnu Orchestra before and will again in the future. The two groups perform in different areas of music, but they go surprisingly well together, considering their differences. Just from a performance at the Century Theater in Buffalo, New York, the group said they liked the acoustics at Haas, and the sound system provided. They did express disappointment at the way the stage lighting was handled. Describing themselves as apolitical, the group feels the important thing is to provide music that the audience can get into the beat and dance to, something that is hard to do in Haas with its comfortable seats. The group performs all its own material, and they said that on a good night, when they are creating for the moment, they receive a tremendous sensation of feeling free. Columbia released *Aerosmith*, the group's first album, three weeks ago. The album, recorded in Boston, has already been a hit pick in *Billboard* magazine and a pick of the month on WBCN, Boston's well-known underground station."

"Many of those present came to hear their local heroes, Aerosmith," wrote the *Boston Globe*'s William Howard, reviewing a show with Mott. "What they got was an hour's worth of extremely loud music from a group that is trying, perhaps a bit too self-consciously, to attain superstar status. Despite protests from the group that they are not imitating The Rolling Stones in their stage act; it all had an uncomfortably familiar ring to it. The derivative rhythm lines, the flailing gesticulations of lead singer Steve Tyler (bedecked in a silver lamé jumpsuit), and the flowers tossed to the adoring crowd did little to dispel their image as imitators."

The pairing with John McLaughlin and Mahavishnu Orchestra was bizarre, with the only connection being that both were on Columbia, and that both were promoting new records, with Mahavishnu's second album, *Birds of Fire*, emerging in March 1973. The pairing did their thing in February, with Aerosmith jumping on with the Kinks in April. Then there was a bunch of shows on their own, with July representing some downtime, during which some recording was done, with Ray Colcord engineering. Additional various billings took place in August and September, with the Mott the Hoople support gig taking place in October, and the New York Dolls along for some of those. November and December was sparse, but there was the stand at the Whisky a Go Go along with the *American Bandstand* taping.

Remembers Tom, "When our first album came out, I remember our manager calling us and saying, 'Look, we just got the reports back from all the local promo guys around the country, and nobody wants to play the record.' We were shocked. And they even made some sheets to give us as a synopsis of all these different guys around the country. We just couldn't believe it. We knew our first record was a really good record, and we knew that from experience, as far as what made a good rock record. We knew what we were talking about, just by the level of our desire and our enthusiasm and all the music we listened to. They released 'Dream On,' and it kind of happened a little bit and then went away. Then the record company would say, 'Your next record better be amazing, or you're not a recording artist anymore.'"

Amusingly, when "Dream On" was relaunched to radio at the end of 1975, it lifted the fortunes of the *Aerosmith* album as well. In fact, success for the song was in the cards. Even before the band's second album, *Get Your Wings*, appeared in the shops, "Dream On" as a single had sold 120,000 copies. *Aerosmith* went gold on September 11, 1975. On April 1, 1976, it had reached a lofty #21 on the *Billboard* album charts. Currently it sits at double platinum, certified by the Recording Industry Association of America (RIAA) for sales of over two million copies. And that really is all down to "Dream On." There are many big bands out there who have multiplatinum albums later in their career, but the debut or indeed first few albums haven't certified at all. It took the courage of the guys to put the ballad on the record, despite worrying that it wouldn't do them that much good live when trying to win over fans who came there to hear the headliners.

Then again, as Tom recalls, "I remember actually, when our first album came out, the first time hearing one of our songs on the radio—what an unbelievable feeling. I was totally unprepared for it. I hadn't anticipated what it would be like. But I was in my car, or in a car, and heard it and realized, oh my God, if I'm hearing it, that means there's thousands of other people listening to it right now, for the first time. Such an amazing rush."

As David Krebs explains, there were a number of appeal points to this band that made them promising, beginning with Steven Tyler. "Big star. Steven Tyler wrote 'Dream On,' I think, when he was eighteen. That's pretty interesting. And he wrote the music and lyrics himself. And if you haven't listened to the song, as you get older, the lyrics become much more meaningful. I think from the standpoint of the writer, it was easy to open up and say the American Rolling Stones or whatever, the way they described it. I was a very, very early and big Rolling Stones fan and saw them a number of times. In no time did I think Steven Tyler was a duplicate of Mick Jagger—singing style, vocal prowess, whatever.

"But like the Stones, Aerosmith had two stars. I always told the other guys, don't worry, you don't want five stars in a band. If you have five stars, you have nothing. A band can have *too much* charisma. Certainly, there's the Yardbirds influence too, absolutely; there's a bluesy stretch to Aerosmith that really works. Aerosmith is just an unusual band. You cannot be around for thirty-some odd years and still do 10,000-plus people, unless you're special. There's no way. I don't think that is true. Frank Marino & Mahogany Rush, they're playing, but they're probably at a club level. I thought as a team and a foundation for Steven Tyler to be the front man, I thought that they were great.

"Remember," continues David, "Steven Tyler had been in a couple of bands not as the lead singer, in bands that had failed but had records. And he was the drummer. Which is, you know, several of the prominent stars were drummers. Phil Collins is one, and the lead singer of the Eagles is another, Don Henley. And there may be more that I'm not aware of. You know, there was magic there. Obviously, it was raw, but they also had written some great songs.

"Plus, they're all in Boston. They all lived together in a house. A gigantic advantage to Aerosmith was, because Frank Connelly was the biggest promoter in the Boston area, he was able to always keep them working and making decent money. Before they had a record out, Aerosmith sold out three thousand seats at a hockey arena, I think, at Boston College, and made $10,000. That would be the equivalent of making maybe $50,000 and you're a local band."

Reviewing the album for the *Daily Breeze* in California, Joseph Bensoua wrote that "boogie at its very, very best is the only way to describe Aerosmith. On its debut album for Columbia this Boston five-some have assembled a foot-stomping package for those who love to turn up the volume and move to a driving beat. Unlike other boogie bands, Aerosmith is not three chords, a beat, and, 'Hello Sue, you know I'll be true' lyrics. The group is an evolved band which encompasses a wide range of driving scores that, when added together, come out pure boogie. Album highlights include 'Mama Kin,' 'Make It,' and a great version of 'Walking the Dog.' Aerosmith is one of the few honestly good boogie groups to come out in a while, and it's worth hearing them."

A couple of months later, Bensoua interviewed the band, with Tom promising that "even though we loved the first album, the production on it didn't exactly knock us out. On the new LP, each individual instrument will stand out. It shows us in a mature light." In any event, they'd come a long way since scrounging around for places to play. "We were about three months due on our rent and living off brown rice, when we decided we better get ourselves in gear and do something. We wanted to practice at the local rock theater called the Fenway, but the manager wanted $50 for its use and another $50 to use the sound system. We told him we didn't have near that amount between the five of us."

"Aerosmith, a new hard rock band from New England, is good enough to become America's answer to The Rolling Stones," proclaimed an uncredited review in Pennsylvania's the *Evening Sentinel*. "Those who doubt that prediction are invited to listen to their debut album, one of the best albums of hard rock by an American band in years. The music is tough, gutsy, blues-tinged rock at its best. The album is not perfect, but it consistently demonstrates such great strengths that the future of the band appears exceedingly promising. The music is almost all original, written primarily by lead vocalist Steve Tyler, who is good enough to hold his own with anyone. Guitar and vocals are very powerful and supporting roles of bass and drums are also excellent. The group's playing is extremely together, even though the group still has rough edges. There are several tunes in the album which could and should emerge, with 'Make It' and 'Somebody' and 'Dream On' the best. Any one could pop, particularly 'Dream On,' a beautiful rock ballad. If Aerosmith can hang together, it can make it big. Five stars."

Added Terry Atkinson of the *Los Angeles Times*, "This young group from Yonkers achieves all that punk rock bands strive for but most miss. Clichéd but properly raw lyrics are growled and rasped by a fine, manic voice. The guitarist packs a Rory Gallagher wallop, especially sounding like the funky Irishman on the great 'Movin' Out.' Irresistible riffs underlie 'Make It' and most of the other songs. Side 2 is a thorough delight, ending with a 'Walking the Dog' that cooks as well as the Rufus Thomas and Rolling Stones versions. The band's longest song, 'One Way Street,' could have been more diversified or simply shortened to good effect, but it's still a good song. *Aerosmith* is a hearty, sensual, hip-shaking serving of hot rock. Play it loud."

And yet, even in context, to my mind the *Aerosmith* album came out the other end of this process as dated and not dynamic, either sonically, in the writing, or in terms of personality. It is a bloodless album. To be fair, fitting the narrative of the band, they are lovers of old, traditional rock 'n' roll anyways, abnormally so for their ages, and therefore the music they wanted to make comes from the same motivation that the Rolling Stones had back in 1964. As well, they were rushed in the recording, and drugs were involved. Actually, we may as well start blaming the drugs for everything. For a band that had been in operation since the autumn of 1970, why was there not an album and a half's worth of originals, concert-tested and at the ready? Indeed, why were there not songs brought into Aerosmith (besides a few bits and pieces from Steven) from all the guys and their numerous previous band situations? And we can't blame youth, because to quote Steven Tyler on "Sick as a Dog," they "really ain't that young."

And back to this business of the British blues boom, if we're following the evolutionary narrative, one might have expected the *Aerosmith* album to represent the next step after Mountain and Cactus, rather than *Little Games*, *Disraeli Gears*, *Truth*, or the first two Led Zeppelin albums. And that's given that it's probably too much to ask that the guys might have learned something from Deep Purple, Black Sabbath, and Uriah Heep, each of them already into a mature phase that was eons beyond the blues, with everybody making exciting, creative heavy music, and all recorded boldly, technically speaking, on at least a record or two at some point before late 1972. Then again, as David Krebs reminds us, Aerosmith weren't aiming to be a heavy metal band.

But sticking with America, even inside this idiom, there was really nothing better anyway. Bang, Dust, Sir Lord Baltimore, and Captain Beyond proved to be also-rans. *Montrose*, which craps on *Aerosmith* from a height of several miles, is still nine months away. *Kiss* is a year away, and only slightly fresher or brighter than *Aerosmith*. Fortunately—for the Aerosmith guys and for the fans and for our story, all of us—the next record would represent a variety of dramatic leaps in quality, rendering the gulf in achievement between a first and second album one of the widest in rock 'n' roll history.

2
Get Your Wings

"The whole process was a win-win."

Get Your Wings almost didn't happen.

"Great first album" begins manager David Krebs, telling the story about how Aerosmith was saved to live another day. "Not all great, but one bad song. But 'Dream On'—genius. On *Aerosmith*, there isn't a weak song. Keep in mind that the price of an album was five or six or seven dollars. Albums were thirty-five minutes. So, Aerosmith's first two albums are like eight songs each. Today, the expectation isn't what it used to be; it's sixty, sixty-five minutes or fill up the CD. You do that and it's almost two albums compared to the old days."

"On the first album, obviously most of the songs are written by Steven Tyler himself. 'Walkin' the Dog' by Rufus Thomas was a great choice, in my opinion. It gave Aerosmith a whole new dimension that was very exciting. The other songs besides 'Dream On' were very simplistic, and it captured them raw and bluesy. Not about anything esoteric or intellectual, but they're like kids writing sort of love songs. I see only one song written by Joe Perry and Steven Tyler, 'Movin' Out.' Okay, so Tyler brings in some good material. Remember, Tyler was in two unsuccessful bands. One of them got some exposure.

"I think we went with Adrian Barber to produce because of his involvement with Cream; I don't remember who recommended this. It could've been Columbia, but I'm not sure. We chose Adrian Barber. And Adrian Barber produced a really good rock 'n' roll record, in my opinion. And like I say, there is probably not one weak song, not that they're all brilliant, on that album. But certainly, it's got many more songs than 'Dream On.' It was a great first record. But if you look at that record versus *Get Your Wings*, there's an incredible sophistication of production that is put into the next thing."

But it was a bit up in the air whether Columbia would continue with the band after the first album.

"Yes. Aerosmith's first album comes out, I think it's done 30,000 copies, of which 25,000 were in the Boston area. And their option is due. And Clive has just left. And because I had done a lot of the business affairs on record contracts, all the business affairs guys I had a relationship with. So the guy who is the head of business affairs at Columbia was Larry Harris, and he said, 'Listen, David, I've got some bad news. We're not picking up Aerosmith's option.'"

To clarify, this is not Larry Harris of Kiss and Casablanca fame. "No, this a different Larry Harris. This is a lawyer. Larry Harris was a promotion guy. Kiss's number one fanatic. And maybe he told me in person, but for whatever reason it dawned on me that if Columbia dropped Aerosmith, it would be blamed on Aerosmith, not Columbia. So I said, 'All right, Larry, listen, here's what we're going to do. We're gonna get you an extra six months' free time; let's see what happens.' The rest is history. In those six months they broke wide open; they picked up the option and onward. I'd never heard of anybody doing this before, giving the label extra time, but that's what we did; we knew we could break this band."

This is the latter half of 1973, and what Aerosmith are doing with this six months is "touring and building fans. Opening up to Mott the Hoople built a lot of fans. Aerosmith doing a couple of dates with

Mahavishnu Orchestra would've been a bad joke on TV. Nobody in Mahavishnu, nobody in that audience likes Aerosmith. But in the end, it's a pickup of the option for the second album after the original deal."

To clarify what David means by giving the label an extra six months, it's like this: Aerosmith had essentially become a free agent when their option had run out. David then said to the label that we'll go away and build the band into a better proposition over the next few months, and we'll still come back to you, Columbia, as if you were our only option, when, moving forward, the band and their management were no longer obligated.

Asked what the advance would have been for what became *Get Your Wings*, David says, "It could've been the same $45,000, could've been a little bigger, I don't remember. I also don't remember . . . see, I don't know what the sales of the first album were at the time the second album came out. I don't know if I have those kinds of records. But Aerosmith was happening. The word on the street, in terms of word of mouth, which has always been the number one factor when dealing with this kind of music—maybe other kinds also—was that Aerosmith was a great rock 'n' roll band on a live level."

Wrapping up tour duties in December 1973, the band set up shop at Timothy's Too in Framingham, Massachusetts, to do preproduction work on this newly negotiated second album. It was to be called *Night in the Ruts*, according to promises Steven had made from the stage at various gigs. Much of the writing, according to Joe, had taken place in the summer of '73 at the band's apartment on Beacon Street. More work took place in the basement of Drummer's Image on Newbury Street and, according to coproducer Jack Douglas, at the back of a restaurant in the North End of Boston, frequented by the local Mafia. Unhappy with the sound of the debut album, the band declined to work with Adrian Barber, agreeing with the label to hire on Ray Colcord for the job.

In fact, things would get ugly with Barber, when in January 1976 he sued Aerosmith for $1.2 million, arguing that he had the option to produce future Aerosmith albums if the debut reached 150,000 in sales and there was a single that cracked the Top 50. Then there were also certain sweeter terms with respect to royalties that would be attached to a second production. The suit quietly went away, and it would be the last we'd hear from Barber.

Back to the new album: Ray Colcord was a session musician, playing keyboards with Lou Reed and Don McLean, and an A&R guy at Columbia. But he was not known as a producer, either before or after twisting knobs for Aerosmith's second album, renamed *Get Your Wings*. Colcord would go on to a prolific career in TV and film composing before succumbing to pancreatic cancer in 2016 at the age of sixty-six. In the end, he'd be credited as coproducer on *Get Your Wings* along with Jack Douglas, who indeed took over the reins. Bob Ezrin would take an executive producer credit, and legitimately so, helping with the acquiring of Jack, checking in from time to time, and consenting to a couple of buddies to help out on the band's cover of the Yardbirds' "Train Kept a Rollin'."

"I just think we were trying to do something that sounded almost as good as Led Zeppelin," Tom Hamilton explained to me. "Our aim was to put something out that made us feel as inspired as when you listen to the Who or Zeppelin or the Stones or the Beatles. We grew up on it, and we were all imprinted with it really powerfully during that period. So when it was our turn to go into the studio, we wanted to hear something that made us feel the same way. That's how we knew we were doing it right. *Get Your Wings* was a fun album to make, but also there was a lot of pressure on us. The label was not happy with how the first record had done, and said that our next album better be bigger or we're going to drop you. So there was a lot of people that were involved on the production side of that record that I felt sort of . . . I kind of resented them. But we had Jack Douglas, which was awesome. He was our friggin' dream producer."

"Actually, that was a really interesting album to make because that was the first one we did with Jack Douglas," adds Joey. "And Jack got very, very involved in the songwriting process and with the band personally, doing that, and that became the first of five or six records we did with Jack. We had a really good time making it, but we worked really hard at it because he turned us on to techniques and required certain things of us to do, which involved a lot of drilling and practicing. I think probably the most important part of that was when we realized that Jack was going to be the catalyst he was, between everybody's vibe and everybody's ideas. He was always the guy that, no matter who had the idea, Jack was always, 'Well, let's try it.' And the end result of that, for the first time, was *Get Your Wings*."

The original plan had been to record with Bob Ezrin, a Canadian, in Toronto. Ezrin had started as a junior to Jack Richardson, and by this point he had distinguished himself with a string of hit albums for Alice Cooper. But Ezrin had decided that the band was "not ready," and the job fell to Jack Douglas, who was going to do the album back home, at the Record Plant in New York City. In addition to the Ray Colcord coproduction credit, chief engineer would be the famed Jay Messina, with Jack and Rod O'Brien getting a cocredit in that department.

Jack had started at the studio as a janitor, working his way up to engineer on sessions for the Who and John Lennon. He'd also been in bands of his own, as a folk musician, joking that he'd sign anything, and wound up contracted to three record labels at the same time. It was his work engineering on the first New York Dolls album, produced by Todd Rundgren, that served as the connection to what Aerosmith was attempting to do. Jack saw similarities between the two bands musicwise, but hooking Jack up with Aerosmith also came from Leber and Krebs, who had both acts under their management umbrella. They sent Jack up to Boston to see the band, and Douglas instantly fell in love with them, given their shared love of the Yardbirds and the Stones.

Recalls David, "Jack Douglas was the engineer on the New York Dolls album, so I must've gotten to know him there. I always liked him, and he was a bass player, and he was a good guy. And I'm getting ready for my second album, and for some reason I decide I don't want to use Adrian Barber. I'm not sure why. And maybe I was wrong, but I guess it wasn't based on what happened. So I say, okay, I'm in a precarious position here. Because if my second album isn't successful, I got a lot of problems, so I better protect what I'm doing in a certain sense. So I try to get Bob Ezrin to produce *Get Your Wings*, or what turned out to be *Get Your Wings*. Bob Ezrin is busy. I don't know what he thought about Aerosmith, but he didn't think enough to do it. And he recommended Jack Douglas. Which, I said fine. But the credits on that album list Bob Ezrin as a coproducer or something, so that Columbia cannot challenge that if the record failed; they certainly couldn't look at us and say you chose a weak producer, you know? And Ray Colcord was an A&R guy at Columbia. He was into the band. I don't know what happened. I've no idea what happened to Ray Colcord."

When I asked him if there was a Jack Douglas sound, Jack said, "I mean, some people will say there is. But I tried to say that if you want my sound, you'd have to get my records. But what I try to do is get the sound of the band. And I still like to record as much live as I can, because that's how you get the feel of the band. So that's really what I always went for. What does this band have and how do we make it sound like the band, to make it sound unique? The only influence I would have would be my feel in it, you know? Probably it was most noticeable in Aerosmith, because it became the most popular thing I did. But I have a bluesy, R&B feel—that's how I feel things. Rhythm is an important thing to me.

"My mission there was to get what was in their heads on vinyl," continues Jack, reacting to my framing of *Get Your Wings* as a quantum leap beyond the debut. "Because what they imagined they wanted to be and what they were were two different things. And that's a lot of work in the preproduction stage before we got into the studio, so that we would really understand what we were going for and what we were doing.

The result was a much more dynamic album, sparkly even, despite the dour cover art. "It was the bright record; it was the totally bright record," laughs Jack at that assessment. "Everyone and everything in the band was just starting to really, really break big. And so, there was so much optimism, and everyone was so happy, and basically there was very little drugs. That was a major album, although my favorite was *Rocks*."

If Jack had been hopeful about the new album, Steven was even more over the moon at the time, declaring himself "blissful" about the new songs, explaining that through the increased amount of collaboration, they reflected the personalities in the band much better than the early material.

Get Your Wings, issued on March 15, 1974, arrived in stores housed in an album cover that wasn't much of an improvement over the first one. The band looks menacing but also kind of sad. It's a dark and depressing shot, giving off Alice Cooper vibes, but this was definitely not a glam band, with the guys' clothes almost disappearing into the black background. Up top, there's a rough, early-days version of an Aerosmith logo, with the "A" designed to look like Steven's favorite part of the female anatomy. Or more likely, tonsils, according to Joe, who also says that the wings looked too much like bat wings, to be corrected later to look more like the Harley-Davidson logo.

Randomly, over to the left is our album title, in red. So we have a black-and-white band shot, plus two colors, red for the title and gold for the logo. As for that title, "get your wings" can refer to having sex with a woman (i.e., the "wings system"), especially in a biker gang context. And given that it's rendered in red, well, red wings means sex with a woman during her period. It also refers to obtaining one's pilot's license. Steven, of course, went with the most extreme definition, explaining in his book that "I came up with the second album title, *Get Your Wings*, after reading a book on the Hells Angels. Getting your wings is a Hells Angels thing. If you give a girl head when she has her period, you are definitely one of the guys, and, my friend, you've got your wings." Of course, more innocently, what it also means, given the name of the band and their new logo, is "Buy an Aerosmith album." But none of this would have mattered if they went with Steven's preferred title: *Bobbing for Piranha*, complete with predictably ghoulish cover art.

Past the wrapper and into the record, first we get "Same Old Song and Dance," where instantly we hear the vibrancy of Jack's production job, as well as the new, evolved, blossomed nature of Steven's singing voice. Jack had most definitely piped up and said that what Tyler had done on the debut was ridiculous, and that they'd be crazy not to present Tyler's natural singing voice to its full potential. Joe remembers coming up with the song's kind of goofy, show-bizzy, circular riff while sitting on his amp in the living room of the band's Beacon Street apartment, with Steven readily joining in on vocals until the song was born. It would turn out to be one of these songs where the vocal melody follows the guitar riff pretty faithfully. At the rhythm end, Tom plays what Roger Glover would call "teenaged eighth notes" while Joey turns in a rock-solid, almost rigid shuffle feel, if that's a thing. There's ample thump to the bass, and his snare drum cracks like a gunshot.

It was Jack who suggested adding in the saxophone, which becomes pervasive throughout. It's in fact a brass section, made up of Michael Brecker on tenor sax, Stan Bronstein (from Elephant's Memory) on baritone sax, Randy Brecker on trumpet, and Jon Pearson on trombone. Despite most of it sounding like sax, all can be heard clearly at various points, with Michael Brecker taking the memorable sax solo. During the halting, almost marchlike break section, there are nice, high-fidelity handclaps massaged in, providing additional detailing. As for the guitar solo, that's Dick Wagner, who did sessions with Bob Ezrin and had been brought in at Ezrin's behest. Curiously, Bob and Jack were in agreement that neither Joe nor Brad was up to snuff yet to do all the solos on the record.

And speaking of solos . . . "'Same Old Song and Dance' is a challenge because I do a semi solo on the end of it," Tom Hamilton told me in 2005, describing a modern arrangement of this perennial favorite. "We go into the ending part of the song and just keep it going and going and going. We build the energy, and what happens is, the band cuts out at the end of the main body of the song. Steven does some cool vocal stuff over Joey's beat. You know, he keeps going, playing twos and fours, and then when we come back in, everybody keeps playing, but I'm playing a lead bass guitar kind of thing. So that's a challenge every night, to make that work and not make it too planned and play off the top of my head but play some coherent stuff. It's also physically challenging because it's all triplets. So, it's kind of an endurance song."

"Same Old Song and Dance" would be picked by the label as the album's first single, issued on March 19 and backed with "Pandora's Box." Tyler was not happy with the choice. The single version represents a bit of a crude edit, with a minute removed from the original 3:53 album duration. It wasn't much of a performer, failing to chart on *Billboard* and reaching #107 on *Cash Box*.

"Uh, I used to, but it doesn't matter any more," chuckled Jack, when I asked him if he ever produced with radio in mind. "Because they don't play them on the radio anymore. Now I work on making them sound good on mp3s and computers. But back then, yeah, we had our own little radio station at Record Plant, which only worked to about 30 or 40 yards in either direction from the front of the studio on 44th Street. It was really funny, because you would be listening to one radio station in your car, and if you drove by Record Plant, that radio station would disappear and you would hear an unreleased Bruce Springsteen song being played, because the guy in the studio is checking it on the radio. And you'd wonder what the hell is this? And then you'd drive another 30 yards or so, maybe less, and that would disappear, and your Spanish station would be back.

"So yeah, we had a little radio station, and that's how we would check. We had an actual broadcast limiter on the thing, and sometimes we would do our mixes or our tune-ups for singles through that. And of course, we would always mix through various small speakers, and we would do separate mono mixes for singles. There was a lot of things that we would do to make the record sound hotter and sound louder on the radio when they got to us. We used to study Motown records. For a long time, we studied Motown records, because they were always louder on the radio. And basically, the trick with a Motown record was that they had no bottom in them—no bass. They must have rolled off at about 100 cycles. There was nothing below 100 cycles, and so the radio limiters didn't hit them so hard, and they just came flying out of your speakers in your car."

Back to they guys not playing certain solos, Brad remembers Joe and himself being crestfallen about the situation, citing this song and "S.O.S. (Too Bad)," while also sounding quite sure he's nowhere to be heard on "Lord of the Thighs." Jack, for his part, assured them that Dick Wagner and Steve Hunter would not be credited on the album and that no one would know. But he acknowledges that Brad and Joe were furious, but also that Steven thought it was a pretty good idea.

Next up is the aforementioned "Lord of the Thighs," a second tough rocker, with the title being a lascivious play of words on William Golding's novel *Lord of the Flies*. This was actually the last track written for the album, with the band holing up in Studio C at Record Plant to knock it out. It's credited to Tyler, who also provides the dramatic, rhythmic piano part. Lyrically, it's about the creepy characters who were hanging around the streets outside the studio, as well as the Ramada Inn the band was staying in at 48th Street and 8th Avenue, with the Lord of the Thighs actually being a pimp. Vocally, appropriately, Steven adopts a sort of slangy, streetwise accent, although he goes full and powerful natural Steven come chorus time. Jack says that Steven was good at this, picking up the lingo of the street, which was a hotbed of vice around Times Square in the '70s and well into the '80s. Also, rhythmically, Joe turns in a novel snare-and-bass combination, although ultimately it's still a four-four beat, straightening out after the intro.

"Spaced" is an interesting, dark, proggy number, written in the studio, with much assistance from Jack. At the lyric end, Steven uses the imagery of an astronaut stranded alone on a distant planet to represent exactly that, along with being spaced out on drugs and just generally alienated and mentally fragile because of it. It's musically just as sophisticated, opening with spooky, extraterrestrial sound effects, a reverse fade, and then we're into the song. The guitars are subtle but weaving like the Stones. Meanwhile, Joey is alternating from a high-hat beat to the bell of a cymbal, likely a crash, given its high frequency. There's a dramatic and rhythmic break section that is first instrumental and then featuring a high, strained vocal. Then we're into a new musical section with rapid-fire notes. Soon we return to the ascending chord sequence of the verse section, followed by a quick return to the swirling second break bit, at the end, accompanied by jazzy piano.

Steven wrote "Woman of the World" with his old Chain Reaction bandmate Don Solomon. At nearly six minutes long, a lot happens. Joey opens the song with a simple, hypnotic beat, and then we get acoustic guitars mixed with electrics, something Kiss would turn into a bit of a trademark, working both with Bob Ezrin and Eddie Kramer. Joe says the song developed further out of the middle section of "Rattlesnake Shake," a Peter Green–written Fleetwood Mac song from 1969 that the band used to play live. Again, guitars weave like the Stones, panned hard left and right. Everything sits perfectly in the mix, inside of a song that is, ingeniously, mostly poppy hard rock but also connects to the blues, mostly through Steven's vocal phrasing. Holding interest are the song's recurring double-time parts. Late in the sequence, we get one of those double-time bits with a sort of Bo Diddley beat from Joey and some harmonica playing from Steven. This converts to a slow fade as the band jam it out.

Side 2 of the original vinyl opens with "S.O.S. (Too Bad)," which stood for same old shit. It also stands for save our souls, and, closer, same old situation, as made famous on the *Dr. Feelgood* album by Mötley Crüe. Curiously, right here on this record, we also have "Same Old Song and Dance." The song arose from the rehearsal sessions at Drummer's Image in August 1973. In any event, "S.O.S. (Too Bad)" is this album's most up-tempo track and hardest rocker, essentially early-days heavy metal and positioned well away from the blues. It has a nice hook, stopping dead in its tracks for the "It's too bad, can't get me none of that" line, sung in unison with the moaning guitar phrase.

The Aerosmith guys always loved the Yardbirds and always loved "Train Kept a Rollin'," with Steven actually seeing the Yardbirds perform the song when both Jeff Beck and Jimmy Page were in the band. Later, when Steven's band had been the warm-up act for the Yardbirds, he found himself standing at the side of the stage seeing the track performed again, but just with Jimmy Page.

As Joe explained to Alan DiPerna, "It was the only song we had in common when we got together. Steven's band had played 'Train,' and Tom and I played it in our band. Steven's band was really tight and played Beatles songs and things like that. The band Tom and I had was just the opposite—loud, noisy, and a lot of feedback and out of tune sometimes. But the common ground we all had was playing 'Train Kept a Rollin'.'

"Proto-metal for sure," continues Joe. "It's a big song, if you follow its roots all the way back. To me, it's as important as 'I'm a Man,' as far as the rhythm goes, the push-pull. I always thought if I could play one song, it would be that one, because of what it does to me. The Yardbirds were definitely taking that blues thing—as a lot of those English guys did—and putting larger guitars on it. They had a melodic sense, you know, with Jeff Beck in the band. They were a pop band trying to incorporate some of that blues edge and still get played on the radio. The fact that Eric Clapton quit the Yardbirds because he was a purist and only wanted to play the blues—you have to scratch your head over that one. Because you look at his career three years later, and what's he playing?"

In that portrayal of the Yardbirds, Joe lays out for us the Aerosmith formula, especially on the first album and *Get Your Wings*. It's the blues, with Jeff Beck's melody and "larger guitars on it." Put those three things together and you have Aerosmith.

As an aside, I wrote a book titled *Who Invented Heavy Metal?*, and I posit in there that the Johnny Burnette Trio version of this song might be called the first heavy metal song ever, albeit for a half-dozen very slight reasons combined. Aerosmith's version is so gnarly and rockin' that always, as kids, we put aside the fact that it was a cover, because it was so dirty and heavy, nearly as heavy as the song before it on the album. Interestingly, the half-time part at the front is almost like a new composition, but then it picks up, where the true headbanging nature of the song is revealed. This reaches a crescendo as the band hammers the track home with a raucous live-style windup.

"We may not have heard all the original versions of it," reflects Brad. "Our real driving force on that was definitely the Yardbirds. We were just huge into Jimmy Page and Jeff Beck—still are. We basically became a two-guitar band just like that. And that song just had Aerosmith all over it. As soon as we started doing it, it had such a powerful riff, and a touch of funk to it." As for the intro piece, Brad says, "I believe we started messing around with that in preproduction, when we were working on the album. And also, being huge fans of James Brown and funk music, I think it just came up in rehearsal one day and it immediately clicked, and we went, 'That's cool!' So, we decided to basically put two versions on it at the same time. I love the slow version. It's just so badass [laughs]."

The song was recorded in two sections, with the fast part rendered faux live, complete with crowd noise at the end piped in from *The Concert for Bangladesh*, which Jack had worked on.

The scandal with this track, of course, is that Dick Wagner and Steve Hunter play the guitar solos on it.

"Yes, and it was tough for them, at first, to swallow," says Jack Douglas, "but they came along. I mean, Steven, really, he was totally down with it. And the deal was this. You can't really play at what you want to sound like, you know? On somebody's solos. No, it wasn't all of them; it was just some choice solos in there that really, of course, are some of the highlights of *Get Your Wings*. But Steve and Dick were guys that we were using on Alice Cooper records, and they were great personalities, and they would always be sworn to secrecy that they would never open their mouths and of course didn't for twenty years. I think Joe let the cat out of the bag, finally. But the deal was this. Not only will they play these selected solos, but they will teach you these selected solos and how to finger them and how to get that sound and everything about it. So that this project is not only we're going to have these amazing solos, but you're going to be able to go on the road now and play these solos, and no one's going to know the difference. And because you can play them on the road, you guys will step up your playing by 100 percent. And so, the whole process was a win-win because it was great for the record and it turned those guys into the players they always wanted to be. And Steve and Dick were the most-gracious two guys I could ever imagine."

As Dick recalls, "It was 'Train Kept a Rollin',' and I played on 'Same Old Song and Dance'; I think I played on four tracks on that album. I haven't listened to those albums in so long; I don't remember the titles." When I asked him if it was because Joe was still a little green, Dick says, "Basically that's what it was at that time. Steve Hunter played on it and so did I. They used us because we were more advanced; we could come up with the stuff more quickly, whatever, and Joe was still learning. I mean, he's a great player now. But you know, it takes awhile to get to the stage that Steve and I were playing at, because we both had been doing it a long, long time. Steve's on 'Train Kept a Rollin'' too; we're both on that track. We're doing the solos, and I think we also play on the rhythm tracks too. But Joe also had rhythm tracks on that song."

"Well, I'm sitting in the lobby of the Record Plant," adds Hunter. "Bob Ezrin was . . . we were in Studio A, which at that time at the Record Plant, that was a great big room. He was doing some editing. So I usually left the room when he was editing, because he really had to concentrate. In those days you had to cut tape. You didn't cut and paste; you had to cut tape. So it got pretty tedious. So I got out of the room and left him alone. I was sitting in the lobby, and right across the lobby is Studio C, and Jack Douglas poked his head out and saw me there and said, 'Would you like to play?' I said, 'Yeah, I'd rather play than sit here.' So he asked Bob Ezrin if he could borrow me for a few minutes. Bob said yes, and next thing you know, I'm in the studio with Aerosmith, they're all in there, and they want me to overdub this, do some soloing and stuff, in the first part of 'Train Kept a Rollin'.' And I think I did a couple of passes, and I was done."

I asked Steve if he thought that Jack was trying to send a message to Brad and Joe to step it up. "I don't know. I really don't know. It happened so fast that I didn't really have time to absorb what was going on. That's happened to me before. People called me in to play on people's albums, and I was told, 'Don't tell anybody; we gotta keep this quiet.' That's happened to me so much before that I just accepted it. I don't really know what the motivation was. I have no idea. Like I say, I came in and played and left, and that's all I knew about it."

Jack explained to me that he didn't have any ulterior motive. And in fact, as he alludes to above, it all worked out great, because when they reconvened to do *Toys in the Attic*, he was delighted to see that the guys had rapidly evolved as musicians.

In the end, Steve was featured on the first half and Dick on the second half. "Train Kept a Rollin'" was issued as a single, heavily chopped down to 3:15 from its original 5:33 album length. It became the second single from *Get Your Wings*, to be followed in February 1975 by "S.O.S. (Too Bad)." None of them charted.

As for "Seasons of Wither," the song arose the same way "Mama Kin" did, on that discarded, warped guitar. As Steven says in his book, he "tried to find the words to match the scat sounds in my head, like automatic writing. The place was a mess, and I moved all the shit aside, put a rug down, popped three Tuinals, snorted some blow, sat down on the floor, tuned the guitar to that tuning, that special tuning that I thought I came up with. One of my highlights of my career was being in Greenwich Village with Mark Hudson and coming across a guy sitting on a rag playing a guitar. His feet were black from the streets he'd walked. He looks up at me and starts playing 'Seasons of Wither' note for note, exactly as I wrote it. Someone was looking at my painting."

At the lyric end, he says the song "was about the winter landscape near this house I was living in with Joey near an old chicken farm. I used to lie in my bed at dawn, listening to the wind in the bare trees, how lonely and melancholy it sounded. I was pissed off about my taxes, and getting mad helps me to write."

Says Tom, "I remember just being in my room and reading a magazine or something, and Steven would be in there, and I noticed he had picked up a guitar, which is rare. And he was playing this neat, sort of haunting arpeggio on it, and just right from the start, it was cool; I loved it. So we developed the song and we were really psyched about it. Those songs are songs we really feel bonded to. As I said before, I remember we had put our first album out on Columbia, and it basically wasn't doing very well, and the record company was pretty disappointed. And they said, 'Okay, you guys, your next album better do pretty good or that's it, goodbye.' And so, when the band first started, before we ever had a record contract, we all lived together. And we made a decision to do that again, and we moved back in with each other, in an apartment. And it was a really good decision. It really focused the band on making an album that was a step forward."

All told, "Seasons of Wither" has emerged decades later as one of the most well-regarded songs on the album. To be sure, it's a ballad, but it's performed mid-tempo, with purposeful but spare drumming from Kramer framing it, complete with flammed snare whacks. Hauntingly, it emerges from the crowd noise at the end of "Train Kept a Rollin'," with the whole sequence sounding like the end of Kiss's *Destroyer* album. There's blowing wind and then this beautiful acoustic guitar coming in through a reverse fade. Then the song lifts to a soar before settling back down to the original arpeggiated premise. There's backing vocals, freight-train slide guitar, splashing cymbal crashes, and all three of its parts are distinct but perfectly dovetailed.

Get Your Wings closes with "Pandora's Box," which once more demonstrates the band's fusion of boogie rock and funk, but in a hard rock context, given the anchoring that takes place with two guitars. At the start, we hear a union engineer at the studio playing "I'm in the Mood for Love" on the clarinet, but the brass section returns for real later, rendered with a proper arrangement on the chorus. There's piano as well, played by Steven, but it's in there sparingly. Uncommonly, the music on this one was written by Joey, who came up with the melody at a rented farmhouse the band had in East Thetford, Vermont, when they had been set up with rehearsal space nearby in New Hampshire. Steven's lyric is themed around women's liberation. It's an appropriate closer, given its building energy as well as its complicated ending structure, an almost progressive-rock punctuation to the song and, as a result, the album.

"If you're going to steal, steal from somebody good," wrote JM in an off-the-wall look at the album in the *Ann Arbor News*. "Aerosmith steals from the best, taking licks from Jo Jo Gunne, the Who, Spirit, and the J. Geils Band (that I can remember), and putting them together in a sound that's about as good as a derivative sound can be. With drummer Kramer and guitarist Joe Perry as the front personnel, this is basically a singles band. There are three excellent candidates for Top 40 land in 'Same Old Song and Dance,' 'Spaced,' and 'Woman of the World.' Unfortunately, those are the first three cuts, and the rest is a slide downhill. The band is at its peak when Kramer takes charge, which he neglects to do on most of the remaining tracks. Steven Tyler's raspy vocals become grating, and you keep waiting for the explosion into something a bit novel. It never happens."

A little more sensible, but humorous for other reasons, is this uncredited missive from the *Blade-Tribune Tempo*: "Aerosmith is well on its way to becoming America's premier hard rock band. This is the group's second album, a strong follow-up to its raw, exciting first. This album is smoother, but just as raunchy and exciting. The group's success is guaranteed if it continues writing and performing material of the caliber of this album and the last. The group's sound is a lusty, hard blues rock. Lead singer Steve Tyler, who writes most of the group's material, will be America's rock sex symbol and the finest singer in American rock if he keeps up his stuff. He out-Jaggers Jagger. The group's sound is that strong, and Tyler's sensual voice is instantly appealing and so richly original that if he can keep it strong, he will be a legend in no time. Listen for 'Same Old Song and Dance' or 'Lord of the Thighs' or 'Spaced' or 'Woman of the World.' Those are the first four songs in the album, and any could be the group's first monster hit. Five stars."

Writing from more of a UK perspective is *Melody Maker*'s Chris Welch—the band hadn't visited yet and indeed wouldn't for a worrying stretch to come. As well, elsewhere in the piece, Chris calls *Get Your Wings* the band's first album.

"Powerful, exciting rock from an intriguing new band of 20-year-olds from Boston, Massachusetts. Their music is thoroughly recommended to all who appreciate a certain panache and skill to the delivery of basic rock truths. They have funk, cheek and glamor, but the instrumental ability is also obvious, rather like a mixture of Steely Dan and the New York Dolls. On 'Same Old Song and Dance' and 'Pandora's Box' they add a powerful brass section. Oddly enough, 'Same Old Song' seems to be related to an ancient Marc Bolan composition, the title of which escapes me, but you'll know what I mean when you've rushed out and bought this cheerful evidence of developments on America's East Coast. Steve Tyler, of saturnine good looks, seems likely to become something of a star, and he evinces much drama on 'Lord of the Thighs,' where he plays piano behind his spitting sensual vocals. This track harks back to the Stones' *Satanic Majesties* period, if only in the echoing, battering piano sound, but there is a certain amount of magic and evil to their music that will earn them a dedicated following here, if they sound this good 'live.' The guitarists too have prodigious technique, with some particularly fine slide work from Joe Perry. Let's hope they make it to these shores, as it would be nice to see if they can match up to the album in a live context. Pity about the name of the band though. Somehow 'Aerosmith mania' doesn't quite have that magic ring."

I like that bit about "cheerful evidence of developments on America's East Coast." It's almost like Chris is rooting for something useful to come out of America, which tended to drop out of the hard rock sweepstakes in the early '70s, albeit soon to come on strong in 1975, with Aerosmith playing a significant role.

As for the manager's assessment of the important second record, David Krebs figures, "Far more sophisticated. 'Lord of the Thighs' is one of the quintessential great lyrics of antifeminism, I would think. I would think women would object to the lyrics of that song today. That's my take [laughs]. I thought 'Woman of the World' was a great song. Don Solomon was an old friend of Steven Tyler's. Here's the difference: Aerosmith was always a heterosexual-attracting group, even though the predominance were men. So, all of these songs with sexual themes are also good, sophisticated songs musically, despite the sexual innuendos.

"Aerosmith was always song poor," continues Krebs. "Whether they had ideas or melodies going back years, I don't know. But my recollection is songs were written for the albums, and there were very few, if any, extra songs that didn't make it, so to speak. I thought 'Train Kept a Rollin'' was a great Aerosmith song which somebody else recorded. I think we see sophistication in 'Seasons of Wither' that we've not seen before. And I always loved 'Same Old Song and Dance.' That's my take. 'Pandora's Box,' I think that was the only song Joey Kramer wrote, from what I remember. I don't remember what the lyrics are to 'Pandora's Box.' It must have sexual innuendos.

"And Jack Douglas, you can see the difference between him and Adrian Barber, which was much more towards a live performance on the first album. This is a giant step forward in terms of what happens in the band at this point, and this is the whole point of this kind of music: The band is becoming big only because of how great it is live. There were no hit singles out through two albums—'Dream On' has to be rereleased. But I think Jack Douglas added a lot, obviously, but Adrian Barber had great credentials. Remember, Jack Douglas came in for Bob Ezrin, who was too busy to do the record, and that's why Bob's got that executive producer listing. He probably made a point or two off that album from that listing."

It would be hard to call *Get Your Wings* a success at the time. Still overshadowed by "Dream On," the album got to only #100 on the charts, although after the success of *Toys in the Attic*, it would work its way up to #74. In fact, on April 18, 1975, just two weeks after the launch of the third record, *Get Your Wings* would reach its RIAA gold certification, en route to its current triple-platinum status, achieved in 2001.

"It was very important," answers David, asked about playing up these certifications. "Because we used those awards to return favors to promoters and radio and print press people who supported the band. Industry people got sent a gold or platinum plaque—they loved getting those things. Plus, we took ads out in *Billboard* and other industry magazines celebrating the fact. Letting people know about those accomplishments also really helped when it came to the concert side of things."

Right away, Aerosmith hit the road playing with a bewildering array of acts, including, just in March, James Montgomery Band, Blue Öyster Cult, Deep Purple, Rory Gallagher, Bull Angus, Kiss, Redbone, and Hawkwind.

Tom says this is exactly what the band had to do to become successful, explaining to Sam Dunn, "So we all moved back in together and worked 24/7 on our second album, which came out really good. We had a new producer, Jack Douglas, and the label really liked it and it did well. But the thing that really put it over the top for us was touring. We just had to go out on the road. Now you would call it viral marketing. You had to play in front of people, get on the best tours we could, opening for whatever band. We opened for some weird people back then [laughs], but it was a crowd. We didn't care. So eventually we just built that up to a critical mass.

"When we first came out, *Rolling Stone* said these guys are just a second-rate Stones rip-off, basically. Oh, I get it, Jagger, Richards. And they, in a way, they were dead-on because we were extremely influenced by Mick Jagger. Steven was inspired by Mick Jagger to the point of going to study the guy, and I think he's got pretty good taste. So that was the initial thing. And also, I think a lot of the sort of college magazines and the press, the rock press that wanted to be upwardly mobile, wanted to hear a bit more of an intellectual component from other bands. We weren't just about rocking out, but maybe they thought we were trivial.

So for the first few years, we didn't get a lot of good press. But again, just touring and touring and touring, and going and proving it onstage every night, started to change that. And after our second and third records, people could hear that what we were playing was not like a Stones record. It really had its own style."

Asked if they were okay with being called heavy metal, Tom says, "When people called us heavy metal, I thought they were completely . . . they didn't know what they were talking about. We really identified more with being a blues band, even though we knew we weren't a pure blues band, because we were into a lot of other stuff. We thought we were more sophisticated than heavy metal. Whoever thought up that term, I think it was maybe in response to Led Zeppelin. Now, if Led Zeppelin is what heavy metal is, then heavy metal is really cool [laughs]. But more and more, we would hear these bands come out that were loud, and they could do that, but they weren't that good, and they were kind of sludgy. So we didn't identify with the heavy metal thing."

There wasn't much of a pattern heading into April either, with Aerosmith sharing stages with Three Dog Night, ZZ Top, Suzi Quatro, Elliott Murphy, and King Crimson. This continued on right through to the end of the year, which was a typical thing back then, actually, where there's not a set tour package going out for weeks at a time. There was a nice close to the year's tour grind, however, with the band playing support to the Guess Who in Honolulu, Hawaii, with the emceeing done by none other than Wolfman Jack.

3
Toys in the Attic

"I started walking around the control room like the hunchback."

In the ramp-up to the third record, Aerosmith had been fueled only by "Dream On," good live notices, and their inherently recognized advancement as musicians and writers. Then both albums started selling, says *Cash Box*, "at the rate of almost 15,000 copies per week," and the buzz about Aerosmith was beginning to pay off. In the early months of 1975, the band regathered and thereby found themselves with an embarrassment of creative riches, to be sure, driven by drugs but also by their wide-eyed recognition of their collective potential. Also, this was to be a record that would benefit from the calluses raised by intense roadwork. The guys were worked in and on point but also arriving with very few ideas, writing basically from scratch outside of three or four songs.

"*Toys in the Attic*, we also did with Jack," says Joey. "We did that at the Record Plant. That was pretty much the same deal as *Rocks*. We had lots and lots of practical joking and kidding around with Jack and Jay Messina. Again, we were having so much fun at the time that it really shows in the tracks. We were having fun, and we were recording that fun."

Adds Tom, "There were people nosing around. When it came time to do the *Toys in the Attic* album, I just wanted to make sure that whatever I came in with in terms of my playing and my songwriting was the best I could. So that we could rule off any possibility of being bothered by outsiders, when we made that record. And being judged by people that weren't friends of ours, basically. So, you know, I worked my ass off, and put a lot of practice in, and put a lot of effort into coming up with some ideas."

Elaborating with Paul Gargano, Hamilton says, "I was determined to (a) do some writing on the album, and (b) take my bass playing to another level again. This was the early honeymoon with stuff like cocaine. I actually had the ability to snort some and then work it out on bass for half an hour and then snort some more and do the same thing. I used it as a stimulant to get myself energy." Asked by Paul if it was helpful, Tom figures, "You know what? I can't say that, because I've always gotten a minor reaming for using the word 'responsible' when I talk about that era. It was an illusion. It was me looking for energy and strength from the outside instead of finding it in myself. And that was about confidence. I always felt the bass guitar has never been something that has come easy for me. I think the reason I'm a bass player is based more on my dream of being in a band, of being involved in music, and living the kind of a life that it is, because I have so much natural ability in that way, and it really is the most logical way to go. I think I fought for every single knowledge and ability that I have."

Management could see that the stakes had been raised. Says David Krebs, "Remember, the environment in terms of the industry was totally different. The whole theory of rock 'n' roll was conquering one city at a time, and you had that ability because you were really in the early stages of FM radio. You could go out, open a show, headline a club, and radio people would be out there and the local programming guy would have the option of picking up your music and playing it. So, a group like Aerosmith, if they had sold 100,000 records, you would probably find half those records were probably sold in three markets.

"Word of mouth has always been a critical ingredient. The first label that we ever had, which was run by somebody who's quite an illustrious name—Cliff Burnstein—it was called Word of Mouth Records. Since we thought that was the essential ingredient in what we were dealing with. That label, I think, lasted for one group. But philosophically, we wanted to have no more than one hit single every two albums. Remember, you were on the outside of culture looking in, as opposed to now you're on the inside looking out. Aerosmith was perceived as . . . what's the right word . . . as not as noble as Bruce Springsteen, in terms of a press sensibility, in the mainstream rock press.

"But Aerosmith broke by themselves," continues Krebs. "Ted Nugent broke off of Aerosmith by touring with them. So, if Ted Nugent did a fifty-day tour with Aerosmith and played before 600,000 people, you were really in the Colosseum in Rome every night, and the thumbs went up or down. For example, there was a package out; a good friend of mine named Bud Carr managed Kansas, and he really begged a favor—to put Kansas as a special guest with Nugent opening and Aerosmith following. And I said, 'Bud, I think you're making a grievous error, because this is not the kind of band that's going to be able to overcome Ted Nugent.' Well, they didn't. But other bands . . . I think the Scorpions broke off of Aerosmith and Nugent, and I think AC/DC broke off of Aerosmith and Nugent. You knew, because we had bands like Artful Dodger that we put out on these big packages, and we warned them that we thought they should play clubs and they convinced us we were wrong, and we turned out to be right. They couldn't deliver, not in that milieu, so to speak."

Tom certainly remembers AC/DC, telling Steve Newton, "You know, we had no idea who they were, but we'd just be in the dressing room getting ready and we'd hear this incredible beat coming through the wall. It started out with people saying, 'Wow, have you heard the opening act? I think they might be good.' Then it was like, 'Wow, those guys really cook!' And finally, it's like, 'Those guys are fuckin' great!' The next thing we know, our accountant took off and became their manager, and the rest is history."

"So really we're talking about '75, '76, at that point," continues Krebs. "Our first hit single was not off of *Toys*. 'Dream On' was a single that came off the first album. It went into the '70s and '80s. After we had the first hit, we beat up Columbia and said . . . one of the theories we utilized, I said there are no rules. So we came in and said to Columbia, 'Look, we know this song failed once; we think it's amazing and we want you to put it out again.' Which they did, and it went Top Ten, I think #6. But that song had come out and failed."

So, to sum up, as the band went in to record *Toys in the Attic*, it was still "Dream On" that was doing the heavy lifting, as well as the roadwork. "Yes, and at this point the two main competitors coming up were Kiss vs. Aerosmith, and I have always preferred the Aerosmith-type rock act for my own taste."

To cook up the songs, the band, as well as Jack, got together at a converted barn rehearsal space that Columbia had arranged for acts on the label; namely, Aengus Studios, in Fayville, Massachusetts, inland from Boston about twenty miles. Next it was over to the Record Plant, February 10 through March 6, where much of the writing occurred, with Jack Douglas now considered something of a sixth member of the band. Engineer Jay Messina remembers the sessions fondly, with Steven's vocals being easy to capture and Brad and Joe working with minimal guitar and amp combinations, a bit of flanger and phaser, with Brad sent to the left channel and Joe to the right. They were recording to sixteen tracks, but as Douglas remembers it, that was no problem for the band because they often played together live, leaving all sorts of extra tracks for ear candy. Joe recalls Steven and himself always being there for the mixes, putting sliders up and down, debating tambourines and handclaps. The mastering of the record took place on March 22, with the band already out on tour again, specifically playing Cincinnati on a strong bill with Styx and Rush, who famously are on record for saying Aerosmith did not make them feel welcome.

Working titles for the record included *Teddy Bear's Funeral* and *Love at First Bite*, which was a line from *Toys* track "Adam's Apple." Joe wanted to call it *Rocks*. As for the album cover of the eventually christened *Toys in the Attic*, the work on that fell to Ernie Cefalu and his illustrious Pacific Eye & Ear company, essentially America's answer to Hipgnosis. The mad *Alice in Wonderland*–like toy scene illustration was done by renowned artist Ingrid Haenke.

Once discussing the design house's ghoulish *Sabbath Bloody Sabbath* cover with Ernie, he told me, "So there, the girl on the left on the back, that's Ingrid, and the guy is Drew Struzan, and the guy laying [*sic*] in the bed is Drew, and then on the right side, she's the first one looking at Drew, who is laying on the bed. And that's actually Bill Garland, who is another illustrator who used to work with us; that's him kneeling there, and then Ingrid is the one standing on your far right. And like I say, she's the one who did the Aerosmith *Toys in the Attic* cover. She's a really great illustrator herself and does a lot of children's book stuff. Really beautiful work."

On the back, the guys are added to the attic, now with real-life photography. Both sides are framed in a calming and anchoring brown that gives the album a distinctive look. What's more, the logo has evolved into the fine piece of branding art that would be used but for this album and the next.

Toys in the Attic kicks off with what would be the band's heaviest-metal song to date, a speedy, note-dense title track of epic proportions, with nonobvious chord sequences glancing off in all directions and modulation intensifying the drama at breakneck speeds. This one was written in the studio, and the energy is off the charts, saliently compared to any and all the songs on the first two records, save for the second half of 'Train."

"'Toys in the Attic' was a big challenge," says Tom. "To be able to play that that fast, on the bass guitar, and have it sound coherent, where you could hear the riff . . . I mean, the thing is so damn fast, and it was just probably a product of us finally making enough money to buy stupid amounts of cocaine. So here we are, like, making good use of it. But yeah, that song is friggin' fast. Geez, too fast. If we recut it and maybe slowed it down a little bit, it would probably be heavier. But that was an example of something that we wanted to be able to do, because that was something Led Zeppelin could do, or the Who. That was us trying to do that and come up with something that was on that level."

That explanation is very much like what we'd hear from Andy Scott describing Sweet's "Set Me Free," where the band was making a plea to be taken seriously, like Deep Purple, as players and both writers of their own songs. It also sounds like Paul McCartney writing "Helter

Skelter," who was piqued at the Who being considered the gnarliest, loudest, most heavyweight band on the market. In this case, it's Aerosmith wanting a piece of the heavy metal pie, proving they could write in that idiom. Finally, as kids, we always paired this song with "Motor City Madhouse" from the first Ted Nugent album, also from 1975. If this was 1980 and we were into the New Wave of British Heavy Metal, both tracks would be called OTT, for over the top.

What's also interesting about this song is how it presents like a series of prechoruses plus a chorus, with the band almost sounding too harassed to sit down and write a defined verse structure. Plus, it sounds like a high-powered jam, taking us on a trip at the halfway mark with Joey switching to ride cymbal in conjunction with a modulation to a solo section.

As Steven explained in his book, "January 1975 in the midst of a spine-chilling, ball-freezing New York winter, we began working on our third album, *Toys in the Attic*. I came up with the title because of its obvious meanings, and since people thought we were fucking crazy anyways, what did it matter? I wasn't hip to the 1960 Tony Award–nominated Broadway play of the same name or its 1963 Oscar-nominated film adaptation. Didn't matter if I had been. This was Aerosmith *Toys in the Attic*, singular, sexy, and psycho sensational. The other reason I came up with *Toys in the Attic* was that I knew we'd made it. I was the kid who put my initials in the rock because I wanted the aliens to know I was there. It's a statement of longevity. The record will be played long after you're dead. Our records would be up there in the attic too, with the things that you loved and never wanted to forget. And to me, Aerosmith was becoming that. I knew how the Beatles, the Animals, and the Kinks did it with lyrics and titles. I saw reason and rhyme in all the lunacy that we were concocting."

Continues Tyler, "Joe was jamming a riff, and I started yelling, 'Toys, toys, toys,' organic, immediate, infectious, fucking amazing. Once again, the Toxic Twins ride off into the sunset, this time, the sunset of the attic. Joe's been my inspiration on more songs that I would ever tell him. Sometimes, just his presence in the room is enough to inspire lyrics to the greatest melody. It's proved itself on every record we've ever done. I'm friends with some of the best, but I'm partners with almost none. He's so much more than the real thing. Coke has nothing on Joe Perry. Like leaves on an artichoke, the more layers you peel off, the closer you get to the heart."

Despite its, young, fast, scientific modern architecture, "Toys in the Attic" somehow evokes the magic of the Rolling Stones, mainly, one supposes, through the ganged-up vocals, less like sober harmony vocals, more so like Steve and Joe standing at a single mic live, hanging on for dear life. In terms of its instigation, Joe remembers Jack, at the very end of the process, telling the guys they needed "one more rocker" on the album, after which Joe, sitting on his amp, started playing the song's circular riff with Steven joining in on vocals, as he describes above. "A benchmark rock 'n' roll song for Aerosmith," remarks Joe. "That kind of fast tune, that was always a favorite of mine. This was sort of the first one. There were many more to follow."

Tom plays rhythm guitar on "Uncle Salty," demurring that "well, yeah, it was just a few simple guitar parts. On the verses, it was a guitar part over a certain bass part that I play. And I knew the parts worked together well, and I was just . . . it was my dream to hear them played by the band. And I realized that the best way to make that possible would be to walk into rehearsals, you know, with a noticeable step forward in my playing and with my ideas. So that's what I set my mind to doing."

This was a song that was in fact written by Tom when the band first got together, and it hadn't made it to the first or second albums. At the lyrical end, Steven was imagining an orphanage and the image of a child crying and being abandoned and receiving no comfort—except from a predator called Uncle Salty.

As Steven described it in *Walk This Way*, more obscurely, it's "just a fantasy I had of being a madame, the boss of a bordello: work with the girls, hire and fire, keep things running. Salty worked in a home for lost children and had his way with this little girl. That's what it's about. I'm the little girl, the orphaned boy. I put myself in that place. I'm Uncle Salty too."

The story (or stories) sits ominously inside the almost suffocating melancholy of the track's melody. Indeed, like the first song but in an entirely different direction, "Uncle Salty" demonstrates a wild sense of creativity—or at least musical style—nowhere to be found on *Aerosmith* or *Get Your Wings*. I often say that the first three Blue Öyster

Cult albums are the only records that sound like the original Alice Cooper band, but I get that vibe from this particular song as well, with the clean guitar, the loose drumming, the ponderous chord sequences. It's not recorded Doorsy like Alice and BÖC, but it's written a bit like a Doors song. Or "Shapes of Things," with the muted clang of the ensemble music behind the "When she cried at night" part. Then there's the half-time psychedelic breakdown, wistful, behind the "Ooh, it's a sunny day outside my window" line. The sum total even has me thinking of commercial Captain Beefheart, from the two unfairly maligned Mercury albums of 1974. In any event, across two tracks, we're almost in a Queen space in terms of width of palette, and although we'll see some funky, boogie rock anchoring along the journey, that sentiment holds up through to the end.

Speaking of traditional rock anchoring, next is "Adam's Apple," which is more the work of a new and improved Rolling Stones than America's Rolling Stones. In other words, this is one of those songs that we as young kids at the time thought of as kicking the Stones' asses around the block. It was a new, younger, wilder, heavier version of the Rolling Stones, the next evolutionary step past "Jumpin' Jack Flash," which we saw as the riffiest thing those old guys could conjure. Joe plays a novel, fluid slide guitar lick, while Steven puts on a lyric that is an amusing retelling of the biblical story. "One of the greatest put-together songs Aerosmith ever did," notes Steven. "Those were my thoughts on UFOs, the theory of evolution, the monkey and Adam and Eve. How incredibly naïve to think that there were just those two people just buzzing around the woods naked, having a blast."

"Yeah, 'Adam's Apple,' that one just sort of had its own vibe," muses Tom. "It was kind of a laid-back thing, but yet it had its own energy. And that was a very challenging song; it had a lot of chord changes in it. So, there's a lot of bass stuff to come up with." Indeed, at the bass end, Tom plays about half these sections somewhat straight, while on others he gets mobile, like John Paul Jones or in fact compatriot Gene Simmons. All the while, Joey is switching back and forth from a high-hat groove to a ride cymbal groove, while the pervasive, structured horn parts make it sound like a party.

Tom makes a good point, because in fact we are now at three songs in a row with sophisticated chord sequences, strewn across three different styles of songs. "Adam's Apple" is one of these songs like "Strutter" from Kiss or "Cat Scratch Fever" from Ted Nugent, where old-school boogie rock is used as connective tissue between fresher ideas, in this case, as part of the second part of the verse structure. Also signaling it as something traditional is the aforementioned added, thoughtful horn arrangement, providing warmth of bottom end.

"That track we were going to throw off the record," says Jack Douglas, of "Walk This Way," the most famous Aerosmith song and for good reason—or many reasons, including its irresistible beat and even more irresistible riff, along with Steve's pioneering "rap" vocal. "We were famous for doing all our tracks but just having scratch vocals with no lyrics. You know, with just sounds, syllables, and stuff, and the syllables would later turn into lyrics, once there was a theme. And so, when we got to 'Walk This Way,' because of the rhythm setup of it, it was really hard to imagine a vocal. It was going to take a lot of syllables to fill and very rhythmic, which in fact makes it kind of the first rap song. But anyway, we couldn't come up with anything for it. What do you do with it? Sounds more like an instrumental. So, it was the last song that we were working on lyrics for and really couldn't come up with anything."

"And what we used to do when we needed words to fill in things, ideas and themes, since we were in Times Square recording, we would go for a walk mostly in the evenings. And New York in the '70s, there was like a battle zone around Times Square. And so we had this route that we would walk up 8th Avenue, which was all hookers, and then across around 50th Street, where there were a lot of bookies and guys placing bets and three-card monte, and then down Broadway, where the tourists and open-mouthed gaping people from Idaho getting pickpocketed are, and then down 42nd Street, the drug dealers, and then back to the studio, which was just off of 8th Avenue."

"Now after making a walk like that, just overhearing the pimps and hookers and the dealers and all these people, you could come back with a collection of phrases and stuff from the street, and we would use that stuff in our lyrics. And this particular day, it was a Sunday afternoon, and we were working on 'Walk This Way,' and somebody suggested that we go for the walk. The whole band happened to be there that day, which was unusual, but I think it was just because they wanted to get Steven to finish the song or forget about it.

"So we went for the walk, and being a Sunday afternoon, there was really nothing on the street at all. And when we got to 42nd Street, there was a movie playing called *Young Frankenstein*, there in one of the second-play theaters on 42nd Street. So I said let's take a break from this whole thing and go in and see a movie. So we went in to see Mel Brooks, *Young Frankenstein*, and we were laughing our asses off. It's a very funny movie.

"And there's a scene where Feldman, who's playing the hunchback, answers the door of the castle and says to everyone, 'Walk this way.' And he walks like a hunchback, and they all follow him and walk like a hunchback. And of course we were all on the floor laughing, typical slapstick, stupid stuff, but it struck us all as very funny sitting there. And when we got back to the studio, we put up the track and I started . . . it seemed like a natural. I started walking around the control room like the hunchback, doing, like, the hunchback dance, singing, 'Walk this way, walk this way.' And Steven said, 'Wait a minute; I think we got something here.' And about two hours later we were doing that vocal. And that's how that came to be. And you know, he managed to get all those syllables in there. And a few years later in the Bronx, in the very early years of rap, the DJs would use that beat. They would use that intro as the thing that they would rap to. And that's why it became a natural to do the crossover, which we did later. So it was Steven and I. We always crack up—we invented rap. We're the white guys who invented rap."

Remarked Tyler, speaking with Steven Gaines from *Circus Raves* back in 1975, "Joe Perry came up with the basic riff for 'Walk This Way.' I just put some words to it. The band jammed and it worked out like magic. Remember the old make-out parties? Remember the chick who was just a little bit older than you were, and showed you where to put your finger? Well, she showed you 'how to walk.'"

"Walk This Way" is indeed blessed with both a beat and a vocal made for rap, and as Jack alludes to, Aerosmith would collaborate on a new version of the song with Run D.M.C. up into 1986. That more hip-hop version of the song would appear on Run D.M.C.'s landmark *Raising Hell* album of 1986. The record, their third, would go triple platinum, and the song would vault to #4 on the *Billboard* charts. The song, notably through its MTV video, is credited with reigniting Aerosmith's remarkable renaissance to come, a second wind that had gotten off to a rocky start with the bare-bones *Done with Mirrors* album in 1985, their first as part of the band's new deal with Geffen, and a reunion album of sorts.

"Well, those guys had been very influenced by 'Walk This Way,' when they were learning," says Tom. "You know, Steven is a drummer, and he thinks very rhythmically. He's very sophisticated harmonically, but really, where he comes from is rhythm. And so that was a part of our style early on, along with Joey saying, let's learn some James Brown songs. So, we loved the idea of being able to play funk and get away with it, being white guys, and not being laughed at, and know that we were coming across. And so 'Walk This Way' was a demonstration of that, and I just love the irony that that became an influence to these guys in the 'hood and adapting that to what they were doing."

Like "Dream On," the song would be issued as a single twice, first as the album's second single, on August 28, 1975, backed with "Round and Round." A year later and into the cycle for the next album, on November 5, 1976, it would get relaunched, now backed with "Uncle Salty." "Walk This Way" would peak at #10 on the *Billboard* charts but, more importantly, become the band's most perennial staple at radio, with "Dream On" and "Sweet Emotion" getting in line behind it, both with a trace of deep track status. In other words, any given Aerosmith fan is a bit pleasantly surprised when those are played on classic-rock radio, but it's kind of expected of "Walk This Way," sensibly, again, given its ingenious design of platinum hookery, of riff, of rhythm, of verse, and especially of chorus.

Manager Krebs summarizes the ascent at this point, explaining that the breakthrough album for the band was this one. "*Toys in the Attic* had 'Sweet Emotion' and 'Walk This Way.' 'Dream On,' as a single, came off of the first album, and I think made it clear to the high 70s [actually, #59] and fell off the chart. So, Aerosmith was not getting airplay except for Boston. We have a situation where, at a particular moment in time, Aerosmith had sold 45,000 albums, of which 35,000 were in Boston, which was pretty incredible. I always saw 'Dream On' as a great hit, and after 'Walk This Way,' I made, not made, but I convinced Columbia to rerelease 'Dream On,' and it went to #6. So, we're talking about how easily one of the great songs of all time might not have sustained in terms of popularity."

What David is getting at there is that if not for "Walk This Way" becoming such a sensation, there wouldn't have been the good will to suggest a second attempt at pushing "Dream On" and therefore no #6. In my many chats with Krebs over the years, I get the sense that he's a bigger fan of "Dream On" than "Walk This Way."

"Remember, if you're a radio station, you want to be promoting the coolest band in town. So ultimately, radio became a fan of Aerosmith. It was a market-by-market kind of conquest. And in the end, Aerosmith had conquered the whole country."

Unlike the debut, with *Toys in the Attic*, "We opened with a rocker," says David, referring to the singles schedule, one that produced "Sweet Emotion" first, then "Walk This Way," and finally "You See Me Crying." "The sound of AM wasn't suitable for rock; it wasn't high enough quality. In addition, I would think that radio at that time was much more pop. FM radio was the home of Led Zeppelin and all those English bands. Except for the Beatles. They were not getting played on FM radio. It was a perfect fit. That's what the nature of what FM was, to discover new music. AM has always been pop hits."

With "Walk This Way," David says, "We thought it was a hit. I want to make this point. A seminal difference between the '70s and today with rock bands, these bands, when they were beginning, it was so small that nobody looked at them. As I said earlier, we always had a philosophy or theory that we want one hit single every two albums. We did not want to be on AM and pop radio all the time. Now, when you turn to Aerosmith in the '90s, you find that they're getting paid millions per album, so there is tremendous pressure to have four or five hit singles. So there's been a total flip-flop in what you're looking for. And I have always felt that familiarity breeds contempt—out of sight, out of mind is an important thing, if you wish to build mystique, which I still think is one of the major attributes of the bands that are special. I think in today's world, maximum exposure is not enough [laughs]. That's what I sense. The labels now, nobody is thinking long term."

I feel like of all the Aerosmith songs where the drummer should get in on the writing credits, "Walk This Way" would be one of them, although Steven also had a hand in the drumming on this one, being there for an initial jam of it.

Says Joey, "I'm not one of these guys who is obsessed with getting the credit. You know, I do my part. I'm in a band. And being in a band is being part of the team, and whatever you can do to make the team better, you do. You know, if people are interested in separate and individual credits, then that's not the place to be. But as far as songs in particular, specifically, I can't think of any offhand. But there's always stuff and ideas that roll into particular songs that aren't credited to the people that came up with it. The only people that get credit are the people that wrote the chorus and melody of the song."

As for the song's germination, at sound check at that memorable Honolulu, Hawaii, gig supporting the Guess Who, Joe starting messing around with a riff inspired by the Meters, specifically "Cissy Strut" and "People Say." Writing in the key of C, he switched to E and then back to C, and by the end of the sound check, the song was sketched out.

At the lyric end, after the trip to the movie house, Steven wrote the lyrics back at the hotel. But on the way to the studio the next day, he'd left them in the cab, to be lost forever. Once arrived, he grabbed a couple of pencils and scurried off to a stairwell to rewrite them before he forgot them all. But having forgotten to take any paper, he wrote them out on the wall of the top floor of Record Plant and down part of the stairwell, after which he had to go fetch some paper and retranscribe them.

What's additionally satisfying about "Walk This Way" is how it sits squarely within Aerosmith's cumulative style, this idea of being a hard rock band with lots of hook and melody, which, again, the guys all figure was part of the Yardbirds. But it's so incredibly funky and groovy too, with Joey's brilliant beat augmented by cowbell and then danced around, supported by Joe's million-dollar riff.

The next track paints the edges of the canvas but nonetheless also speaks to the evolution of rock 'n' roll, and how it might wind up at Aerosmith, given paths taken at certain decision points along the way. "Big Ten Inch Record" is a cover of a naughty song written by Fred Weismantel and first recorded by Bull Moose Jackson in 1952. It came Aerosmith's way through one Zunk Bunker, who heard it played on Dr. Demento's popular KMET (and elsewhere) radio show, focused on amusing curios through time. It was decided that Aerosmith would cover it but render it faithfully, again illustrating where Chuck Berry boogie-woogie rock 'n' roll came from, along with the R&B and the British blues boom from the '60s and early '70s. Essentially, it's a shuffle, a swinging shuffle.

With horns provided once again by Michael and Randy Brecker, along with Stan Bronstein, again, the song evokes the spirit of Queen, who gave their own history lessons with their regular exquisite constructions that sounded like dance hall songs from the 1920s. Adding further authenticity was the honky-tonk piano work of Scott "Professor Piano" Cushnie, a Canadian who had played with Ronnie Hawkins as part of the Hawks. Like "Toys in the Attic," it also has parallels to *Ted Nugent*, sitting somewhere between that record's oddball "You Make Me Feel Right at Home" and semihit single "Hey Baby," although that sounds more like a mid-temperature *Get Your Wings* track.

Recalls Tom, "Yes! Dr. Demento. We had some friends that lived in California, and they said, 'You've got to hear this Dr. Demento,' and we said, 'Well, we don't get it in Boston.' He played a lot of weird, different kinds of stuff. So they used to make us tapes. And we heard this song, 'Big Ten Inch' by . . . I forget who it was. So we decided to learn it, and it was just a novelty thing, and we just did it for the fun of it. And as we got into the sessions in New York, and we recorded the songs that were sort of our A-list songs, we still had 'Big Ten Inch' and we thought, oh, what the hell, let's put it down. And Jack Douglas had had this friend of his fly in from Canada, Toronto, this guy named Scott Cushnie, who was this blind white guy who was this brilliant honky-tonk, rock 'n' roll piano player. So we cut the song with him playing piano, and it just drove the song. His influence on us, at that moment in the studio, made that song happen. Otherwise, it probably would have just been replaced by something else. But Jack thought, wouldn't it be a great time to have him come and see what he would play, over what we're working on. And I know we were working on it and thinking what the hell is the song about? Some old rhythm-and-blues song. But it just happened to come out so great that the thing just blew up into one of the fan favorites.

"The bass part came to me during *Get Your Wings*," begins Tom, on the immense classic that is "Sweet Emotion," perched dramatically (and sensibly) as the opening track of side 2 of the original vinyl. This is a spot in the song sequence generally saved for the epic of an album that is too self-assured and quietly confident to require the spotlight of side 1, track 1. At least that's how I like to imagine it.

"We were beavering away, and we had all moved back into an apartment together, and it was twenty-four hours a day, get the band together and make a record. And so, I had that bass part, which is the intro to the song. But I wasn't really able to get a lot of attention. So when it came time to do *Toys in the Attic*, I wanted to make sure I had something maybe that was more developed, so that if the moment came up, I can stand up and say, 'Hey, check this out.' So I just worked really hard on coming up with some other parts of the song, like the sections between the verses, the instrumental parts between the verses, where it sort of went into a high-energy type of thing. There was an album by Jeff Beck called *Rough and Ready*, and I just loved the bass playing on it and thought, oh my God, I wish I could play like that. And so, I overcompensated. It was inspired by that, and I came up with those sections between the verses."

"And we recorded the basic tracks for *Toys in the Attic*, finished a day early, and we had a day free," continues Hamilton. "So Jack said, 'Hey, anybody got anything? Let's hear it.' And so, I said, this is it. This is my chance. So I said, 'Yeah, I've got these song ideas.' And so, we put it together and then did the arrangement, and then later Steven wrote those amazing lyrics. That was like wow. So that would've been one of the very last songs we did for the album. And again, it would've been something that never happened. But we had that extra day, and happy to have Jack Douglas producing us, because Jack was very good at making sure that everybody got attention for their ideas."

For Tom, this was definitely a confidence builder.

"Yes, myself, I was a little lacking confidence in my ability, my musicianship and everything. The band was starting to make it, starting to be on the verge of getting really big. So all of a sudden there were people around on the business side, and decisions being made for the sake of business, that I didn't necessarily agree with. But I didn't feel I was up to that challenge. I just wanted to be in my jeans and my T-shirt and playing guitars with my buds; that's what being in a band always meant to me. But at the same time, I wanted to be in a band that made it big. So I wanted to go with it. But then we got to do *Toys in the Attic*, and that was really awesome, together with Jack Douglas, hammering out these arrangements in rehearsal, and then going to the Record Plant in New York City and having a blast recording it."

Again, like "Walk This Way," the guys find a way to be both funky and heavy on this master class in songwriting. Tom's psychedelic parts are there to set up the funky bit—namely, the verse—and then it's back to the textured recline of the chorus. For heavy metal spice, there's the setup to the verses, and here—and throughout, really—is where you can hear Hamilton aspiring to what Clive Chaman was doing on *Rough and Ready*.

"It has a heavy aspect," agrees Tom. "It has big guitar riffs and drum parts, and you've got the verses, which are kind of like angry or sarcastic sounding. And then you had this very sweet thing, with this intro that actually starts on the bass. That's how I wrote the song, originally. I had no idea back then what made it sound so delicious, but I think I could probably analyze it a little bit better now. The notes that make up that part are the simple basics of the chord. They are the notes in a chord that everybody loves to hear. It just feels good to hear it. And so, you combine that melodic aspect with sort of the anger and the intensity of the other parts, and you can hear this texture. It's like crunching on the outside of the creamy center [laughs]. Really, the texture of it is what it's about for me.

"Because, you know, when I was listening to the Who, when *Tommy* came on, or *Live at Leeds*, what I was really focusing on was the texture and the intensity. My playing, my actual chops, were pretty crude back then, and maybe it's because I wanted to be a good instrumentalist. But the main thing I think I was going for was how it felt to hear certain notes. If something is made up of very simple elements, that was fine with me."

Said Steven back in '75 about the lyrics, "It's about how much pain you put out for the joy of it all. About life on the road, good reviews and bad reviews. The chorus screams for the sweet emotion of it all, but the verses get into the debts."

Helping elevate the track's arrangement is the use of bass marimba, played by engineer Jay Messina and doubled. Jack also appreciated how Joey inverted the beat, calling the rhythmic feel of the song "magic." There's also the overt use of talk box, an ear candy hook that helped perk the ears of prospective radio listeners. This was done by Joe, using a now-discontinued device called The Bag, made by Kustom Electronics. Because there were no maracas available, Steven shakes some packets of sugar, while he also plays some vibraslap.

As far as Kramer goes, there's an element of playing behind the beat to this one, with his spare fills coming a millisecond late, and the surging effect accentuated by the opening and closing of the high hat. The actual reversing that Jack is talking about comes with the circular riff with no vocals, where Joey's whacking the snare on one and three, then collapsing back into his deep, Stonesy groove as this section ends. Further painting the corners rhythmically is the use of shakers, triangle, and reverse recording, the latter resulting in an infectious whoosh sound, also (and only) on the reversed bit.

As Tom told Alan DiPerna, "Steven had the idea of taking that intro riff, which became the chorus bass line under the 'Sweet emotion' part, and transposing it into the key of E and making it a really heavy Zeppelinesque thing." Counter or additional to the above quote, Steven's lyric is considered, in part, a subtle dig at Joe Perry's wife, Elyssa, who had been causing problems.

"Remember, we didn't know how to end it," adds Tyler. "We got into a big fight, blew [cocaine] all over the place. It was late, and we were at the end of our rope. Finally, I said, 'Just fucking play a drum fill, and we'll go into [sings outro riff].' And we did it. It was such a magical moment."

Indeed, this "false ending" closing section, a full minute of the totality, is so detached that it sounds like a new song. Essentially, it's a jam, a vehicle for guitar soloing, but also rhythmically complex, with a strange shuffling thing going on with the high hat, perhaps mixed with some shakers. Then they end the song for real, using a lengthy slow fade. Again, it adds to the complexity and element of surprise we experience regularly across the album.

Says Joe, "We knew it would be killer live—a showstopper. So then the fucking record company gets it, and they say, 'What can we maul to get this on the radio?' You listen to the single version of 'Sweet Emotion' and it's pretty chopped up. They edited it down to just the melodic element. But that's how it was done back then."

Shortened or not, the song was picked for lead single, after which it worked its way to #36, making it the band's first Top 40 placement.

"Yeah, it was amazing," continues Perry. "And we didn't get that, really until our third album. That's when 'Dream On' became a hit, from our first album. So, all at once, the whole thing just gave way, and we were this big band. And a lot of it was that by the time we did our third album, our confidence in the studio and our knowledge of how the studio works was so far beyond when we did our first record. If you listen to the difference in the production, between the first and the third album, that's not a very long time, but things were progressing so fast then, and *Toys in the Attic* just reflected that. And it reflected our new relationship with Jack Douglas, who was our producer, our mentor, and our coach. Here was a guy who was totally there for everybody's ideas, no matter how strange or off-the-wall. And we would try stuff that was really off the beaten path, and it would work and become a cool sound to use on the record. Yeah, he loved to do that."

The single issue of the song was backed with "Uncle Salty," meaning that nobody was thinking the B side was ever going to overshadow the A side. In this format, "Sweet Emotion" is only 3:09, knocking a minute and a half off the album version. Gone are the intro and the guitar solo section at the end. Credit to modern radio, the single edit is rarely heard anymore, replaced by the majestic slow burn of the album version.

"No, I don't see that," answers Tom, when I suggest that "No More No More" is one of the Stonesiest songs the band has ever done. "That's interesting, because if I listened to it now, I would probably hear it. But no, that's not where that song is from. That's a close relative to 'Seasons of Wither,' because it starts with a really nice arpeggio based on a detuned guitar. And for me, that pulls me right in, because I love music that chimes and drones and has percussion in it. So that riff, it starts the song, where Steven was playing in his room, when I remember him starting to work on that."

Noted Brad about "No More No More," "Songs like that came about through long hours of the writing process [laughs]. We'd just all get in a room, and it starts off with a riff or something, and we'd just bang it out from there. It happened to be a great rock anthem. I love playing it."

As Joe remarked in the *Pandora's Box* liner notes, "I still love the song because of Steve's lyrics. It's not one of those stupid, generic 'I love rock 'n' roll songs' that some bands do. It's a real song about the rock 'n' roll lifestyle, or our rock 'n' roll lifestyle. I don't know if it's the definitive song about life on the road, and I don't even care. It's like a page from our diary." Seconds Brad, "This is one of the songs I really liked where Steven does his little storytelling bit about life within the band. It's him talking honestly about an interesting slice of the Aerosmith story."

Remarked Tyler, to Steven Gaines, "It's basically about life on the road. Sometimes I start thinking about having a wife and child, but the group is my carriage pulling me right along, so I have no time for that now. Maybe we'll be tremendous one day. If the way the crowds are reacting is any indication, that could be happening now. We play well, don't wear glitter to detract and hide, and put on a good visual show. We play our asses off every night, and we sound like it too."

As usual, Steven packs so much imagery into short lines, and also, as will be a growing theme throughout the catalog, the story that Steven tells of the band is one of trying to please both the girls and the boys. In between, there's the aspiration and the exhaustion, all wrapped up in a line like "Never get a second chance / For the dance to the top of the hill."

Two clichés come to mind: "sex, drugs, and rock 'n' roll" and "born to rock." It's like Steven has three hobbies he's excited about: rock 'n' roll, sex, and drugs, foremost being the curse of committed communion with the arts, at the expense of cultivating family and friendships. It's too bad, too sad, but nobody ever talked about Steven as being a really nice guy, and then at various levels and for various reasons, there was an element of that with everybody else in the band, with second place definitely going to Joe. To be sure, in later years it was in large part due to how devious heroin makes you. But all along, again, it's like these guys were born to rock, tunnel vision, one mission, no time for being considerate. When there's only twenty-four hours in a day, there's not much time for anybody else's needs. Credit to them, though; they loved the job so much, and they so dearly wanted to make good records, with the respect of their peers foremost in mind and not just pleasing the casual listener.

Muses David, "They definitely were fans of rock 'n' roll. Were they fans of anything beyond that? I'm not sure. My recollection, in terms of those days, keep in mind this: I don't think there were any college graduates in Aerosmith, for example. So therefore, in terms of discussions where it would be all of us or I would be with one or the other, it's about music, it's about rock 'n' roll or the competition; it was about that. We didn't sit down and talk to the members of Aerosmith about the economy."

That "born to rock" pathway is baked into the way the guys would tell their grim origin stories. Also, in the interview with Steven Gaines, Joe explains that his first guitar was a $14 Sears Silvertone, because "they were so cheap, that's what your mother would buy you when she really wanted you to be a doctor. Parents are never sympathetic to a rock career. They just want you to go to school. They don't want to know about musicians.

"I never fit in with anybody," Perry continues. "I never had any friends; my grades were always terrible. The few things I liked, I did all right in; I just hated school. My parents decided they would try to do something to get me into college. So, they stuck me in a prep school, where I really got flipped out. That's when I was first exposed to a lot of weirdos, you know, New York weirdos. I started to really hate the system at prep school. Every time I picked up the guitar, people would yell at me. They wanted me to cut my hair, but I kept it as long as it could be. I learned all the tricks. You don't wash it for three weeks, put Brylcreem on it, and stick it under your collar. On the weekends, when I went home, I would wash it. I quit prep school with only a month to go to graduation. At my parents' insistence, I reregistered into my hometown high school, but the principal insisted I cut my hair, and I never graduated."

Then, in an amusing parallel with what they say about the forging of hard rock in Detroit and Birmingham, England (i.e., how steel factories helped cause this music), Joe took a job at a foundry.

"I had to deal with all the redneck greasers who worked there. They really gave me a lot of trouble. Nobody spoke English, and the only people who worked there were people who couldn't find any other job. It was a jungle of red-hot steel and sand. Every day after work, I would blow my nose, and the dirt I had been breathing into my lungs all day would come pouring out. My hair was constantly filled with sand. I spent two years in that horror show."

In the same article, relating a famous early-days incident, Steven says, "I was going to Yonkers, and they put a narc in ceramics class. He sold grass to 12 kids in school and then busted us. We made the front page of the local newspaper, and I was thrown out of school."

The following year, Brad told Stephen Demorest, "I went to Berklee College of Music for a year. It taught me a lot, but there were too many musicians there. Everybody had their own ideas, and finally I said, 'No more.' I think it's really good for you to work in the clubs and just play five or six sets a night. I went out to play, and then I met these guys."

Like I say, born to rock.

Back to the album, I can still picture the Stones playing "No More No More," with Mick and Keith crowded around one microphone singing a lyric that I can envisage as one of Mick's as well. The connection is underscored by the return of Scott Cushnie on pumping Jerry Lee Lewis—or Ian Stewart, or Nicky Hopkins—piano, as well as the massaging in of acoustics with electrics. Apparently, the version we hear on the album comes from a single take, specifically the eighth jamming of the song.

"Just a great riff that Brad came up with," says Tom, asked about "Round and Round." "We did a lot of that stuff tuned down a half step. I don't know, maybe I'm thinking more of *Rocks*. But I'm thinking we did it on *Toys in the Attic* too, just to get at more weight. Brad came up with these great parts, and it really represented something menacing and heavy. And that's where Jack came in, as a producer, with some of the really neat overdubs that are on there. There was one point where Brad is doing like this guitar part that was an ascending part, where the guitar just keeps going up and up, up and up, a half step at a time. And I'm thinking, my God, he's so far up the neck, how is he ever going to keep going? So we recorded that part, and Jack had the idea of putting his amps out in the back stairway to the studio. So being out there, it was outside of the soundproofing of the studio, and the whole frigging neighborhood was complaining about, you know, lead guitar booming out, on that particular block in New York City. Yeah, it's right at the end. It's in the end, and it's maybe not really out front, but if you listen, it's there. You'll hear it going up, you know, one note at a time, just building so much tension."

What's interesting is that it's arguably weirder hearing Aerosmith do doom metal than it is purist swing jazz like "Big Ten Inch Record." Again, it's like hearing Queen roll like a tank through "Son and Daughter" from the first record or "I'm in Love with My Car" from *A Night at the Opera*. We talked about "Toys in the Attic" being the heaviest Aerosmith song to date, but of course this is the downright weightiest and most Sabbath-like, in other words, heavy of a different nature, and not so much like "Hard Loving Man" or "Burn." Additionally, with respect to the way we've already talked about Queen, here we are late in the album, and Aerosmith is turning in a song wildly left field, widening the palette much further. Might there also be a harkening back to the huskier, lower-register singing that Steven rued circa the debut? Truth be told, despite the heavy metal heft of this song, there's a connection to the blues similar to that of "Dazed and Confused," "How Many More Times," "Heartbreaker," and "When the Levee Breaks," even "Whipping Post."

At the lyric end, that hint of rock 'n' roll exasperation permeating the previous song has turned into full-blown crisis here. Already the character—essentially Steven autobiographically in both songs and speaking for the whole band—is decrying how the dizzying lifestyle has corrupted him, and how what was once fun has him now going round and round. Having to deal with the business end of things—and increasingly hung over and coming down while doing it—results in a song with the same harrowing bad vibes as Black Sabbath's *Sabotage* album, also issued in 1975.

Continuing with our arguably unwarranted comparisons with the *Ted Nugent* album, I also saw "Round and Round" as this record's "Stranglehold." And while we're at it, "Adam's Apple," No More No More," "Just What the Doctor Ordered," "Snakeskin Cowboys," "Where Have You Been All My Life," and "Queen of the Forest" all sound like *Get Your Wings* songs.

Toys in the Attic closes with "You See Me Crying," which is closer to the blueprint of the power ballad—as well as the Aerosmith power ballad—than was "Dream On," given that song's twists and turns and fulminations. One would have thought it was a natural to become a smash hit upon issue on November 11, 1975, following the success of two rock tracks as singles, but it didn't quite catch on. Like "Sweet Emotion," it was heavily edited for wider consumption, losing two minutes. On the B side was the ferocious title track, which just might be played more often on classic-rock radio these days than the polite and perfectly palatable "You See Me Crying."

The song features heavily arranged orchestration, suggested by Jack Douglas and conducted by Mike Mainieri. It's something Bob Ezrin would become famous for, moving forward into Kiss, on *Destroyer*, and solo-era Alice Cooper, beginning with *Welcome to My Nightmare*. Like "Woman of the World," this was a cowrite between Steven and his old Chain Reaction bandmate Don Solomon. Brad takes the two main guitar solos instead of Joe (who does the middle piece), and by all accounts it was a difficult, time-consuming song to put together. Yet again, and way up into the end of the album, Aerosmith adds yet another track that widens the palette, making for a greatly varied album in the spirit of Queen or the band's heroes, Led Zeppelin.

"The world hardly stood up and recognized Aerosmith when it came out with its first album a couple [of] years ago," writes Joseph Bensoua, providing context in his review of the album. "But East Coast rockers like Blue Öyster Cult and J. Geils Band have a way of catching fire once given a chance. But when Aerosmith first came out, it was on fire. The East Coast knew it. All people had to do was listen. Although Aerosmith is hardly the type whose brazen hard rock would receive a lot of airplay, its first hit, 'Dream On,' helped open the door to radio.

"Word soon spread of a hard-hitting band which had as much rock to offer as it had roll. With the Boston group's second album, *Get Your Wings*, the rock world was ready to admit it had a new power to contend with. Recently, that album went gold. Not bad for a group who, only prior to receiving a recording contract, couldn't pay $50 a month rent on a practice hall, was three months overdue on house rent and surviving on rice and beans. Now, Aerosmith has its third album out, *Toys in the Attic*. As great as its other albums are, its latest is the best by far.

"Just when you think you've heard it all before," continues Bensoua, "Aerosmith's music comes out like it's been shot out of a cannon. Its highly imaginative rock 'n' roll carries on its powerful tradition of boogie rock without the frills or pretentiousness. Its scores are highlighted by the dual guitar artistry of Joe Perry and Brad Whitford and the strong vocals of Steve Tyler. If you ever tire of rock 'n' roll, just listen to Aerosmith. The band has a way of revitalizing the whole scene. They're to rock 'n' roll what Joe Louis'[s] one-two combination was to boxing. There's no fooling around. Put on their album, listen to 'Adam's Apple,' 'Uncle Salty,' 'Walk This Way' or 'Sweet Emotion,' and by all means, hang on to something. They'll blow you right out of the room if you don't."

Writes Chris Welch in *Melody Maker*, in a review that finds the legendary scribe continuing to look on curiously from afar, "Aerosmith bring hope from America. They're not a new Steely Dan or even yet another variation on the Doobie Brothers, yet they are most people's idea of what a good rocking band should be. Probably the key to their growing success, they're not attempting to lay anything on us, but have an energetic, refreshing approach to music-making with their roots in the British group sound of the '60s, but with modern refinements. Listen to the contrasting beats and heavy rock of the tongue-twisting 'Walk This Way,' where new star vocalist Steven Tyler chicken-walks against the howling guitars of Joe Perry and Brad Whitford.

"Aerosmith know just how much to give away, so that as Joe and Brad begin to heat up their solos, the engineering department cheerfully fades them out. But to begin though, there is no denying the similarity between opening track 'Toys in the Attic' and a certain Led Zeppelin riff—the day bands stop copping licks from each other, the pyramids will reveal their secrets. 'Toys' is a fast-jumping tune with Steve employing one of his favorite devices, unison singing with Joe Perry's lead. And Joey Kramer's drums have a simple bounce, all cymbal and clipped snare drum that typify British rock drumming before the age of super-heaviness."

After going through a few more tracks, he continues with "If I gave the impression Aerosmith ain't heavy here, the powerhouse playing is real equipment-wrecking stuff. 'No More No More' has a lot of minor chords and is less destructive, while 'Round and Round' has Steve yelling in throaty mood over Joey's rock-steady pulse with the bass drum souped-up to Bonham-ish proportions. Lots of echo on the guitar and despite further Zeppelin influence, it's a titanic performance designed to move mountains and mass audiences.

"'You See Me Crying' is a ballad vehicle for Steve, who shows just how many styles he can encompass and how much vocal technique he has at his disposal. An orchestra is added, which rather devalues the Aerosmith concept, and the piece obviously hints at some future Steve Tyler solo album. I hope the band does not race ahead too fast before their three albums receive proper appreciation here. It would be nice when Aerosmith come to Britain, if they played a few small gigs like the Marquee and Friars Club, rather than launch immediately into concerts. It would give a chance to establish contact with their potential audience here. And if their albums are just half representative, they have a lot to give."

As additional context, it's worth noting that just as *Toys in the Attic* was appearing on store shelves, Blue Öyster Cult had just issued their double live album *On Your Feet or on Your Knees*. They were a New York band going places, and Jack Douglas would engineer the live album.

Not an accident, says BÖC's Albert Bouchard. "One of the things that helped Aerosmith was that they had a great sound, and I think Jack Douglas had a lot to do with that. But I also think that they had an awesome work ethic. They really worked hard, and, I mean, they just got better and better up until *Toys in the Attic*. Each record, to me, is better in leaps and bounds than the one before it. Our live album was around the time when Aerosmith was coming out, and we heard Jack Douglas, Aerosmith's sound, and we said, well, we have to get Jack Douglas to mix the next record, which was *On Your Feet or on Your Knees*. And I don't know if you can tell, but the sound actually changed at that point. And then the material changed for *Agents of Fortune*."

Adds brother Joe, "I mean, we were always sort of jealous of Aerosmith's success. Because we would go platinum and they would go double platinum. They were always like twice ahead of us. But there's probably other reasons for that. You know, they made nice records, and Steven happens to be an inspired singer."

Also, as context, in 1975, both Deep Purple and Uriah Heep were falling to pieces, and Black Sabbath hadn't issued an album since 1973, although *Sabotage* was just around the corner. Kiss had just put out *Dressed to Kill* and a buzz was building, while the New York Dolls were gone. Super-important, Led Zeppelin had just issued their masterful double album, *Physical Graffiti*, and their Swan Song label mates Bad Company had just put out *Straight Shooter*. From Canada, Rush was on the ascendance with *Fly by Night*. Alice Cooper had just gone solo, issuing *Welcome To My Nightmare*. Besides Aerosmith, April 1975 would also see records from ZZ Top, Nazareth, Journey, Bob Seger, and Black Oak Arkansas. There'd be no Stones album this year, but the Who would follow up *Quadrophenia* with *The Who by Numbers*, and Ted

Nugent, a Leber Krebs act, would issue his hit first solo album in 1975. If there's a trend there, it's the waning of British hard rock and the ascendance of bands from America.

Toys in the Attic would rise to a lofty #11 on the *Billboard* charts and certify gold on August 11, 1975, en route to its astounding current counting at nine-times platinum, very much achieved by the high rotation of two hit songs over the years (and only moderate hits at the time) and not much else, although a record that big is bound to produce other radio songs, with the title track and "No More No More" seeing some on-air consideration throughout the ensuing decades.

Hitting the road, Aerosmith were now headliners, with Rush opening a lot of shows, as well as Kansas. Late in the year, both Slade and Mott (i.e., without Ian Hunter) played warm-up in the Northeast. They also supported for ZZ Top and for Bachman-Turner Overdrive. They finally got to Canada, but still there was no excursion to Europe. Toward the end of the year, that new Leber Krebs act we talked about, Ted Nugent, started supporting. Soon he'd be as big a deal as Aerosmith.

"Well, we did a lot of touring together," says Brad. "We just happened to be a great package, Aerosmith and Ted Nugent on the same bill. That's really how they presented it. And that's how Derek [St. Holmes] and I met. I wouldn't say there was any competition. It was two different approaches to the same thing, and it certainly helped both of us."

4
Rocks

"Every part of it would be true to itself."

"Even to this day, somewhere off in the distance is the magic that made the old stuff so good."

Says Tom, as frustrated as I am with the overthinking of modern-day Aerosmith records: "That's always there. It's always implied but seemingly unattainable. We want to hear a record that sounds like a *Rocks* or a *Toys in the Attic*—that's Aerosmith. You know what? Those records defined this band. Obviously, we have our years where we've had the hit singles and did a lot of music that sat outside of what we were known for. But if you come to an Aerosmith show, it all goes together as a hard rock show. Onstage is where gravity takes us to where we really are, and I think when we play, we rock out."

Adds Joey, "*Rocks* was one of those records we did with Jack, and we were doing a lot of experimenting. Brad and I and Tom did an extreme amount of drilling for that record as far as getting down the arrangements. We recorded that at our own warehouse and brought in a mobile truck from the Record Plant. We had a lot of fun doing that record, a lot of practical joking, lots of kidding around, lots of laughs. And that's why that record came out that way, because we had a good time doing it. When you have a good time doing it, and it's not work, it always comes out great."

Indeed, the team shook up the process for *Rocks*, recording at the Wherehouse in Waltham, Massachusetts, with a Record Plant remote backed up to the band's spacious facility. As Kramer alludes to, the guys were in good spirits. Each of the first three albums had certified gold, and *Toys in the Attic* would have surely been awarded platinum, had such a thing existed—1976 would change that, with platinum being invented in that year, and diamond to follow in 1999.

Speaking with *Circus* back in 1975, Tom was enthusiastic about the making of the new album, framing it as a new era of sorts after a three-month sabbatical.

Calling it "a complete turnover of the band's repertoire," Hamilton says, "We want to develop a new generation of Aerosmith material. We haven't had the time to get off the road and do that for ages and ages. Everybody's got little things that they've been fooling around with and maybe not showing them to other people. It's amazing how a little idea can start in the morning, and as we start jamming, all of a sudden, a new tune comes together.

"I hope we can record enough material for two albums," says Tom (egregiously erroneously, as it turns out!). "That's what I'd really like to do. That would give us more time for the road. One thing that we've really never been noticed for is that our material is pretty diversified. We can deliver drivers like 'Toys in the Attic,' but then we do something like 'You See Me Crying' and we're pretty good at doing R&B, like 'Big Ten Inch.' It's just a matter of staying within certain stylistic guidelines."

Contradictory about where it's going, Tom says he feels "pretty strongly" that the next record will be heavier than *Toys in the Attic*, "but it's going to show the same kind of diversified material. I think that's the personality that's going to emerge from Aerosmith, is going to be one that people can't so readily identify with being heavy metal, that power chord connotation. We're going to be more R&B, more of the classical elements, like the blues beats, although it's not going to be a blues album."

Also something they wouldn't get around to: "I'd like to do something this year, put together some kind of relationship between us and the Bicentennial, try to stimulate kids into realizing where they live. They've got to realize more about the world they live in. It's sad, but it seems that it's unfashionable to have any kind of national pride. I'd like to see Aerosmith, as an American band, be able to do something to turn those kids back toward being proud of where they live."

"The mission with *Rocks* was to capture exactly what was going on with the band at the time," says Jack, with the benefit of hindsight (unlike Tom above). "And to create a record that sounded like every word . . . that the sound of the record and the chords in the record and the harmonic structure and the lyric all met each other and were all—in today's vernacular—on the same page. For it to be one thing that sounded like it was one thing, and not that each song sounded the same but that each song, every part of it, would be true to itself.

"And so in doing that, we ended up working in the Wherehouse up in Waltham, Massachusetts for . . . and it was going to be a very, very long . . . I think it was a two-and-a-half-month preproduction, working on these songs. By now the band was so busy on the road that they would come to preproduction with a song and it would just be one lick. That would be the song, and we would have to build it from there, But every day—and this was a big warehouse—we would set up in there in a really cool way, where the amps were and the drums were. Every day I would go in there before the band, and I would do something to make the room sound better—hang a rug somewhere, put a ladder in the middle of the room with a big drape hanging off it. I would treat this, treat that, put some pillows somewhere. Every day for two and a half months, I was doing something to that room.

"And what was happening, as we were doing this, the writing was being affected by the environment we were working in. Certain chords, structures, and things were sounding good in there because of the way the room was sounding. And so when it came time to actually record the album, I knew I wasn't going to leave the Wherehouse. And keeping true to everything, I just brought a truck in and recorded it the way it sounded there. And I think that's why . . . drugs weren't a problem yet, but drugs were part of the picture. But I think that's why it all worked out so well. It's really my favorite album."

But you have to picture recording the album in the dead of a Northeastern winter. They got it as comfortable as they could, with the road crew fashioning a tent around the truck, which managed to keep it warm. Inside was a DeMideo console and a couple of sixteen-track machines. Outside and into the band's clubhouse was a lot of cement, which made for booming sound captures. And the brief really was, beyond the loftier and more obscure philosophy laid out so eloquently by Jack, that this would be a harder rockin' record than the last.

Which fit the spirit of the times. I mean, even Columbia was on board, when famously, in the beginning upon signing, the band was skeptical they'd found the right home.

"Well, let's see; let's take a look at who was running the ship there," ponders Jack. "We had Walter Yetnikoff [Of note, Clive Davis was ousted amid a financial scandal, shortly after signing Aerosmith]. The thing with hard rock was, in the '70s, hard rock was the money-making machine. And Columbia and Atlantic were the most aggressive at signing hard rock bands. Atlantic came to the table a little later because they were basically an R&B label, but Columbia I think was the most pop label, and by pop I mean popular music and whatever would sell. But the thing was, during that time, the label was considered the enemy. The establishment. And the producers who were not A&R men were considered part of the band, or with the band. So there were two sides. There was always the label, who wanted to do things their way, and the artist and producer, who were trying to protect what they were doing and felt what they were doing was precious and right. So what went on at the label internally, we had very little insight. They considered us pretty much the enemy too."

But to reinforce, Columbia, along with sister situation Epic Records, was having a good time of it with hard rock. Columbia had Aerosmith and Blue Öyster Cult, and now a new baby band in Leber Krebs artists Rex. Epic had Ted Nugent, Cheap Trick, and their own baby band in Ram Jam, whose ferocious second album, 1978's *Portrait of the Artist as a Young Ram*, was expressly made that way to compete nose to nose with Aerosmith.

Blue Sky Records, a subimprint of Columbia, had Derringer, who, again, soon had a second record, 1977's *Sweet Evil*, which sounds like

Aerosmith (while Rex sounded like Aerosmith too, very much so, on both their albums). In fact, *Sweet Evil* plays, in its funky heavy metal totality, very much like a lost Aerosmith album, which makes sense, because it was recorded at Record Plant and produced by Jack Douglas.

But that's one thing with Aerosmith: Despite lots of garish goings-on and scandalous stories because of drugs, the tight relationship between managers David Krebs and Steve Leber and the label, just down the street, meant that relations with Columbia didn't throw up the usual amount of roadblocks—and *Rocks* was going to make them just that much happier.

They weren't above spending either. To commemorate the first three albums going gold, Columbia put together a promotional box with all three albums in it called *Pure Gold from Rock and Roll's Golden Boys*, which was then given to supporters from the industry who had pushed the rereleased "Dream On" and kept *Toys in the Attic* in the charts.

A signed cover letter written by Columbia sales manager George H. Ryan, dated March 1976 and included with the package, reads as follows: "Just three short years ago, a local rock band came onto the scene anxious to impress record-buyers, radio-listeners, concert-goers, and everyone else in our area with their unique style of music and presentation. Of course they aspired to national recognition eventually but at the beginning they had to make a significant impact in their home market first.

"*You* took Aerosmith into your own personal world of radio, records and print and launched a super group that has conquered audiences not only here in this country but now all over the world! All three of their Columbia albums have been certified gold! *Toys in the Attic* is now over 800,000 pieces nationally and is headed for 'platinum' (one million units)!

"We have packaged their albums in a special gold box to present to you as a small token of our appreciation for the important part that you played in helping us to establish Aerosmith as 'rock and roll's golden boys.' Their new album will be ready for release very soon and we're confident that it won't take long for it to go gold just as the rest of their catalogue has."

For the *Rocks* album cover, Columbia went with a classy shot of five diamonds. Diamonds are called rocks, hard drugs can come in rocks—Chinese rocks, as Johnny Thunders might say—and Aerosmith "rocks." In fact, all of this is telegraphed by the placement of the title in double quote marks, which is usually ignored when talking about the album, myself included.

In his autobiography, Joe wrote that the purpose of this album "was to re-identify us as America's ultimate garage band, with blistering guitars, blistering vocals, balls-to-the-wall smash-your-eardrums production. The cover showed five diamonds, one for each of us. We saw that record as a jewel, the culmination of all our angst and anger and excitement and joy as go-for-broke rock and rollers." Perry's line about "five diamonds, one for each of us," is also manifested in the idea that the band considered calling the album *Aerosmith Five*, even when they were on only their fourth album.

At the tactile end, the original cover was textured and embossed. Included was an inner sleeve featuring a cartoony illustration of the guys playing live, with big heads and skinny bodies. This was done by a friend of the band named Teresa Stokes. There was an earlier version that was lost in a fire, but Steven insisted she redo it. The plan was to use it as a backdrop on tour, but then Steven decided he didn't like it. Instead, they'd go with a simple logo, which somehow managed to look kind of evil, making the stage look like an opium den. Everywhere we saw song titles and credits on the album, the regal feel of the front cover was maintained. Everything about the front and back covers of *Rocks* looked important, like we should be treating the enclosed music with respect.

Opening the album is "Back in the Saddle," which was also suggested as a title for the record. It's a well-worn phrase, and a catchy one to use as a title, gaining popularity in a musical sense first through Gene Autry and his old-school country-and-western hit song with that title.

When asked by Alan DiPerna why he played six-string bass on the song, Joe Perry responded that "one of my favorite guitar players—Peter Green—used to play one. I don't think he ever did a solo with one on record. But he would, live. In the middle of the song, they'd just do this little segue with him playing six-string bass. So in the back of my mind, I always thought that was a cool thing. So I found a six-string bass and started playing it. I liked the way it sounded."

Speaking with *Circus* back in 1976, Joe remarked that "Jack Bruce used to use one, but it's kind of hard. The strings are halfway between bass and regular guitar, and you can get some really flipped[-]out sounds out of it. I'm going to use it on stage."

"I was very high on heroin when I wrote 'Back in the Saddle,'" continues Perry, back to the DiPerna chat. "That riff just floated right through me. Drugs can be a shortcut to creativity. All throughout history, medicine men and priests in all those primitive cultures used drugs to get to that spirit place. Ask any writer. You get to that place where your fingers are flying on the keyboard; you know, the stuff is just flowing through you. But for a lot of writers, getting to that uninhibited place is difficult. So it's a shortcut just to have a beer. And it works for a while. But then you reach a point where it takes two beers to get there, then three. And after a while, it's not working for you anymore, and your liver's going, and the doctor is saying, 'If you drink anymore, your nose is going to turn into a cauliflower.' That's just us excessive bastards, you know. But with all the drugs, you burn out on them, for different reasons. With heroin, your body just caves in. After a while, all you care about is getting that buzz. Then you don't care about picking up a guitar. So it ends up blocking your creativity rather than helping it."

And true to form, making *Rocks* was just a little more blocked because of drug use than *Toys in the Attic* was. The creativity came, and it was wonderful, but it was a tougher process, most notably in terms of getting lyrics out of Steven, which actually delayed the finishing and subsequent release of the album. After the Wherehouse sessions, the team moved over to Record Plant for overdubs and vocals, which of course required getting lyrics out of Steven. Jack says that he and Steven would rent living quarters together for this process, with Jack kick-starting Steven's morning with a coffee and a cassette, telling him to start writing.

Jack admits that drugs were a problem, but he's also adamant that they were encouraged by the label, with a rep actually delivering them. He says the label thought if they could keep the band gacked on coke, they'd deliver the album faster. Eventually it became a scandal, and people were fired over it.

Tyler's lyric for this opening track is all about a cowboy's hankering for (paid) sex after working the mother lode, but metaphorically, it's about being back in the saddle, spurs on, ready to tackle the next record and tour cycle. As Joe alludes to, he's playing six-string bass (a Fender

Bass VI) on the song, but it was also written on the instrument. In fact, the closest thing to a riff on the song is played on the Fender Bass VI. It's heard in the chorus, and the chorus starts the song—that is, after a dramatic and ascending intro, which features horse hooves clopping like the cavalry arriving to announce the coming of *Rocks*.

Once we get to the verses, we're into something more like a Stones weave, a song built of fabrics one laid upon the next. Think "Bitch" or "Jumping Jack Flash," which are riffy for the Stones, but then again, the Stones get only so riffy. It's Brad who plays lead guitar on this one, taking the solo as we move toward the conclusion, when the trotting returns as well as yelps and cracking of the whip. The guys spent hours trying to get an actual whip to crack, but in the end, defeated, they wound up using a 30-foot electrical cord combined with shots from a cap gun. The hoofbeats came from Steven banging coconuts together, and the spurs were tambourines and bells stuck on Steven's boots by David Johansen and Joe Perry. Tyler has said that he wanted the song redolent with nostalgia, like his memories of "spaghetti" westerns. Additionally, the song is considered one of the most extreme within the catalog with respect to Steven's vocals, featuring a number of throat-shredding screams.

"Back in the Saddle" would be issued as the third and final single from the album, on March 22, 1977, backed with "Nobody's Fault" from further up the album. The first single, "Last Child," didn't do much (reaching #21), and nor did the second single, "Home Tonight," which stalled at #71, representing a second shot at following "Dream On" that went kaput. "Back in the Saddle" continued the moribund results, reaching only #38. However, over time, it's become one of the most important and celebrated of Aerosmith tracks, a perennial live favorite and the most regularly visited song from the album on classic-rock radio. It is indeed the representative composition on *Rocks*, now fifty years old, and therefore the most redolent in terms of nostalgia. In that respect, Steven got his wish, only now the nostalgia factor inside the song is experienced by aging Aerosmith fans.

"Off of that, it's funny, they played 'Back in the Saddle,'" recalls Jack. "That was the big one in terms of airplay. There were stations that we lived or died by in Detroit and Boston and New York. And they really loved radio, and they loved the deejays, and you made sure that they kept a good relationship with everyone there, their staff. They made sure that when they came into town that everybody there got tickets and merch, and that people were up at the station. Radio for us was our lifeblood. If you didn't get radio play, you weren't going to sell, and really radio was everything. Before MTV, it was everything." And as discussed, many Aerosmith songs enjoyed a second life through the concept of classic rock, especially at radio. "Yes," says Jack. They went away and now they're back, classic-rock radio stations. I still hear just tons of our stuff."

Also, crucially in dalliance with radio would be our second track, "Last Child," which was issued as the first single on May 27, 1976, backed with "Combination." It's a cowrite between Steven and Brad, with Whitford explaining that "'Last Child' just grew out of the end of a rehearsal day. Everybody had split from rehearsal except me and Steven. I started to come up with the basic skeleton of that song, and he sat down and started to play the drums until we had sort of a lock on it. And that was it; we pretty much had it right away. And then Steven came up with those great lyrics. Sometimes they just come out like that." Adds Tom, "I remember putting it together at the Wherehouse. It was a big room with a high ceiling. We hung up all these drapes. We were basically like a bunch of kids building forts."

Suitably, Brad plays the solo on the song, and Steven even credits Brad with the lyrical hook, both the "Take me back to sweet Tallahassee" and the "Home sweet home" bits. All told, it's a paean to country life, with the character burnt out by city life and wishing for all the comforts of home sweet home. As discussed earlier, the guys indeed were not exclusively city folk.

Steven had high hopes for the song, thinking it might be some sort of a disco hit "played everywhere." In actuality, it's more like slow funk rock, with some semblance of that genre's chirping or "chicken scratch" guitaring. Helping frame Aerosmith as a hard rock band, when it comes to the prechorus, they go heavy and not pop or more purist funk. It might seem like an obscure point, but you can compare all these '70s bands and look for which way they turn from a verse. With Aerosmith, the math churns out more heavy turns, especially if they've delivered something dangerously light for a verse. And case in point, the new music behind the solo section is also more of a grinding hard rock thing than the verse. Apparently, Paul Prestopino plays some banjo on the song, although I couldn't find it, other than a hint of a trace of a semblance for a few seconds at the 2:33 mark and again at 2:45. It also might be doubling the verse riff.

Remarks Jack on "Last Child," "Yeah, it was tried as a single, absolutely, because they thought it was the follow-up to 'Walk This Way.' Because it was funky. But it was really 'Back in the Saddle' that got the play. It was the most infectious song on the album."

Actually, I've always had it in for both of these songs. I've never been a fan of the chords in "Back in the Saddle" and their part in its ascending structure, or even that bass riff, which sounds like something out of a Gene Simmons song in the '80s. I feel like the familiarity of the intro music plus the sound effects went a long way toward making this song a hit, but I've always found it kind of murky and turgid, sort of hookless like some of the fever dreams on *Draw the Line*, in particular "The Hand That Feeds." And then, "Last Child" is just too funky and R&B for my tastes, and yet, ironically, awkward of rhythm, like it has a leg injury.

But the song's groove suited Joey Kramer just fine, who told Stephen Demorest back in 1976, "That's where my roots are. Before I joined Aerosmith, I used to play with the big, black soul revues—the Unique Four, the Turnpikes—and they turned me on to a lot of things, like Kool & the Gang and The O'Jays. I had to go to every rehearsal to help the singers with their choreography. I don't really like fancy drumming. I like the stuff that's real solid, like Bernard Purdie."

Next up is "Rats in the Cellar," another candidate for heaviest Aerosmith song ever. Originally titled "Tit for Tat," this one also has a connection to early-days live staple "Rattlesnake Shake," written by the old Fleetwood Mac. It's framed by a manic panic of a drumbeat. Remarks Joey, "Drums is really about, for me, emotion. And as far as Aerosmith goes, the way a song feels is pretty much going to get dictated by the drum track. That was what it's all about. Feel and emotion in a song is what it is. And a good drum track is going to dictate that, so everyone else can lie in there. It doesn't appear like that on the front page, but that's what everything lies upon in order to make it feel good."

Tyler calls the song a "tip of the hat, or an answer to 'Toys in the Attic.' Meanwhile, in real life, 'Rats' was more like what was actually going on. Things were coming apart, sanity was scurrying south, caution was flung to the winds, and little by little the chaos was permanently moving in." It's a cool comment, because, first off, indeed, it's a note-dense fast song, a clear sister track to "Toys in the Attic," and equally framed by very rhythmic guitar playing. Also, one can imagine the drugs working better on the preceding album, lending the band an attic high as they played—comparatively and innocently—with their toys. Now the drugs are getting darker and so are the songs, a sentiment that has been readily recognized by Jack.

In tandem, New York isn't exactly improving. So now there are rats instead of toys and a cellar instead of an attic. I wouldn't say there's appreciably more darkness on this album versus the last, but it is indeed heavier overall, with about the same number of dark songs each, essentially threeish. Plus, I'd say that *Rocks* sounds more urban, more decadent, with *Toys in the Attic* indeed evoking a rural vibe—I never really thought about it before, but I suppose I always pictured that attic as the attic of a farmhouse.

Reinforcing the back-ally vibe, Tyler has elsewhere indicated that the lyrics to "Rats in the Cellar" were inspired by the possible murder of the band's dealer and his girlfriend in and around March 10, as the guys were finishing up *Rocks* at Record Plant. Typical of the junkie's devious self-absorption, all the focus in the song is about what happens to the customer when he loses his connection.

At the music end, to push the comparison, it also has the same sort of long vocal notes utilized in "Toys in the Attic." It's hard to pin what the chorus is, because "rats in the cellar" isn't part of it. Unexpectedly, the first solo taken on the song is Steven on harmonica, which is then nearly mimicked by the guitar solo. Later, the song modulates up for some new music and another solo section, kicked off again by harmonica, soon joined by freight-train guitars and some nice instrumental chatter or dialogue. The energy builds and builds for one of the most dramatic, violent, and careening end-of-song windups from anywhere in the band's catalog.

Next, "Combination" is most definitely another dark one on the album, and again, despite the song's uncompromising heavy metal stance, through Steven's and Joe's duet vocal there's a clear connection to the Rolling Stones. Joe, with his bedheaded similarity to Keith Richards in both look and voice (and job description), can be heard clearly, sullen and laconic, against the more powerful Tyler. This one is credited solely to Perry, and at the lyric end there's yet more allusions to the band's drug use and also to the fracturing relationship between Steven and Joe, who was getting increasingly frustrated about how painstaking it was getting lyrics out of Tyler.

What's most impressive about this dark-horse track is how sophisticated the songwriting is, both musically and lyrically. Ted Nugent and Kiss couldn't hold a candle to the nonobvious chord sequences and surprise arranging that goes on in this song. Although Thin Lizzy could write heavy metal songs this smart, and so could UFO. At the top of their game, direct competitors Blue Öyster Cult might be able to get here too—think "Tattoo Vampire." But it was rare for an American band to sculpt early-days heavy metal this erudite. Inside Aerosmith, "Combination" represented significant growth, for there was nothing on the first or second albums like this, and really, only something like "Sweet Emotion" or "Toys in the Attic" from the last record aspired to the cerebral maneuvering that takes place throughout the alleys of this song.

"They're still listening to Zeppelin," laughs Jack. "That's their main influence at this point." And yet, there's still a portion of the song, the "I forgot my name" passage, that circles back to the Rolling Stones, a prime influence, albeit in a flagrantly heavy metal direction. I love the octave-jumping bass playing from Tom as well, which can be heard during the "I found the secret, the key to the vault" portion of the song. After the second round of that, an entirely new musical motif kicks in, as heavy as everything before it, jamming, noisy, but atop an odd sort of hard rock samba beat. It cuts off violently, followed by the lurch of a guitar, and an Aerosmith classic with immense gravitas has been born.

Speaking with Johnny Angel from KNAC.com, Jack brings up a great point about how the guitar tones made *Rocks* sound so much heavier, something most evident on the very powerful power chords of "Combination."

"We cut all the basics at their rehearsal space, the Wherehouse, in Boston's suburbs. A big, metal, roaring, huge room. I used stage monitors in with them to blow the sound right back at them. And that's when they started to stretch out. Joe would ask what he ought to be listening to, and I'd hip him to John Coltrane for solo ideas—and he'd try to get that! Even in preproduction, I knew it was great. I have cassettes of the evolution of every song on that record, and you should hear 'Back in the Saddle' as it evolved from Joe's basic lick to the monster it became. Wanna know what the secret to *Rocks* was? Distortion. Everything is totally overloaded. When I brought it to the record company, they panicked at first, but not for long."

Side 2 of *Rocks* opens with "Sick as a Dog," this writer's second-favorite Aerosmith song after "Draw the Line." Upholding the balanced collaborative milieu of the album, this one's credited to Steven and Tom. "That was similar to 'Sweet Emotion,'" Hamilton told me, "except where I started out on the bass in 'Sweet Emotion,' I started out with guitar on 'Sick as a Dog' and came up with those chord changes, that sort of jangly arpeggiated part of the intro. It's a very simple song. There's only three parts, and then another thing for the bridge, which was Steven's idea. Everything I brought to the band back then, especially, was very simple, because I just didn't really feel like a sophisticated musician. But one thing that happens is, when you have a very simple structure for a song, it leaves room for a lot of really amazing overdub ideas and harmonies, and it also translates better when you play live."

All of that is true, except the modest assertion that the song is simple. There's actually a lot that goes on, and, fair to Tom, maybe the complexity was added in the overdub stage. Once again, this is the greatest song the Rolling Stones never wrote. It's in the multiple vocals, the dovetailed harmonies, and it's in the sublime guitar riffing, not to mention the marriage of electrics and acoustics. As for the acoustic intro, Tom had been inspired by "Mr. Tambourine Man" and the Byrds in general. Also on the vocals, Steven turns in a sharp, exacting performance, exquisitely combining vocal fry with vibrato. Jack is there to capture him perfectly and place him, with complexity, soft sometimes and loud sometimes, inside the mix. The song modulates up for a solo section over which Brad places a sophisticated "song within a song" type of solo, which deftly mixes electric and acoustic, like the intro passage. Late in the sequence, there's a chill break section featuring just drums and riffing guitar, after which the band meets up again for one of the most sublime and joyful song outros in all of rock 'n' roll, all freight-train guitars and Mick an' Keith vocals, and all of it augmented by glorious handclaps, which is the last thing we hear because Jack left it up in the mix while the rest fades.

Back in 1976, Tom said that Jack "always has time for what people come up with. I wasn't sure about it, but playing it for Jack, I realized it had a lot of potential. We recorded it last and I'm glad, because everybody was hot by then." On the subject of arranging, he adds, "That's one of my fortés. But Steven has a certain veto power, because he has to sing these things." Tom plays rhythm guitar, while Joe plays most of the bass. When he switched over to do his guitar solo, it was Steven who took over the bass playing for the outro section. "Sick as a Dog" began life as "Uncle Tom's Cabin," and it's weirdly fitting that an Aerosmith offspring band of sorts, Warrant, would have a minor hit with a song called that in 1990.

Continuing to work as a team, Brad gets a second writing credit on the record, coming up with the music for the pounding and sinister "Nobody's Fault," with Steven, as usual, doing the wordsmithing. Brad also wrote "Round and Round," which could be considered the bookend track to this complex, textured doom classic.

"Well, those two were sort of our nods for my love of really heavy stuff like Zeppelin," says Brad. "I wanted to hear that really big riff-based music with gigantic drums and all that sort of thing. And I think we really accomplished that on those two songs."

Steven says the song is about earthquakes, which freaked out the band, along with flying. Sparking the idea, the guys had been reading an article about the severe 7.5-magnitude quake in Guatemala on February 4, 1976, with Steven remarking at the time that "they found another fault in New Jersey; it runs right by an atomic plant. Isn't that crazy?"

The drums sound like an earthquake too, bashing, booming, chaotic, slipping and sliding, and it's no surprise that Joey considers it one of his best performances on an Aerosmith album. He's heard front and center doing some pretty inventive stuff during the myriad stops and starts in the song.

Meanwhile, Steven puts on a vocal showcase, thespian, halting and spitting in spots and then stringing long, sighing notes over the mayhem elsewhere. It's a suitably dramatic presentation of a lyric that goes well beyond tremors and into the apocalyptic, with Tyler suggesting that the earth is shaking because mankind screwed up. Brad takes the guitar solo, and over a thumping rhythm he plays suitably dirty, with a bit of a wah-wah effect, taking it close to what Tony Iommi might do on a song like this. There's more of this as the song rumbles to a close, ending in a slow fade, tremors over—for now.

As for its origins, "Nobody's Fault" evolved from a February 1975 jam the guys were calling "Soul Saver." It's on *Pandora's Box*, and it's quite hard to see the connection. But as Tyler says, "When you listen to each other and have a little perseverance, even a really shitty riff can become a great song."

Next is "Get the Lead Out," and we're back to the standard Tyler/Perry credit, the so-called Toxic Twins, the brothers cursed with each other and with heroin. It's a song that carries the weight of all of rock 'n' roll history, and it's the work of these two rock 'n' roll animals who live for two things, the unparalleled high of making music and all the secondary highs that go with the lifestyle. Those are the two things this song is about, and somehow the charming riff we hear in the verse says all that without Steven having to sing about it. The chorus riff keeps the conversation going by being a variant of the verse riff, and then the "No no no no" section takes us to a completely different place.

Up into the solo section, harmonica comes back to harass the guitars, followed by a truncated late verse and then more of this sighing "No no no" stuff, with Steven scatting and bouncing between the left and right channel and Joey playing some tasty fills. Then, unexpectedly, things go atmospheric and dark, with some volume-swelling guitar effects topped with some intersecting high notes from Steven, drifting in and out of the miasma. Jack puts the song to rest with another slow fade, filled at the end with new but disappearing ear candy.

"Really vibrant guitar stuff, and a lot of bass and guitar; I love 'Lick and a Promise,'" says Tom, and indeed "vibrant" is the perfect descriptor of another one of these songs such as "Adam's Apple," "No More No More," and, most stridently, "Sick as a Dog" that position Aerosmith as a replacement Rolling Stones. It's the second song in a row where the word "boogie" comes quick, and like "Get the Lead Out," it's about the magic of rocking as well as the side benefits, which, again, is very much Aerosmith's raison d'être. Most poignant is the surprise late verse (a great device on its own), where Steven has Johnny's mother concerned about him "pacing the floors." But then, "He grabbed a guitar and a couple of beers / And the crowd keeps screaming for more." That's the young punks in Aerosmith in a nutshell, getting kicked out of school, then using that "combination" of drugs and rock 'n' roll to get adoration from the girls as well as the boys. Also like the last song, the guitar riff says all this without Steven even having to open his big mouth, especially the euphoric wind-tunnel guitar signature we hear behind the "He gets his woman every night for free" line.

Come solo time, it's Joe who takes the honors, and what's cool here is that after a perfunctory initial stab, plus some more vocal parts, we get to an outro passage where we hear a version of Joe's evolved style from the '90s, more lyrical, more rhythmic, and also searching for fresh tones.

Closing the album is "Home Tonight," which creeps closer to the Platonic ideal of power ballad, beyond "Dream On" and "You See Me Crying," en route to the hit songs that Aerosmith would have others write for them, rather than use their own noggins. There's almost nothing to the lyric here, which allows the band to breathe, to stretch out, and to embody the power in the term "power ballad." Steven even belts out a few screams. It's a fitting loud arrangement on an album that had volume and power as part of its thematic being. As a result, even this rote and almost maudlin "Auld Lang Syne" type of song (Steven called it "a goodbye song") doesn't stick out particularly against the rest of the selections, at least when checking the meters.

Built on piano by Steven, the song also features Joe on lap steel, and Jack, Tom, and Joey in on backing vocals, with Joey notably drumming hard. The solo comes from Brad, and it's surprisingly aggressive and distorted, again driving home the point that this is a power ballad, meaning no changing anything onstage for it, other than, theoretically, the ostentatious wheeling out of a grand piano so Steven can be Freddie Mercury.

Issued on August 27, 1976, as the record's second single and backed with "Pandora's Box," the song failed to catch on, stalling at #71 on the *Billboard* Hot 100. Perhaps this was proof that Aerosmith wasn't supposed to play it safe. Indeed, back to weirdness, before we'd see "Back in the Saddle" as the third and last *Rocks* single, "Walk This Way" would be trotted out again, reprising the "Dream On" narrative. This time it would be backed with "Uncle Salty," and this time the song would reach #10 and stay on the charts for seventeen weeks.

In a nice summation of the band's journey thus far—from *Aerosmith* to *Rocks*—Jack explained to Stephen Demorest back in 1976 that on the first album, "they just played and Adrian would say, 'Oh, that felt good. That's a take.' There are a lot of mistakes and wrong notes on that first album, although the energy was right and the band was excited about doing it. When we started with *Get Your Wings*, there were many hours of practice just getting them to sound professional. By my standards, they were a young band—in fact, they still are—and they were afraid of the studio. It used to be that as soon as the red light went on, they'd choke and make mistakes. Plus, we had some hassles, because we had some people there that shouldn't have been there."

"*Toys in the Attic* was better, and by this album, once we started to cook, there was no problem. Now, it doesn't mean anything to them that it's going on tape. Now, when the guys do their leads, they do them right in the control room. They just sit next to me, and we run lines out into the studio, and I put on the effect that's going to be on so they can hear what they have to do. I can talk to them—I can even yell notes right into their ears while they're playing. Brad Whitford is not a rhythm guitar player anymore. No way. He's a great lead guitar player, and he's getting better in leaps and bounds. Same with Joe Perry, the whole band. Joey Kramer has always had good time, but he's gotten more confident. He's playing less fills, but they're tastier. I didn't have to get on his back much; in fact, neither did Steven. Steven used to be always . . . well, this time he didn't have to."

Rocks certified gold on May 21, 1976, and then this new thing called platinum, on July 9. It currently sits at four-times platinum, again, driven there by the live experience more than anything, and no big hits of its own but much classic-rock radio play over the years. Also helping was the perennial single status of "Dream On" and "Walk This Way," the release schedules of which sent the message that these songs were timeless.

Mused Joe on the *Rocks* experience, "I'd have to say that, you know, every band that goes through this and is lucky enough to have a career, long enough to put out multiple albums, there's an ebb and a flow to the creativity, just like any other art. I mean, there are times where you can sit in front of an easel and paint your heart out, and you're still not getting it. And there are other times where it just flows right through you, and you don't know where it comes from. You're a writer. I mean, you know, there are days when it just comes out, and there are days where it's like work. And same thing with writing songs. It's like, sometimes it just flows out and you don't know where the hell it came from. And then there's other times where you can beat it to death, and it's just not up to the standard that you know you can get. But, you know, you gotta keep doing it. If you stand around waiting and waiting for inspiration, you wind up with one or two albums for your forty years [laughs]."

In his uncharacteristically awkward-reading review of the album (see above Joe Perry quote!), *Melody Maker*'s Chris Welch makes the point I was making earlier about the early 1970s being fallow years for American hard rock.

"Since Led Zeppelin first smote the music biz on the far side of the Atlantic back in '69, America seems to reel somewhat under the pressure. And when we followed up with ELP, Yes, Genesis, Pink Floyd, and the heavy metal men, Heep, Purple, Sabbath, and so on, Americans preferred country rock singer-songwriters—almost anything except the type of arranged music with glamorous lead vocalist package. There was Grand Funk Railroad, of course, but nothing quite like Queen to add to the long British honors list.

"That was until Aerosmith. I suppose it was the mixture of instrumental prowess, musical attack and dash of flair that attracted me to the first Aerosmith album when it arrived on our shores, virtually unheralded a couple of years ago. I'm still not a rabid fan of the band. We haven't even had a chance to see them yet, and of course, they are bound to upset most critics by appearing to follow a time-honored course. Dull stuff for rock writers, really, just another group that appeals to the vast mass of kids. I can almost see the heads bobbing to the beat of 'Back in the Saddle' at the Odeon Hammersmith.

"Even now, what have this hugely successful combo (in America) got to offer then, I can almost hear resentful skeptics sniff with hostility and suspicion, a certain je ne sais quoi. Steven Tyler is the arrogant, ill-tempered lead vocalist of the saturnine features, who looks as if he might give Freddie Mercury a severely slapped wrist if they crossed laser beams. But most impressive is the relentless riffing guitars of Joe Perry and mighty Brad Whitford. While Steve is shouting out the vocals on 'Last Child,' listen to the Whitford guitar (he co-wrote it with Steve) dig into as nasty a riff as has been blasted forth since Jeff Beck was hooked up with Carmine Appice. Not to put too fine a point on it, they cook, and the guitars send those icy fingers along the spine.

"Dig the way the high-hats belt in a la John Bonham on the fast 'Rats in the Cellar,' a kind of tribute to the canyons of New York City. Solid vocal harmonies, driving guitars—what more could a simple rock fan request? And for more laid-back tastes, there are the chiming chords and Who-like aggression of 'Sick as a Dog,' a most listenable stomper, followed by the even more raucous 'Nobody's Fault,' with Tyler getting almost apoplectic. Joey Kramer is the man in the engine room, a blur of flailing crash cymbals and detonating tom toms, and he kicks along a boogie epic like 'Get the Lead Out' with angry vehemence.

"Depending on your philosophy, it's irresistible stuff that will get knees pumping in the three-quid seats and groans from scribblers in the freebies. But at the risk of being cut dead at the annual rock writers convention, I find the sensuous rhythms and animal pulse of 'Lick and a Promise,' just one of many erotic selections, a strangely heady brew. They could keep up this eclectic hullabaloo based on the familiar backlog of rock riffs all night, and I'd feel no pain."

Not sure what album Dana Sue Jackson from the *Detroit Free Press* was sent, but in her *Rocks* review she figures that "they had 'Toys in the Attic' in their last album and come up with 'Rats in the Cellar' for this one. Big deal. There's nothing on this release that has the tender tension of 'Dream On,' the instrumental hook of 'No More No More,' the momentum of 'Train Kept a Rollin'" or the bratty charm of 'Walk This Way,' all songs that made their earlier albums sure hits. Once Aerosmith was innovative, even when they stole their main ideas from other bands. Now they've slipped into the lazy habit of having Steve Tyler shout a few lyric lines with the rest of the band shouting back the title as a one-line chorus. Too many of these songs sound alike. Lead guitarist Joe Perry isn't playing up to any sort of professional par. I've heard guys in local bar bands play much better. Tyler's rock ballad 'Home Tonight' is acceptable at best. The catchiest cut is 'Sick as a Dog.' That's a dubious achievement, since the whole idea of the song is repulsive. At this point, Aerosmith is a drag, and that's not the way rock ought to be."

In yet another review full of awkward turns of phrase and stilted rhythms—does *Rocks* cause mental impairment?—the *NME*'s Max Bell wrote, "This is a far better album than the surprisingly feeble *Toys in the Attic*—more juice from producer Jack Douglas and concentrated concert atmosphere from da boys. They've evolved their own 'sound'; it's loud, they play with as much vim as the hard rock fraternity in England. If we're going to count units, then they're also beating Zep, Bad Co., Queen, and Mott at their own card game.

"Steve Tyler rants and raves raucously. Brad Whitford and Joe Perry strike off planet-weight, mass-density, leaden guitars, meaty axes, I should say, and the rhythm duo, unfunky Joey Kramer and Tom Hamilton, race the beat through all manner of unconnected time changes and structural idiosyncrasies designed to confuse you and open up the guard for the kill. *Rocks* might even be a concept in that it takes the live overview design. It begins with 'Back in the Saddle,' obviously a fine way of detonating the wolf pack, and ends with 'Home Tonight.' See what they're getting at? Tactically, Aerosmith are not dumb. Their records get less subtle as their importance grows accordingly. They play with flame and come out unsinged. Now and again, the fuse lights off its own ignition spark plug. 'Rats in the Cellar' busts the metronome in your brain. Sounds like The Tubes on a heaving metal send-up. 'Combination' seems to be a pretty safe number too. Brad and Joe slice necks on the breaks. At least it ain't background stuff. Qualitatively 'Sick as a Dog' and 'Lick and a Promise' are all right movers. They actually keep the solos under control, and Tyler must be getting close to carrying off the muscular vocal cord award usually held by Robert Plant.

"Ultimately, Aerosmith are nothing special. Plenty of spit and polish, but studio-wise, they don't storm the rink as serious contenders for any crown of creation. I see the appeal, the ordinary nature of American speed brat rock, defying the listener to ignore the beat. Very masculine punch, plus Steve for the ladies. It's all to do with sex. Surprise, surprise. 'Get the Lead Out' and that 'Lick' thing are mindless teen anthems. You just get absorbed in the cacophony and let it drift over your skull. Maybe I've missed the point. Aerosmith are exploding like acne, and yep, they do have their moments. I still like those bits between the tracks best though."

Baffling reviews aside, the first slate of tour dates for *Rocks* was postponed as the band struggled to finish the album, with Steven joking that he didn't even know what he was singing about on the last four songs. Opening multiple shows were the likes of Angel, Henry Gross, and

Mahogany Rush, with the latter being another Columbia act and another band that was part of the Leber Krebs stable. Starz supported as well, with Jack Douglas producing their Aerosmith- and Kiss-like debut as well as the fine *Violation* album of 1977, with both being recorded at Record Plant. Into July and August, we'd see Derringer supporting, out promoting their self-titled debut. Into September, Jeff Beck and Spirit would enter the mix, with Beck kind of miffed to be part of the undercard.

Lisa Robinson from *Hit Parader* caught up mid-tour with Joe Perry, who offered some musings on the trip so far, including the recording of *Rocks* plus thoughts on touring.

"In some cases, it was rushed, and in others it went just right," begins Perry. "It sacrifices some things because of the way we put it together, but in others, there were really good things that came out of it. At the last minute we decided to record it in Boston. We did all the basic tracks in Boston, and we finished at the Record Plant. When I walked into the Record Plant, I hadn't been in there since *Toys*, and it was like putting stale gum in my mouth. I just said 'ech.' I can't stand another three months in this place. I wanted to do it in one of those warm places; we would have done it in Jamaica if it was a little cooler down there, you know. Now the place is being burned down, so I figured the next place that would be decent would be Criteria, in Miami. We just couldn't get it together with the production schedule. We finally just had to do it. We ended up doing seven or eight rough tracks in Boston, with a mobile, but the sound was really good. You can tell the difference, which tracks were done there.

"When we first started, the whole scene was different," reflects Joe, now in a big band. "The huge places we're playing now, well, the Beatles did it, and the Stones did it, but now it's commonplace to do those places. All I cared about at that time was playing; if we played the Tea Party in Boston it was a big deal."

Asked by Lisa if it's gotten out of hand, Joe responds, "Yeah, I suppose it has. Especially huge outdoor places like Pontiac Stadium, like that. You can go out there and play good, but it isn't the same as you would in a small place. I mean when we went to Madison Square Garden, after having been in Pontiac, well, the Garden was like a club. It was like, wow, it's good to be back in a small place again. It's bad enough when we play 20,000-seat indoor places; now we can get that together. But the bigger ones . . . what can you do though? There are so many places, so many kids. The reason we haven't played in Boston for so long is that no outdoor place will let us in. We have to go into Boston Gardens for something like four nights. We avoided it this summer because it wasn't air-conditioned. It's one of the oldest facilities in the country. The reason they won't let us into the outdoor places is that we have a very bad reputation."

Proposed by Robinson that there's a certain element of violence to a live show, Joe figures, "Sure, like vicarious violence. That's why Kiss, or Ted Nugent, are so good. Ted said it a while ago in an interview; he goes up there and projects all this violence, high energy, and the kids are like watching a violent movie or something. It gets played out for them. That's what rock is you know. It's energy. I'm basically a rock fan before anything else, and I get off on bands that play like that. That's why I get off on the Dolls, I get off on Kiss, the MC5, the Who, all of them. All the high-energy stuff. That's how I judge our music. I don't listen to see if I'm playing or not. I listen to see if it gets me off on a gut level. I suppose that's why my music will never get to the point where it's flowing along. It's like so many guitar players, they lose that, they just get caught up in the studio, in the technical end of it. I don't enjoy that. I would rather feel good from it in a different way. I listen to rock 'n' roll in the morning to wake up because it gets me moving."

Somewhat incredulous at how big the band has become, Joe says, "Yeah, I spend a lot of time thinking about that. I think we were just turned on by something and now we're just a lens of whatever that energy was. I don't know. The format has always been there. It's been there for twenty years. We were turned onto whatever it was that turned us on in the 1960s, and now it's just coming through us again. I'll never be as good as Chuck Berry, or doing new things, or channeling old things. But on the other hand, five years from now, there may be someone who would think, 'Well, I'll never be as good as Aerosmith.' I don't think there's ever anything really new, but there are some people who put more of themselves into it. You can always see the roots, but some people sound more unique—like Hendrix. I mean, you could see where the roots came from, but the guy was a genius. Once you get to that place, you get set free. He just went on until he burned out. Like a meteor, all of a sudden, 'ssshooo.' It's too bad. But then, if he'd been another kind of person and he'd really been cold about it, he might be alive today. But he never would have been as hot as he was when he was hot. You can't be totally unique, you know. You always have to use the medium, and that's rock. I don't know, I don't think we sound as derivative as some bands do. There are some songs that are pretty unique that we do."

Remarked Steven, also speaking with Robinson, "It's a little bit boring when you're off the road, and especially when you think you're not going back on for eight months. In those two hours that we play, it takes me four or five shows to get back into shape. That's why I jog around and stuff before we go out. That's why I have a jump rope here with me. I almost passed out twice, because there's no air, man, when you're up there on that stage. There is absolutely nada oxygen. That's why we have the fans up there. Plus, there's a rush, seeing all the people. You're in the dressing room and the doors swing open and there you are in front of 19,000 people—bingo."

Wrote Steve Millburg from the *Omaha World-Herald*, reviewing the band's Nebraska performance on August 20, "It wasn't a night for subtlety. Aerosmith, Rick Derringer and Starz kept the music hot, heavy and relentless at the City Auditorium arena Friday night. Aerosmith, the main draw for the sellout crowd of 11,300, is from Boston, but has had its greatest success in the boogie-happy Midwest. The group features two guitars, bass, drums and lead singer Steven Tyler, the main showman. Tyler, with his shaggy hair, pouty lips and some sort of long-sleeve, multi-hued jumpsuit, looked, pranced and, at times, sang like Mick Jagger. He was almost constantly in motion, flinging his streamer-festooned mic stand around him when he wasn't singing into it.

"When drummer Joey Kramer or lead guitarist Joe Perry were [*sic*] soloing, Tyler helpfully held his microphone up to the drums or the guitar speaker. Neither needed the extra amplification. When Tyler wasn't dancing around them, goading them into motion, the others in the band stood still and played elemental rock. Aerosmith does nothing fancy musically. They just keep the beat fast and insistent. The closest thing to a slow song all night was 'Dream On,' which starts relatively calmly but builds to a screaming climax that Tyler's voice wasn't quite able to pull off."

But it was sometimes touch and go with the band live at this point. Remembers David, "It really became apparent to me the level of the drug problem I had to deal with when they were headlining at the end of '76 in Anaheim Stadium. When they were supposed to go on to perform, Perry and Tyler were both drugged out, sleeping on the floor. Robert Kelleher was Aerosmith's road manager for some time, in '72 or '73 till sometime in '78, and by the end he was in as bad shape as the band. But yes, my first major understanding of how deep Aerosmith's problems were was when we were headlining in '76, Anaheim Stadium, 55,000 people, sold out. I don't know who was under us, could've been Ted Nugent and other acts. And it's Aerosmith's time to go on, and I think Kelly and I go backstage, and there are Tyler and Perry laid out on the floor, stoned on heroin, out of their minds.

"There are some rules in rock 'n' roll. One is, if you want to do a bad show, you never do it in London, New York, or L.A. It's just not smart. You can do a bad show in Cincinnati—nobody's there, in the sense that your reputation is going to suffer. So we are forced to act. Because it dawns on me, if the headliner does not appear for a reason like this, we may have to pay for the 55,000 tickets. So we force the two guys up—I don't remember how we got them to go onstage—and of course they did a bad show.

"And after that, I began to try to figure out how to deal with heroin, which I basically failed at. Because of certain reasons, one of which is, as silly or simplistic as it sounds, at that time, in the early '80s, when they recommended, we'll get Steven Tyler sent away for rehab, you'd think, oh, that's a good idea. But you need to send his girlfriend, who is also addicted, with him. Because if he cleans up and comes back and she's still addicted, you achieve nothing. So, looking back, I spent from that period until March 1984, when Steve Leber and I split from Aerosmith, trying to figure out an answer to this problem. And did not succeed."

In October, Aerosmith would execute a foray into Europe, where, like Kiss, the band was shocked to find themselves playing much-smaller venues and not selling out either. To have left it this late and for the tour to comprise only a handful of dates . . . in the end, that really did contribute to the fact that Aerosmith would remain very much an American band doing much of their business from coast to coast, and notably all over the Midwest and the Rust Belt, where their "blue-jean army"—often jeans and no shirt—faithfully gathered for battle any time the Toxic Twins came to town.

5
Draw the Line and Live! Bootleg

"Not laid-back, but wallowing"

Come *Draw the Line*, the songs came much harder, and when they arrived, they weren't as good.

"God, I don't know," Joe Perry told me back in 2014. "Again, it's democracy. When you're in the studio with five guys, everybody's got a different take on what it should sound like. A certain part works or it doesn't work, or it's a mistake, or it actually adds something to the song. It's always been kind of a battleground. Steven is a perfectionist, and he wants to fill in every hole, every spot, everything, and I sit there next to him and try to steer it back towards the roots. That's been the thing. It's a partnership, when we're writing, when it *is* working, the magic that it is. Unfortunately, there's a few elements, basic elements, that were missing from that partnership. In order to have a partnership, you gotta have some trust. And that kind of went by the wayside. But when it's working, it's definitely a give-and-take that makes it Aerosmith."

"I think there were some really cool riffs on *Draw the Line*," says Joe, this time from our 2005 chat. "I think the production was kind of sloppy and murky, just because of the times. We were going through kind of a . . . not laid-back, but wallowing. I think we were waiting for the next thing to hit us. It was disjointed. I just remember making that record in kind of a fog. Even though there are some really cool riffs on it. I think there are a couple of songs that are 90 percent there, and if we had made a couple little changes, it would have brought it up to the level that it should have been. But again, because of the times, it took too long, and we were under pressure to put it out. I think it might have been a better record if it had been remixed. Maybe if we did a couple other songs for it. But there are some cool things on it."

Much like with *Rocks*, the band began work on *Draw the Line* elsewhere, with good intentions, but had to move over to Record Plant to finish the job. This time it was the Cenacle, a mansion, or manor, in Armonk, New York, just north of the city. Beginning in March 1977 (after a first tour of Japan, in February, and some time off in Hawaii), the months dragged on, with Brad, Tom, and Jack picking up some of the slack because, as Joe put it, "Steven and I stopped giving a fuck." Also, on April 13 the band lost their first and biggest supporter, Frank Connelly, who finally had lost his long battle to pancreatic cancer.

"It took a lot of time and there was a lot of money spent unnecessarily," recalls Joey Kramer. "We were up in this place called the Cenacle, which was an old mansion that we built a playback room into. Again, there was a lot of practical joking going on, but we were all living in the house together, so there is a lot of clowning around going on. That was at the time when we became drug addicts dabbling in music as opposed to musicians dabbling in drugs."

"We were well on our way to blowing it, at that point," Tom told Sam Dunn. "We had reached a creative pinnacle with the *Rocks* album, but we had also gotten to the point where we all had our own houses and spent a lot of time thinking about buying cars and drugs and getting wasted. And coming back off the road wasn't something where we came back off the road and, two weeks later, we were at it working again.

There would be this indefinite period where everybody needed a break from the road. Because we got burned out on the road. But it allowed us to get into a lot of real decadent stuff that let things really slip away. That's what happened with *Draw the Line*. There are a lot of people out there who really love the album, so I don't put it down like I used to, but it was a fiasco, and it was a very difficult thing to get finished."

"Aerosmith was completely burned out," says David Krebs. "Working from '72, '73, through '78, in '77 with *Draw the Line*, you start to see that the drugs are really getting in there [laughs]. And then between '80 and '84 or '85, even the first Geffen album, the quality of Aerosmith's songs is very much undermined by whatever is going on internally in the band, on a personal level. But back to 1977, keep in mind this: An album was thirty-five minutes. When we turn into CD time, initially, everybody said, 'Well, let's give them seventy minutes.' I think we learned, after a few years, it's foolish to fill an album that is full of mediocre songs that is basically two albums of the '70s. And now people put forty, forty-five minutes on a CD. And they had a rigorous schedule. We would do an album, they would tour, do an album, and every year, in '73, '74, '75, '76, '77, five albums, followed by *Live! Bootleg*, which was to give them some time off [laughs]. That was the idea."

"You see, even though the key to your success is the road, the road is a very boring existence, filled with people coming up backstage saying, 'I have a gram for the lead singer' or whatever. And if you really think about it, in twenty-four hours, the band is not occupied that many hours. So you fill the void, kind of thing." It was Krebs's idea to record at the Cenacle, to get the band away from temptation. Which of course didn't work, with Steven reminding us that drugs can be imported.

Reflected Tom, in conversation with Paul Gargano, "There was a period there when things were . . . even with drugs, it was the honeymoon period, and we weren't suffering the consequences of it. We were doing the first album, and *Get Your Wings*, *Toys*, and *Rocks*, and everything was on an ascending curve. The quality of the music, quality of the shows, our ability to go out on tour and feel better about mastering the idea of playing in the huge hall, that was all on an ascending curve. And then a certain amount of money came in, and then it got really corrupt. It wasn't about the quest anymore. It was about the quest for the rewards of the music. We didn't set out to glamorize it. I think that that's the right context for back then."

Plus, there were growing fractures. "One of the painful things that comes along, I remember, or one of the moments for me that was really a painful event, was when we were playing in Chicago, and me and Joey and Brad were in one room, and Steven and Joe were in the other room having a talk with our manager. And you can hear him through the walls telling them, 'You guys are the stars; those other guys are along for the ride.' Just thinking about all the work that we had all done together. It would have been nice if someone with that perspective could have sat everybody down and said, look, you know, those guys are the face of the band. Steven's the singer, Joe's the lead guitar player, but you guys are important too. Because we know we are. We know what role we play in the band. The public and some people in the press especially see it kind of from the most obvious, and don't look beyond the face. It's something that I had to learn over the years. To put in perspective, there are degrees to everything. I never got to the point where I sold all my belongings to pay for drugs. I think even though daily drug use was something that I reveled in and loved and was really unhealthy about, habitual about, I was blessed not to have that compulsion that leads you to think that it's the most important thing in your life, that any sacrifice is worth it to get it. I still have my 1974 Dino Ferrari, which is the first thing I rewarded myself with when the band started making money. Yeah, we went from this really beautiful mansion down to this little condo, but we always had somewhere nice to live."

From my own chat with Tom, he explains that "the Cenacle was a former nunnery, in upstate New York. And I was just up there, the engineers and a couple of other people, Jack Douglas. Joey and Brad and I had already done about a month's rehearsing, just the three of us. Steven and Joe were kind of unfindable during that period. But then we all moved into the Cenacle—everybody was there. People talk about a band's self-indulgent period. That was it, where we had a couple of successful albums and we were really wallowing in the sort of rewards of the flesh, if you know what I mean. That album took a ridiculously long time to make, and the sessions started at ten o'clock at night. It was just disorganized."

Illustrative of the fragmented sessions is an unused instrumental jam called "Krawhitham," which can be heard on the *Pandora's Box* compilation. As Brad explains, "That's the sound of Joey, Tom, and I entertaining ourselves while we were waiting for Steven and Joe to wake up and get their shit together." Adds Tom, "Usually those two didn't even come down from upstairs. So we'd drive our Ferraris around Armonk, New York, for a while, then jam and record. We had a good time, but then again, we didn't."

Another outtake on the box set is a cover of Otis Rush's "All Your Love," with Tom remarking that "we weren't into covering like the hits of the day—we were just choosing the songs that we loved. That's just a typical electric blues sort of thing from the '60s. We were formulating our style by who we covered." Adds Joe, "This was one of those songs we all played in bands before we played together. There were only a handful, because, like, Steven was playing the *Abbey Road* album while Tom and I were doing the MC5. But we both were into ones like that and 'Train Kept a Rollin'."

Both these tracks would have made *Draw the Line* worse. One is an unremarkable song they didn't write, and the other is more of a bad riff idea, where the melody is sour and hard to pin down. Granted, a smart band like Aerosmith would have selected only a chunk or two from "Krawhitham" and put the hammer and tongs to it until it was unrecognizable, and then used it as a break or something. Nonetheless, it goes to show that the muse is not always cooperating.

The Cenacle was part and parcel of the Rose Hill Mansion, situated on 100 acres and built in 1904 for Broadway star Billy Rose. As Tom alludes to, following Rose's death in 1966, the place was taken over by the Congregation of Our Lady the Cenacle, but then it fell into disrepair, having been acquired by a couple of doctors who planned to turn it into a youth center.

As Steven related to Alan DiPerna, "What I specifically remember was not being present in the studio because I was so stoned. In the past, I always had to be there and hear every note that was going down—who was playing what and were they out of tune. But for that album, I was so stoned on Tuinals. Heroin doesn't come close to what Tuinals do to you. You take two—whether you eat them or shove them up your ass—and you're fucking gone. Sorry. You're over the line immediately. And that line is Fuck-All Land. I just don't care anymore. To be honest with you, it was really only when I didn't have my drug of choice, which was cocaine, and I started messing around with [barbiturates] like chloral hydrates and what everybody in America takes today: Xanax. I tried to take as much of that as I possibly could.

"*Draw the Line* is when it got to be a habit of being so stoned that I had to be doing the mondo salute—because I was seeing double, I'd just hold my hand over one eye. I'd just get so out-there that my eyes would cross. Instead of passing out, I'd be cross-eyed. See, I grew up in the '60s. There was no such thing as stopping. If you couldn't do all the drugs on the table and still walk out the door, you weren't cool."

And back at the Cenacle, the guys had the age-old problem of getting lyrics out of Steven, who'd sequestered himself in his room, experimenting on himself. In his defense, however, Tyler writes in his book that "I write exactly to the music, and when the music ain't coming, neither were the lyrics."

And as he told Lisa Robinson at the time, "We're putting the finishing touches on it, just like all the other albums. It's not that it's delayed, it's just that a lot of the tunes for this album were written as the album was being put down. Why does it take me so long? Because I'm not Patti Smith, who sits down and writes poetry every time something comes to my head. Perhaps I should. I have to write exactly to the music. I don't keep a diary or anything like that. A tune gives off feeling; it almost speaks itself. You can't sit down with a song and expect to write all the songs to an album in one week. It's gotta come from somewhere. It's hard. It doesn't come out unless you sit down and think about it and fill the fireplace up twenty times at least, with paper."

Asked if he could do more of it when on the road, Tyler says, "Oh, you can try, but you've got the likes of Perry, and Kelleher [road manager Bob "Kelly" Kelleher], and Tyler, all in the same hotel, with a little bit of Whitford and a pinch of Tom, and a dash of Kramer. And that's just 50 percent. There's the rest of the road crew."

Steven explains that for the *Draw the Line* cover art, "the cartoonist Al Hirschfeld came up while we were there and drew the caricature of the group that's on the cover of *Draw the Line*. He really nailed us. We look like freakish botanical specimens pinned under glass. *Draw the Line*—it was the perfect title for the way we were living. I always went too far and was often reminded that I never knew where to draw the line. I hated to hear that, but that's how it was. Say 'Don't do it,' and we would do it. 'Cause I knew that if you don't know where to draw the line, then your choices become infinite."

"I'm pretty sure that was my idea," notes Krebs, with respect to commissioning Hirschfeld. "I thought it would be cool. I thought Aerosmith had reached a level that they could . . . Well, think of it this way: It's sort of a way of moving you into the mainstream. Like here's a big, well-known artist. Al is doing a cover for them. They're no longer this rock 'n' roll . . . however you want to describe them, inconsequential if you don't like this kind of music. He gave them a little cachet, let's say, artistically."

Says Joe, in his book, "We were elated when Hirschfeld agreed. When he came to the Cenacle, we weren't sure what to expect. This was, after all, our first experience working with an artist of his caliber. He was a friendly older gentleman in a frumpy suit. We discussed music and art. He told us how he liked to ride the New York subways and sketch people by putting his hand in his pocket and, without looking, drawing them on a small pad. After an hour of fascinating conversation, we asked him what he needed us to do. Should we pose? Did we need to do a sketch? 'Oh, no,' he said, 'I have everything I need. Give me a week and I'll send you the drawing.' We were amazed. He didn't make a single note or sketch a single line. We were even more amazed when the drawing arrived. Al Hirschfeld caught the essence of each of us. He did exactly what we'd hoped for. He drew the line. The cover was brilliant."

This isn't entirely accurate, because there's a portrait shot reflecting that exact pose, done by professional photographer Ron Pownall. The band is seated outside on a sunny day in front of a brick wall. In any event, what was also brilliant was the band illustration used on Rainbow's *Long Live Rock 'n' Roll*, which, if you were a metalhead in the late '70s, you'd be amused at the similarity between the two album covers.

Not every edition of *Draw the Line* had the logo on it, but those that did feature the now fully evolved winged logo we see today.

"Well, we never set out to have one," reflected Tom, speaking with Sam Dunn. "We never thought okay, we need to get a graphic artist in here, or we need to draw something. But somebody within our immediate circle, the people around us that were helping us out, drew this, made this crude drawing, and we thought wow, that's pretty cool. I get it—

Aerosmith, wings, makes sense. And why that meant something is an interesting question. You know, why are symbols so compelling to bands? We were still in the Cold War era; World War II had ended, maybe thirty years before that, and at least Joe and I were totally fascinated with everything about that period, that war, the technology, and just the magnitude of it. Sometimes I wonder if people's way of being affected by the magnitude of that made the music have this magnitude, being deafening, and being powerful. It's something you just wanted to hear and be part of that overwhelming and almost out-of-control sound. Maybe it was left over from those weird years of the war, you know?

"God knows, there were a lot of symbols and logos in that war. You have the American Air Force logos on the planes, the Germans went crazy with logos, and the Japanese had the big red circle. There are people that study that. These things go very deep into the psyche for some reason, and I think somebody put something on paper that was a symbol representing the band and we loved it, and then it started to develop and evolve over the years.

"And you have the idea of the brand being a marketer's term," continues Hamilton, "and figuring out how to get people to give you money for what you're doing. But why is a brand compelling? It's a symbol that describes a whole type of music, a whole personality, a whole attitude. So the idea of a brand does have a very legitimate thing in terms of how people want to collectively enjoy something. People were wearing logos on their T-shirts. The whole T-shirt thing really didn't get going until we'd been around for a while. We had a guy that had actually started out as a guitar player in the band, Ray Tabano. He was in the band for like the first eight or nine months. And even after Brad came in later on, he came back and worked for us and said, 'I've got this idea; we can get these T-shirts made with your logo on them, and we can have a mail order business and people can send in money, and we send them a shirt with your logo on it.' And we're like, 'Sounds cool; go ahead and try it.' But our manager said, 'No, a T-shirt . . . that's never going to be anything but a promotional item,' and so the whole thing went south. We could have had our own mega, multinational T-shirt conglomerate [laughs]."

Fortunately for the fans, the guys stayed as musicians, and there's no reward bigger than the first track on *Draw the Line*, issued on

October 28, 1977. Of course, it's the title track, which is arguably the greatest song these guys ever wrote. "Draw the Line" is almost insanely energy infused and at the same time it's complicated of riff, as sort of an update on Led Zeppelin's "Celebration Day," given the little added tail on what is an oddball riff to begin with.

"It's really a diamond in the middle of a lot of nothing," laughs Jack, telegraphing what will turn out to be the narrative of the album as a whole.

Steven's descriptions over the years of the lyric provide the sense of running on fumes that we get from the song's thin-air euphoria. He calls his words here "scrambled eggs" and understands full well that people sometimes can't tell what he's talking about. But as he says in his book, "Joe had this lick on a six-string bass that was so definitive, the song just about wrote itself. It reached down my neck and grabbed the lyrics out of my throat." And on the subject of Steven's throat, there's a passage near the end where he goes abusively beyond what he did on "Back in the Saddle," ripping the hell out of his vocal cords as if he's about to throw the mic down and retire off to some drug den until death do us part.

"It was a statement of where we were at the moment," reflects Tom. "Joe was really into the punk thing. You can hear that in just the flailing of 'Draw the Line.' It took the longest time. That song was . . . we never really played it, and we just started playing it again. Well, we've played it for the last seven years, and it serves its purpose. It's really fun for the band. You flail away at your guitar. It's very simple. You can play it on one string if you want, and actually I'm going to try it on Sunday night. You can like strum away on the string and play percussion on the bass. But it's fun for that, and it's rah rah energy, and Joe does the spectacular slide guitar solos. So, it's just an energy moment."

As for Steven's famous scream, Tom says that live, he has a way of not having it be fatal. "Yeah, sometimes when he does that, it's kind of a falsetto scream. So, he's not actually pushing it. It's not like he's ramming his vocal cords against the wall, trying to get them to hit a high note. He can go into a falsetto thing."

Says Tom in the *Pandora's Box* notes regarding "I Wanna Know Why," "We were going down to the wire on *Draw the Line* and a lot of stuff was coming down on Steven. I always thought this song was Steven's reaction to all the shit he was getting into at the time."

"I Wanna Know Why" is a strident, traditional rocker, boogie based but with enough chord changes to make it sophisticated. Scott Cushnie returns on barrelhouse piano, and Stan Bronstein returns on brass, specifically saxophone. Both are massaged into a thick, active, urban mix, creating a sculpted, incestuous sound picture that represents a next level of urgent atmosphere, sorta like Aerosmith in a desperate New York Dolls place. And that really goes for the composition as well. It's a traditional, rootsy rock song, but also maybe a bit druggy.

"Critical Mass" continues the tarry substance of this record's sound, in fact emerging out of a reverse fade of reverse recording. Then we're into a stiff sort of shuffle, with distant, drowned, drifting singing, effects everywhere plus harmonica. Once more, we have a song that sounds like it emerges out of the weight of traditional rock 'n' roll history, but there's not much in terms of particulars to anchor it to that sentiment. There's waves of guitar licks rather than a riff, Scott Cushnie is in there somewhere, and Steven's vocals sound in the round, but loose and casual. Curiously, it sounds like the cover art, where we see five versions of Casper the Friendly Ghost. It's an album that is more apparitional than inspirational.

Notes Tom, "I remember writing it on bass like I did 'Sweet Emotion,' then writing a guitar part around it. In those days we'd always record the basic track without any idea what the song was about. And I thought the song was bizarre at first, but I came to really like it. It's like a chant with a great production."

The lyrics come courtesy of Jack Douglas, who wrote them about a dream he had at the Cenacle—which makes sense, because the whole song ebbs and flows like a fitful, druggy dream. And yet again, if over the course of the previous couple of songs one is starting to think that some of this album might be undercooked in terms of songwriting, at the positive end, there's more of an intriguing *Exile on Main St.* atmosphere that's been obtained, in fact over and above any Aerosmith album to date.

And yet, the lyrics to "Critical Mass," along with the others, are dense and imagistic, impressive all-around. Indeed, Jack stylizes like Steven on this one, and its succinct stabs of imagery, again, along with myriad others by Steven, serve as a metaphor of the music and the *Draw the Line* experience in total, this idea of everything moving too fast to stick in pronouns and verbs and turn things into sentences. In other words, the literary side of the album is adjectival, action packed, in a hurry. Plus, there's a lot of drugs, being on them and just as much coming off them, but it doesn't sound like it was written on drugs.

The vibe continues on "Get It Up," which opens with simple tribal drums, a dirty riff, and some even dirtier slide. This one's funky Aerosmith like "Last Child," and to underscore the R&B nature of it, Karen Lawrence from L.A. Jets joins in all raspy on the chorus.

"There are lyrics that show that the band is not happy," remembers manager David Krebs. "'Draw the Line'—where my royalties? So now we're into a heavier period. See, with *Toys in the Attic* and *Rocks*, the lyrics are upbeat, boy/girl stuff, good situations. But with *Draw the Line* and *Night in the Ruts*, it's negative, depressing. The old lyrics were sleazy and testosterone fueled, which is what their fans wanted to hear. And now they're getting 'Get It Up,' where the lyric goes '*can't* get it up.' Let's not forget that the Cenacle was a nunnery, so here's this transgressive band there recording an album, and there are bad vibes. They also found babies' bodies buried under the place, so talk about negative vibes."

Closing side 1 of the original vinyl is "Bright Light Fright," sung very capably by Joe Perry, who gets sole writer's credit on this uptempo heavy metal rocker. Geometric chords provide sturdy, capable framing, with Kramer slamming out a fast, almost punky beat, inverted, with snare on one and three. It was inspired by the Sex Pistols, and when Joe presented it to the band, it was a hard sell.

As Joe remarked to Lisa Robinson at the time, "I wrote 'Bright Light Fright' and you can really hear that it's me singing. I sing a couple of verses alone. I did it a different way in my house, but I really dig the way the band does it. It's kind of like Dave Clark Five. And we have Stan Bronstein playing sax on it. All the songs this time we'll be able to do onstage. There won't be any songs that are too high for Steven to sing."

Bronstein's thrilling sax solo recalls what Buddy Bowser did on "Human Being," from the second and last New York Dolls album *Too Much Too Soon*—there really are all manner of parallels between the two bands, across the four guitarists, through to the Jagger-like mugs on the front men and over to the two taller blonds on bass.

"I think after all of these albums, if he was only interested in singing on one song, we got away with murder," chuckles Krebs. It's a prescient point, because as we would find out, he'd be singing on more songs moving forward, and with less acceptable results. The reason it works here is he's asking of himself to push a lot of air. I've always said that about these singers where the voice isn't that interesting or where singing doesn't come naturally—the results are often best when the guy is forced out of his dull or shaky lower range and then puts his shoulder into it. That happens here, and lo and behold, Joe's first vocal becomes his personal best of the entire catalog.

As alluded to earlier, the story painted in the lyrics is of sheer exhaustion, with Joe blown sky-high on booze and fast-making drugs, predictably with sleep not coming. You'd think that with that title it's a song about stage fright, but Joe's actually scared of the day.

Side 2 opens with "Kings and Queens," which is this band's "Achilles Last Stand"; in other words, something of a "forced" epic (on a concurrent white album) that winds up working famously, with both songs largely appreciated by the respective fan bases. My point is that this doesn't feel like an Aerosmith song, not the slow, dark verses, not the lyric, and not the mid-tempo heavy bit with its dark, ponderous chords. But it's a rich addition to the canon, especially when a chunk of this album is clumped around the core mandate—wayward enough, mind you—of a band that does hard rock or heavy metal with a connection to the blues and funk. "Kings and Queens" is none of that. It's more like a muscular half ballad that would be on a Rainbow or Thin Lizzy or Uriah Heep album—very British.

This one gets a crazy credit, enveloping everybody in the band except Joe and adding Jack Douglas. On the subject of splitting guitar duties with Whitford, Perry told me, "Not much has changed. We don't really talk much about that. That's one of the things. We just had a kind of natural affinity for that kind of communication. We listen to what each other is playing and make adjustments as we write songs. Right down to, well, what is Brad playing on that? He's using a Strat; I'll use a Gibson. Little things like that. If he has a certain feel for his part and he wants to go with a certain tone, I'll work with what I need to make my thing work with what he's doing. Or if I'm playing a certain kind of open tuning and playing a certain way, he'll make adjustments around it. It's a real natural, kind of free-floating thing. So we don't really talk much. The music pretty much chooses the way."

Offers Brad, "I just like it old school, pure vintage tones, basically plugging in with not a lot of effects. My reference points are Eric Clapton, Stevie Ray Vaughn, people like that; I don't like it very colored. Just give me a good clean tone, something that's as good as I can possibly get. I love that tonality of the Gibson Les Paul or Fender Strat. It's not rocket science. I like bands that basically plug in and don't use a lot of effects."

A song like "Kings and Queens" is significantly complicated but still within a four-four framework, but as Brad says, "I don't know if it's difficulty we're after. Certainly, I wish we did more things outside of four/four, which would make it interesting, add some intensity. But there's also a real beauty in what Nirvana did. You know, it's nothing complicated, so fresh and straight-ahead. Like Tom Petty—those songs are simple, yet they're so fucking amazing. You play them in the context of a band, and you find out how complex those songs can be. My reference is to try to be old school, but it's incredible when we get in the studio, we create a lot of music, put a lot into the songs. We like coming up with stuff that you can put headphones on, that just makes you go, 'How the hell did they get that sound?' or 'Holy shit, where did that come from?!' Certainly, you have to get comfortable in the studio. We have that idea that this stuff is going to live on in history. What you lay down is forever. That can freak you out, but you settle down, and that's what we try to capture. Whether it's myself and Joe writing, or myself and Steve, we work very organically. It just happens. You get in that zone. We find we can be very creative."

Jack Douglas is in the credits because he was in on the lyrics, grinding out the words with Steven. He also plays mandolin on the song, with Paul Prestopino adding banjo. For the recording, the band set up in the chapel, with Joey's drums on the altar and the rest of the gear on the floor, with the pews removed. Brad plays both lead and rhythm guitars on the song, with Joe providing only rhythms. There's definitely some electronic keyboards in there as well, pervasive, uncredited.

"I've always had a fancy to do songs about anarchy and the church and the government," said Steven, for the *Pandora's Box* notes. "This is not the only one. There's also something like 'St. John.' The band comes up with the licks, and then the music talks to me and tells me what it's about. This one was just about how many people died from holy wars because of their beliefs or non-beliefs. With that one, my brain was back with the knights of the round table and that shit—I do a lot of fantasizing."

"Kings and Queens" was issued as the second single from the album, on February 21, 1978, backed with "Critical Mass." True to tradition with this band, it was heavily edited, losing a minute of the plot. It didn't do much, managing a #70 placement on *Billboard*. This followed on "Draw the Line" as the first single, which got to an also middling #42, although both tracks are now highly respected as Aerosmith classics and find their way onto classic-rock radio fairly regularly.

"Another old one that I think would be great to be playing more live," offers Tom, in closing. "It's got a real, dramatic, powerful vibe to it. Very melodic and musical. Yeah, we play it once in a while, and every time we do, I'm just so proud to be up there playing that song."

Next is "The Hand That Feeds," which vibes along the lines of "Critical Mass"; in other words, floating along, half written, half sleepwalked. Even the intro tells you that it's something of a jam. Again, like "Back in the Saddle," there's more of a riff structure to what Tom is doing than there is to the guitars. In fact, my lifelong vague dissatisfaction with "Back in the Saddle" is for this very reason—because it feels like all the parts are in preparation for better parts that never come.

As Joe says, "Brad and Steven wrote 'The Hand That Feeds,' which I didn't even play on because I'd stayed in bed the day they recorded it, and Brad played great on it anyway." The credit for this one matches "Kings and Queens"—Jack plus the whole band except Joe. Take a huff of the lyrics, and the thought crosses your mind that Steven's in too much of a hurried and harried state to keep up with what the music is telling him.

"Sight for Sore Eyes" is credited to Steven, Joe, Jack, and New York Dolls singer David Johansen. It's a sort of thrashed-about funk rocker much like "Get It Up."

"You know, maybe that was reparations," says David Krebs. "Remember, the following thing goes down. Probably in '73, '74, my guess, Steven Tyler has an affair and steals David Johansen's wife. And we managed both these acts. And Steven Tyler moved to New York for several years. Because he's married to Cyrinda Foxe. And that's when

I become very close to Steven Tyler. And I think until March '84, he lived in New York. Joe Perry had a long-term relationship with Elyssa, which I think was very solid. Steven Tyler went from one girl or woman to another. It was always Elyssa and Joe, and Elyssa was on tour all the time. So Elyssa was queen of Aerosmith in a certain sense. And when Elyssa introduced Cyrinda Foxe to Steven, who fell in love, got married, had Mia, Cyrinda became the queen of Aerosmith. Because the lead singer's wife, if she knows what she's doing, could easily be the queen. So that could've caused some friction. Especially because the Perrys were very friendly with David Johansen and Cyrinda. So this breakup must have embarrassed them a lot, certainly. And you can imagine what it was to be a manager of both bands and have to deal with this kind of stuff. I mean, it was not fun."

This one's a bit of a low point on the album, almost too polluted, like a hungover version of "Last Child." It's awkward and it flails and ultimately flounders, and, oddly, that's kind of the vibe I get from the first two David Johansen albums. As for a further connection to Johansen, Joe plays rhythm guitars on "Not That Much" and "Cool Metro" from David's self-titled debut, recorded at the Record Plant and issued in May 1978.

Draw the Line closes with a cover of a Kokomo Arnold song called "Milk Cow Blues" but made famous by Elvis Presley as "Milkcow Blues Boogie." The King's version has a false start of sorts, and so does this one. Elvis and band start it slow and then he stops it, and they go fast. Aerosmith's false start is more of a "You guys weren't ready" thing. Also, Aerosmith emphasizes the riff, and it becomes a hard rock song, like "Walkin' the Dog," like "Train Kept a Rollin'," and like "Think About It" on the next album. As a result, it dovetails nicely into the mayhem of the rest of the record, which, noticeably, has no ballads other than the verse structure of "Kings and Queens," and even *that* is full band and then double time and heavy later in the song.

Relates Joe in his book, "Elvis had sung it and so had The Kinks. I was doing it way back in the days of The Jam Band. For years Aerosmith had been using it as an encore song. It rocked, and now we were recording it because our creative well had gone dry."

Brad takes the first solo, and Joe the second. There's harmonica, and by the end we have a song that underscores one of the band's chief mandates as a new, heavier version of a blues boom band, serving today's teen males from the great state of Indiana. But really, it's not much different than how the Kinks did it, other than a couple of extra kerranging chords in the brief bit that serves as the chorus.

"You can begin to see something happening," says Krebs, in summation. "Let's assume you are drawing an arrow that was continuing to go up from the first album through *Rocks*. *Draw the Line* represents, to me, that you've hit the peak and you're starting on the way down. 'I Wanna Know Why,' I think, is a song of dissatisfaction. I love 'Critical Mass.' I think that shows a different side of Aerosmith. 'Kings and Queens' has a Jack Douglas credit. Which is interesting: Jack Douglas begins to write songs. He's on four of them. So you can now see that the addiction is taking over. Because when one analyzes the difference in the sections of Aerosmith's career, that's the price you pay with drug addiction, especially heroin, from what I can gather. It undermines your ability to write the most-brilliant lyrics by yourself. So I think this shows up in that way."

Reflects Joe, charting the course from being this wiped and mind-blown to more of a sense of clarity later on, "I know there's been a lot made of the drugs and all that stuff, and the Toxic Twins. And frankly, we were never named the Toxic Twins until after we were cleaned up, in the '80s. It's kind of funny. But this is what it takes to keep it together. And especially when some of our arguably most successful years, to the public, were some of the most tumultuous years. When we were sober, that's when people's personalities really get a chance to come through. There's the old thing, like, everybody's all fucked up on drugs and they fight and they talk, and they don't talk and they don't deal with their problems. So once you take the drugs away, two things happen. You learn that you can write songs without being fucked up and having time for hangovers every day. But also, the real personalities show through, and you have to learn how to deal with that."

"Yeah, well, that's a nice way to put it," chuckles Tom, summing up, when I call *Draw the Line* a frantic version of *Rocks* and a "running on fumes" version of *Rocks*. "Yeah, that album to me was, you know, I'm glad we got it out, and I understand there are a lot of fans of that record. But I remember what it was like to make it. It was hell to make it, and compared to the direction we had set with *Toys in the Attic* and *Rocks*, we were going off the rails. You know, I'm always surprised. There are tons of people with Aerosmith T-shirts with that cover artwork on it. We have people that really are attached to that album."

"Let's start it with some kind words and maybe I'll get in the mood," beings *Hit Parader*'s James Spina, reviewing the record for the Aerosmith-faithful mag, albeit many months after issue. "The Hirschfeld cover drawing is wonderful and ties right into the title of the record. Hirschfeld works his daughter's name into every drawing he does. It is 'Nina.' Look for it yourself. And now the music. Don't get me wrong, especially since I've been a fan for years. Maybe I'll get all of that admiration out of the way first. Way back when I wrote for a mag called *Rock Marketplace* (since replaced by *New York Rocker*), I was raving about the finer points of this little old band from Boston. I bought the first album the same day that I purchased the first New York Dolls album, and it was a toss-up as to which one I liked more. Aerosmith popped on the scene in some transitionally lean times. There wasn't much happening back in those days, and the band deserved more credit than they initially got."

"All that praise still goes, but *Draw the Line* brings me down," continues Spina. "The beat at times resorts to some uncalled-for heavy-handedness, which in turn finds Tyler resorting to sickly whining (most noticeable on 'Kings and Queens'). And when will we have a built-up ballad to replace 'Dream On'? They never tried it again. And that's a pity because we all know just how powerful the song could be. I love when a sturdy group like Nazareth takes on a slowboat such as 'Love Hurts.' Aerosmith needs to pull that off at least once per record, but they don't.

"My last complaint is actually a left-handed compliment. The best song on the album is Joe Perry's 'Bright Light Fright.' Perry actually even takes lead vocals on this ode to ghastly confrontations with a TV set while on tour in a never-ending string of motel rooms. The song hits like when Keith steps out on 'Happy.' Perry has one of those painfully endearing non-voices. He screams the hell out of this song and as an added attraction, Stan Bronstein lets fly with a scorching guest sax solo. It just makes me want to hear more of Perry even though I know that that could raise hell within the concept of the group. So, I'm not completely thrilled with *Draw the Line*. I expect more from them, and as we all know, these are times when no established group can expect to sit back and bide their time. There's tons of new stuff happening out there, and I don't want to see Aerosmith lost in the shuffle. Perhaps it will grow on me."

"Crunch rockers Aerosmith wins the award for noisiest record of the year," proclaims Larry Kelp of the *Oakland Tribune*, "which sounds like you're actually at the concert, thanks to feedback, sound bouncing everywhere, echo, screaming voices and guitars that add up to the quintet's best album. There're even a couple of listenable cuts on it. Of course, they still can't play, and lead vocalist Steven Tyler has never attempted to sing (probably wisely), but they haven't lost their hard-driving energy, and that's why this record is already on its way to selling a couple million copies. 'Critical Mass' is easily the best song, though, and the minor key guitar tag on 'Kings and Queens' is an interesting change of pace. Almost home-free, Aerosmith had to blow it by doing a remake of 'Milk Cow Blues,' which exposes all the band's weak spots, of which there are five."

Writes Conrad Bibens in the *St. Joseph News-Press*, "Aerosmith's fifth album, *Draw the Line*, is erratic. When its material works, the group is probably the best American hard rock band today. When it doesn't, Aerosmith sounds like just another boogie outfit going nowhere. The five members of the band consciously try to look and act like The Rolling Stones. They're at least as homely as the Stones. For what it's worth, lead singer Steve Tyler does have more than a passing resemblance to Mick Jagger, though it's been said you could confuse Tyler with Carly Simon just as easily.

"But on record, Aerosmith is closer to Led Zeppelin. Tyler's leering, screaming vocals are similar to Robert Plant's, while the guitar work of Joe Perry and Brad Whitford recalls Jimmy Page. That would be fine if Aerosmith showed the latter band's variety. Zeppelin has always been willing to experiment occasionally, doing all-acoustic numbers that complement the heavy metal. Aerosmith won't take that chance. They've made it to the top by rocking without quarter, and they're not going to mix it up now that they're near-superstars. Tyler and company are giving the people what they want, not what they might need.

"Jack Douglas, the band's producer, has a heavy influence on Aerosmith. He co-arranged all the songs and helped write two of them. He's mainly responsible for the group's wall[-]of[-]volume approach. The production is purposely sloppy. The music comes out of the speakers like a stiff wind that makes it seem as if the band is rehearsing in the next room. Besides the drums, it's hard to distinguish between the individual instruments. Even Tyler's snarls begin to sound like guitars. That style isn't necessarily bad. On the title song, which opens the album, Aerosmith is at the top of its form. The band cruises along like a well-tuned sports car, and the momentum carries over well into 'I Wanna Know Why.'

"But by the last song on side 1, 'Bright Light Fright,' it all becomes a blur that taxes one's endurance. 'Kings and Queens' opens side 2, and it might be the best song Aerosmith has done since 'Dream On.' It's more of a ballad with gothic-like fantasy lyrics that make it seem mysterious. Two forgettable rockers follow. Then the album closes strongly with 'Milk Cow Blues,' which features a blues beat surprisingly similar to something the original Allman Brothers Band would have done. *Draw the Line* will suitably please Aerosmith fans. Still, it isn't as good as the group's previous album, *Rocks*. That effort may be [as] good as these guys are ever going to get, as long as they stick to their present formula. So, if you dislike hard rock, you'll hate Aerosmith. But if you like your music loud, rowdy and ill-mannered, this band is for you."

Bibens makes a number of excellent points. "Erratic" is apt, because "Draw the Line" is as great as Aerosmith would ever get, but there's also a good bunch of "going nowhere." He gets both the Stones and Zeppelin comparisons right, although greater dynamics and variety on an album isn't automatically a plus. You have forty minutes, and trying something experimental mathematically takes away from more time exploring one's core style. In other words, maybe another solid Aerosmith song turns out to be more productive than something like "The Crunge" or a song with just acoustic guitars and vocals. I love how he describes the white-knuckle production of this album, especially the part about all the sounds bleeding together, including Steven's vocals. I think it works great here—urgent and street-heated—whereas way into the future, sort of *Get a Grip* forward, that exact thing is going to happen, only it'll be because of too many tracks used, an overworking of everything that expensive studios have to offer. It results in muddy, noncommittal guitars and lead vocals augmented by multitracking plus professional nonband guest singers. Worst of all, certainly from *Get a Grip* forward, we get drum performances that sound like a clumped conglomeration of world music percussion instruments, handclaps, programming, sampled snare, and some amount of Joey playing an actual drum set.

Also making some excellent points is *Crawdaddy*'s Toby Goldstein, who articulates why *Draw the Line* elicits this vague sense of dissatisfaction.

"Aerosmith's best riffs invariably became their hit singles. When *Rocks* scored with nothing as spectacular as the early 'Dream On' or even their cover of 'Train Kept a Rollin',' the band was remotivated to the lure of a well-constructed catchphrase. *Draw the Line* certainly boasts a panorama of those hypnotic repetitions. Unfortunately, it rarely has the accompanying melodic strength needed to make those foundation lines memorable. *Draw the Line*, almost two years in the process, contains many tunes that will be ignored on disc, though they may well be tailor-made for copying by high school cover bands. To its credit, however, the album closes with the best arrangement Aerosmith have ever recorded, even if they didn't write it.

"*Draw the Line* begins optimistically with the title song reverberating like high-powered chimes. Tyler's fine-tuned vocals have at last broken away from sounding like either Mick Jagger or Robert Plant. He spends the bulk of the song in a comfortable yet still punchy register. Only in its reprise does he come back screeching, and one has the option at that point of concentrating on Joe Perry's tasteful slide or enjoying a call-and-response between Perry and Hamilton.

"Commencing with 'Critical Mass,' the band shows a deadly wear and tear on their creativity, which doesn't abate until the album's closing minutes. Solid passages leading inevitably to neat repeat lines are abandoned in favor of repeat lines alone, to the extent that even Tyler does more rhythm accompaniment than lead singing. Without necessary vocal continuity, songs like 'Get It Up,' which reeks of the Stones' current output or 'The Hand That Feeds,' never become more than bombastic chants. In fact, what sounds like an original hook on 'Draw the Line' is re-used in a mirror image for 'The Hand That Feeds,' discrediting both songs."

Good stuff there, with Goldstein telling us how and why some of these songs sound underwritten, how there are Songwriting 101 things missing from them. And I like that comparison of the two riffs at the end as well. Still, Steven's never sounded like Robert Plant or Mick Jagger (or David Johansen). He's mostly incredibly unique and loaded with personality, but if there's anyone we might compare him too, it's James Brown.

In one final review, Dennis Hill from *Press of Atlantic City* says, "Highlighted by 'exploding' guitars and powerful vocals, Aerosmith's *Draw the Line* offers new life to hard rock music. Steve Tyler is in rare form, showing his strength on the cuts 'Kings and Queens' and 'Milk Cow Blues.' Although at times his voice does become a bit experimental, most of the vocals on *Draw the Line* are enthusiastic. This Boston-based group has followed each of its previous albums with material that outclasses past endeavors. The strong point of Aerosmith's music is that it never goes beyond its audience. Joe Perry and Brad Whitford hold true to form with some very exciting guitar work. The driving force that keeps all this music together is drummer Joey Kramer. His drumming first caught my attention on the infamous song 'Dream On' from Aerosmith's first album. Since then, his work has never lacked power or imagination. Of all the hard rockers, Aerosmith has remained the most consistent band around. The same holds true with *Draw the Line*. If one American band can deserve to rate as stars, Aerosmith belongs in that category."

The Aerosmith Express Tour began before *Draw the Line* would show up in stores. Kicking off in June 1977, support would come from Nazareth, already a couple of years past their *Hair of the Dog* career peak. A short, chaotic European jaunt would take place in August before it was back to the safety of America's Midwest B cities in September. Into October and toward the end of the year, support would come from Styx and Wet Willie, respectively.

Asked about Europe, David says, "They were big, but they got up to the point where they were selling out Madison Square Garden, and I had to put them on their first European tour, and I was really hesitant about how they were gonna flip out when they suddenly had to play these smaller shows now. The only way I could get them to do it was to fly them around on a private plane so they wouldn't complain."

I asked Tom about the very real Midwestern heartland bread-and-butter anchoring of the band, along with this whole Blue Army situation.

"Well, first of all, it would've been really smart if we could have called the tour the Blue Army Situation—I wish I would have thought of that [laughs]. The Blue Army, originally that phrase was actually something that somebody thought up, probably Joe, back in the '70s, when we would pull up to an arena and there would be a long line of people waiting outside to get in and all wearing denim. So they would all be in blue and looking like they were all wearing uniforms. That would be the Blue Army. So we started using that term, the Blue Army."

As for the first part, Aerosmith's positioning as a sort of "flyover state band," Tom says, "That's a really good question. I think you're right, at least as far as connecting that term 'Blue Army' with the Midwest. When I think of it, I can picture pulling up to a gig right now, in my head, and it's probably some arena we played in the Midwest. Because we'd just play the heartland. That's where we really went and made our name. Obviously, we started in Boston, and then we made it in Detroit, and that was huge for us. And I think that's where the word really started spreading, in the Midwest, after we broke in Detroit.

"You think of the gigs on the coast, like Boston, New York City, Philadelphia, and then Atlanta, Miami, a lot of those cities; you think of the audience being a bit more jaded than Fort Wayne, Indiana, or Dayton, Ohio, or Cincinnati, Ohio. Ohio's like a country, because there's so many big cities. And then, you know, out in L.A., finally we broke out there, and L.A., we used to play in this venue in Santa Monica called the Santa Monica Civic Center. We must have done that place a bunch of times. San Francisco, and then finally up to Seattle and Portland, Oregon. But yeah, the Midwest, when I think of the Blue Army, that's kind of where I'm thinking. It's funny; when we decided to use that term for the recent tour, I'm thinking, gee, I hope there aren't a lot of people down south that are pissed off. It's like the Blue Army is like the Yankees."

Ted Nugent was in a similar situation. So was Kiss.

"Well, Ted Nugent, being one of Leber Krebs's bands, they were pretty much soldered to us for a lot of that," says Tom. "We did a ton of touring with Ted opening. And then with Kiss, what happened was we got into a rivalry situation with them within the first couple of times playing with them. And they made it really fast. We played down in, I think it was Delaware, and it was the first show that they opened for us. They showed up in the afternoon, around sound check time, and they were just a bunch of long-haired guys like us. And then that night, the roadies were coming out to the dressing room saying, 'You gotta come out and see what's going on out in the hall.' We went out there, and there's a frigging drum riser ten feet in the air with smoke and friggin' red and blue lights flashing, and these guys dressed up in their outfits and their makeup. We're like, 'What the fuck?!'

"And so we figured, oh my God, we're going to have to be on our toes to get out there and claim our territory. We had some dates around the Midwest, Detroit, where there were rumors of fights between the crews. It was not very long before they were off on their own headlining. So we didn't do a lot shows together. I mean, they were good guys. Paul Stanley is one of the nicest guys you'll ever meet, and Gene is such a character, fun to talk to. You can't complain. I mean, we were having a lot of success, and they were having a lot of success. There wasn't a lot of basis for that feeling. But yeah, anytime we were on the bill with them, we wanted to blow them off the stage, if possible."

Detroit-based Promoter Nick Caris (and dear friend of David Krebs) says the rivalry was bigger between Aerosmith and Ted Nugent—a.k.a. Deadly Tedly, the Whackmaster, the Tedinator, or just plain ol' Uncle Ted—but more for management attention.

"You couldn't judge a Nugent's or an Aerosmith's strengths just by record sales. 'Dream On' didn't hit until eighteen months after that album came out, or some ridiculous thing like that, which today seems crazy. But they had honed their skills. Aerosmith had opened up for ZZ Top, I remember, in Pittsburgh, and just different tours like that. But we built bands live. When you saw Aerosmith or Ted Nugent or Scorpions, regardless of the hit songs, the whole set was made from songs they had been playing live for years. I remember that the first time I saw Aerosmith was when David called me and said, 'Let's go—we're going to Boston.' The first time I saw them, Steven Tyler was playing the drums. I mean he was singing lead also, but that was the very early days. And I said, 'I don't know about a lead singer being the drummer, David.' And then David and I, we continued on with them for quite a long time. But we were always close. It was like me and David, me and David, all the time.

"But yes, back to your question, it was more a rivalry for David's time," continues Caris. "That's what happened with the Scorpions too. They were used to seeing David on the road with Aerosmith. He didn't have to babysit Nugent as much, because he had us covering his ass on that. When you get used to seeing him all the time, and then as

David got busier and Scorpions got bigger, there wasn't as much on-the-road daily involvement that they thought there should be. I knew they thought that David wasn't paying as much attention to them as he had with Aerosmith. But with Aerosmith, it was more like being, I don't know, a babysitter, in that era. Steven would walk in the office with his girlfriend or wife, whatever, and she'd want ten grand, and they'd give it to 'em. And then of course Joe Perry's wife or girlfriend, whatever, would see that Steven's wife got a big ring or something, and she'd want that. It was a game back and forth. It was that love/hate relationship. With Ted Nugent it was easy. Everybody got along with Nugent. And the crew, Nugent's crew, us, everybody, we'd been all together since the '60s. So it was much more of a family thing."

"Aerosmith broke Nugent, and they both broke AC/DC," explains David, in defense. "And Nugent probably helped break Scorpions or whatever. No, I don't think so. I would've heard that, and I don't remember hearing that. There may be occasions. I think there was an occasion at Pontiac Stadium where there was some asshole in production. But that was Nugent supporting Aerosmith, and Nugent opening for Aerosmith gave Nugent untold thousands of fans everywhere."

But then again, he does concede that Ted and Aerosmith were competing for attention from management.

"Of course. But they were both like our children, so to speak, even if Aerosmith was our first child, so they might have been our favorite by a little bit. Nugent was benefiting dramatically from this. Look, it's only when Nugent became a star that the forces around Nugent started to play out, whatever they could do, to diminish the managers, because he lived in Jackson, Michigan, and we were not on tour with him every day, and we were based in New York building a company. So, once you get to the top, there's a whole set of different soap opera games that go down where other people say, 'Now you're a star; I can manage you' [laughs]. I mean, to me, the applause should go to the managers who are there until the first gold album, basically."

Asked by Dave Reynolds about Deadly Tedly, Steven says, "He can be very intimidating. At least he's intimidated the fuck out of me a couple of times." Adds Joe, "Ted has a very strong ego, and if you walk around like you're fuckin' king of the castle, being a rock star, then you're gonna run into problems with him. Ted is a real person. But you

Chain Reaction promo photo, with Steven (*far left*). *Michael Ochs archive*

"Dream On" as a Dutch picture sleeve, German promo and 1975 US reissue

Early-days Columbia Records promo shot. *Left to right*: Steven Tyler, Joey Kramer, Brad Whitford, Joe Perry, and Tom Hamilton.

Get Your Wings ad from *Rolling Stone*. *Martin Popoff archive*

From the Ozark Music Festival, held at the Missouri State Fair in Sedalia, Missouri, July 20, 1974. A couple of dozen acts played over the three days of the fest, including America, the Eagles, Ted Nugent and the Amboy Dukes, Bob Seger, and Lynyrd Skynyrd. Emcee for the occasion was Wolfman Jack. © *Rich Galbraith*

1973 print ad for a Cleveland gig, sold out at roughly thee thousand in attendance. The next night the band would play Toronto, representing their first Canadian show ever.

US promo 7" of "Train Kept a Rollin'"

Get Your Wings CD reissue ad

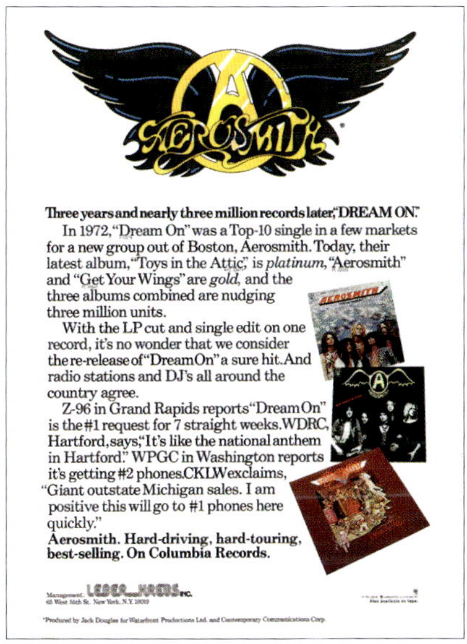

Creative *Toys in the Attic* ad that ran in the UK. *Martin Popoff archive*

Leber Krebs ad congratulating themselves and the band

Japanese 7" picture sleeve issues of "Walk This Way" and "Toys in the Attic"

The unsung Brad Whitford, who by this point in the summer of 1976 had contributed to the band "Round and Round," "Last Child," and "Nobody's Fault." © *Rich Galbraith*

The Run D.M.C. remake of 1975's "Walk This Way," issued July 4, 1986. It scored platinum success as a single in both the US and the UK.

A *Toys in the Attic* ad that ran in *Rolling Stone*

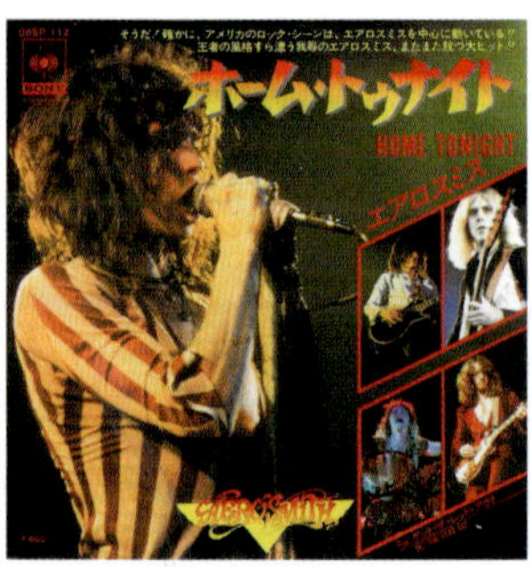

Japanese singles for "Last Child" and "Home Tonight," along with a German issue for "Last Child"

Elegant two-page ad from *Billboard* celebrating the success of *Rocks*

The Toxic Twins, Tulsa Assembly Center, Tulsa, Oklahoma, June 22, 1976. © *Rich Galbraith*

The iconic *Rocks* ad featuring the white album cover, along with an industry ad that ran in *Billboard* and a summary UK ad from the *NME*. *Martin Popoff archive*

A couple of more from the *Rocks* campaign, Tulsa Assembly Center, Tulsa, Oklahoma, June 22, 1976. © *Rich Galbraith*

Mono promo issue of "Home Tonight" from *Rocks*

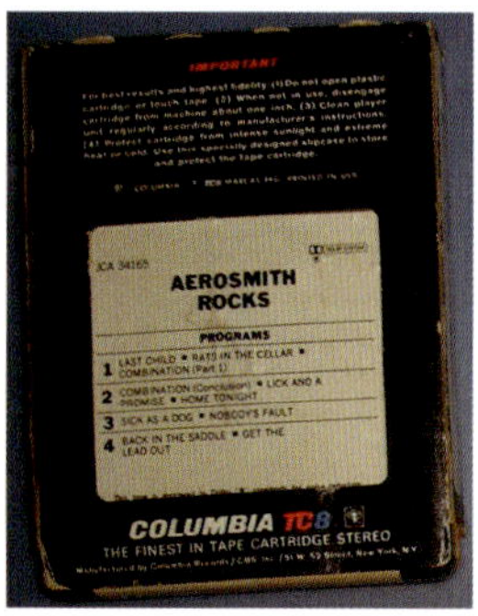

Back of a *Rocks* eight-track tape

This Seattle festival show attracted a crowd of 51,000, who enjoyed performances by Jeff Beck, Derringer, Starz, and headliners Aerosmith, although the heroes of our story went on at 11:30, a half hour late, and, judging from reviews, looked and sounded disinterested.

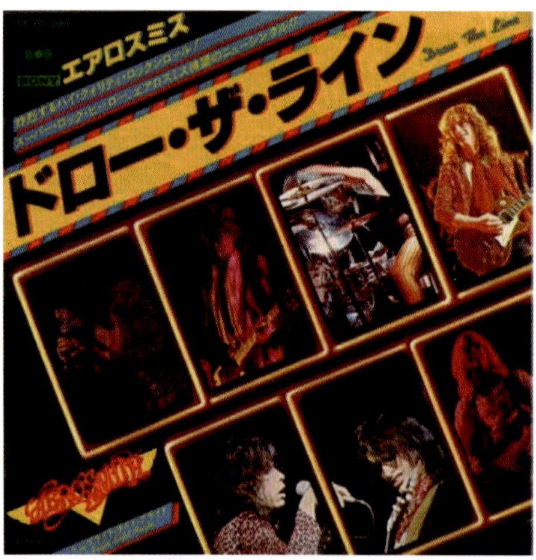

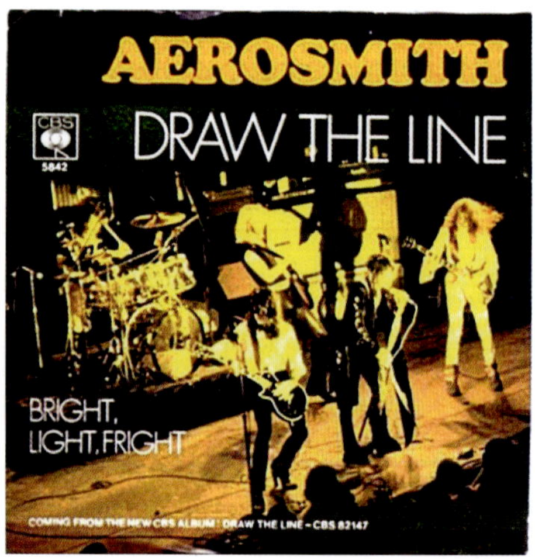

Dutch and Japanese picture sleeves for "Draw the Line"

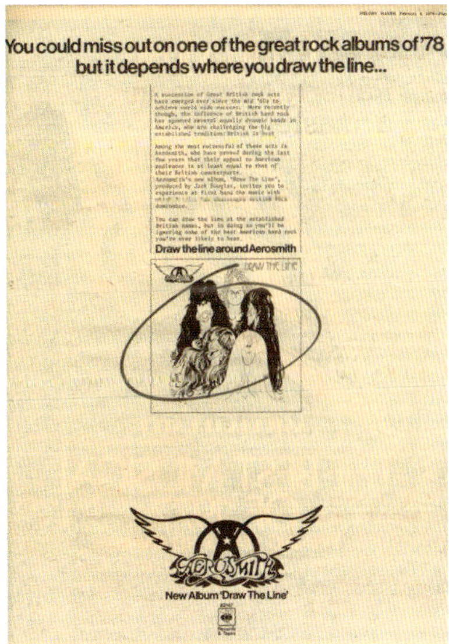

US and UK ads promoting *Draw the Line*

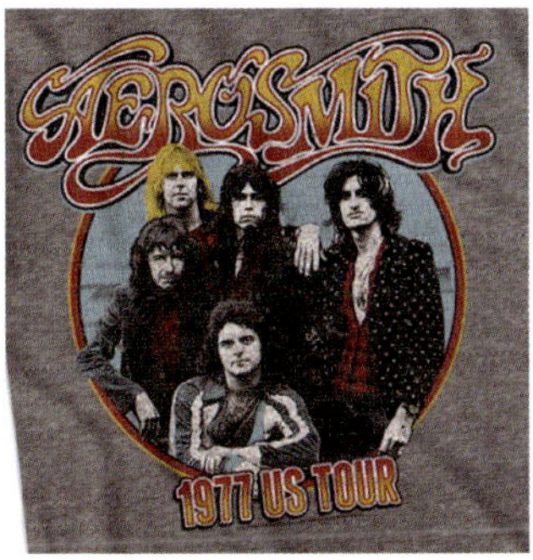

An assortment of classic '70s-styled Aerosmith rock tees

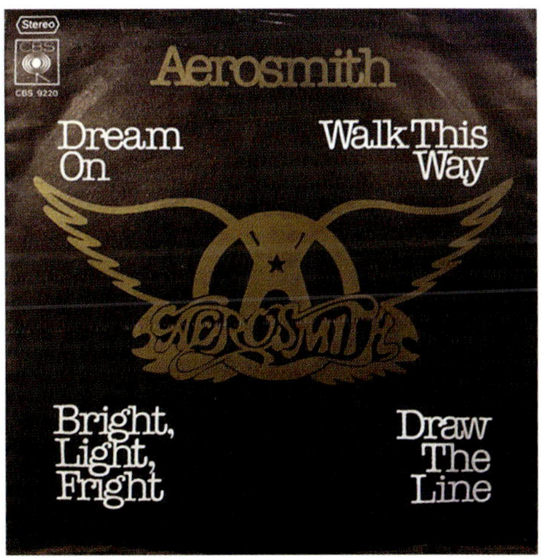

Dutch issue of "Come Together," along with yet another permutation of "Dream On" in the 7" format

Two US ads for Aerosmith's first live album

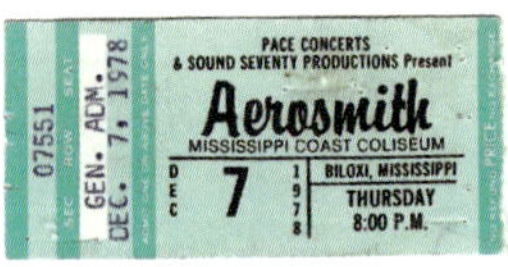

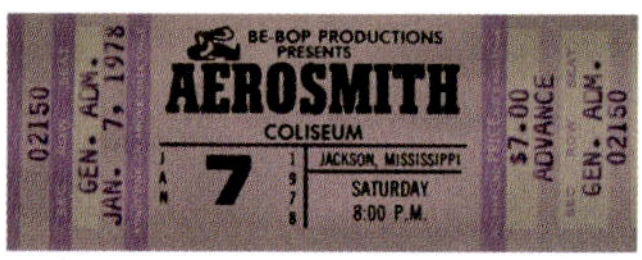

Vintage tickets, along with a satin backstage pass

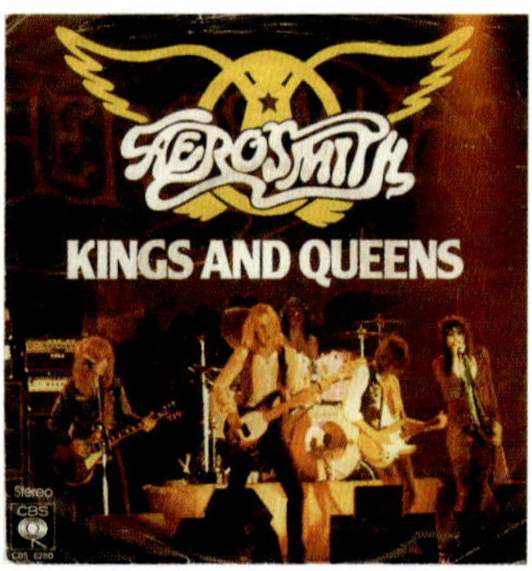

German-issue "Kings and Queens"

Japanese *Draw the Line* (and Neil Diamond) ad. *Japanrockarchive*

US promo studio version of Richie Supa's "Chip Away the Stone" song, as interpreted by Aerosmith

Ad for the *California Jam 2* album, along with promo materials for the concert and its sister fest

Myriad Convention Center, Oklahoma City, Oklahoma, October 12, 1978. Supporting were soft rockers Exile. Attendance was about 10,000 in a venue that held 15,000. © *Rich Galbraith*

A few more from the Myriad show in Oklahoma. © *Rich Galbraith*

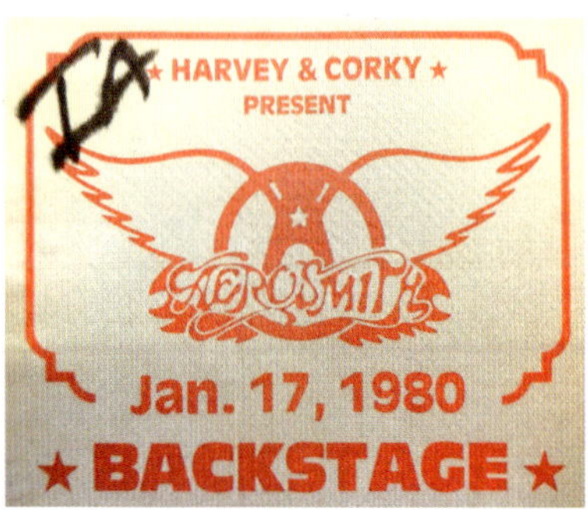

A few shirt designs and a backstage pass

Victorious golden-era Columbia Records promo shot

A couple of appropriately grimy-looking *Night in the Ruts* ads

A *Night in the Ruts* eight-track plus the Japanese single issue of "Remember (Walking in the Sand)"

The twelve-times-platinum *Greatest Hits* album plus an ad for it

Let the Music Do the Talking, *I've Got the Rock 'n' Rolls Again*, and *Once a Rocker, Always a Rocker*

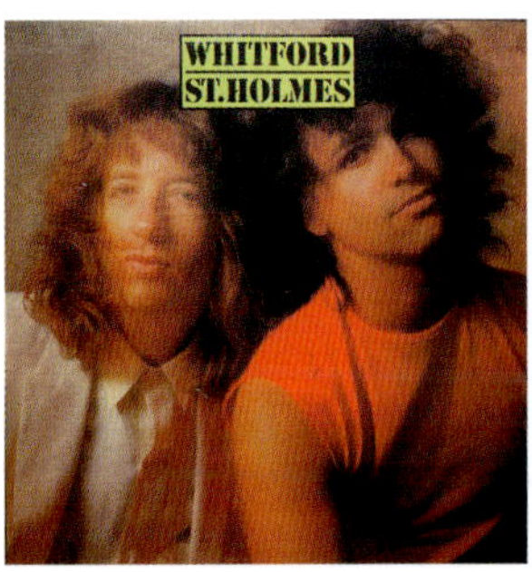

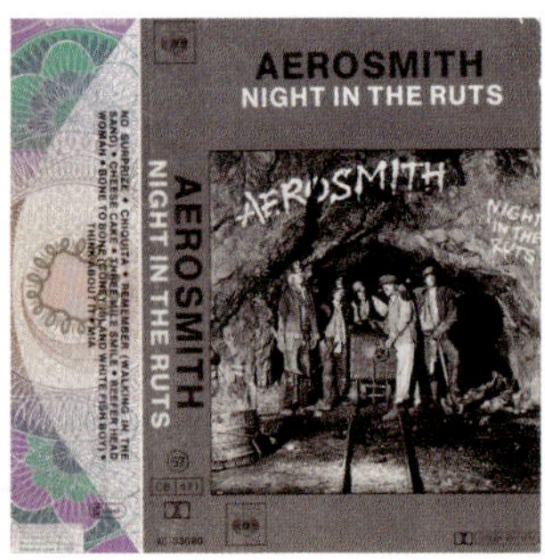

The *Whitford St. Holmes* album, along with a couple of cassette issues of *Night in the Ruts*

Maple Leaf Gardens, Toronto, Ontario, December 9, 1982, with Rose Tattoo and Nazareth as support. There were 15,000 people at this show, but Nazareth would have sold a lot of those tickets, given how popular they were across Canada. © *Ricky Jay*

Rock in a Hard Place as Japanese vinyl and American cassette

Baltimore Civic Center, Baltimore, Maryland, February 16, 1983, with Pat Travers as support. © *Rudy Childs*

Left: Record label 8" × 10" promo glossy of the vagabond *Rock in a Hard Place* lineup

Right: "Five star rock from America's finest"

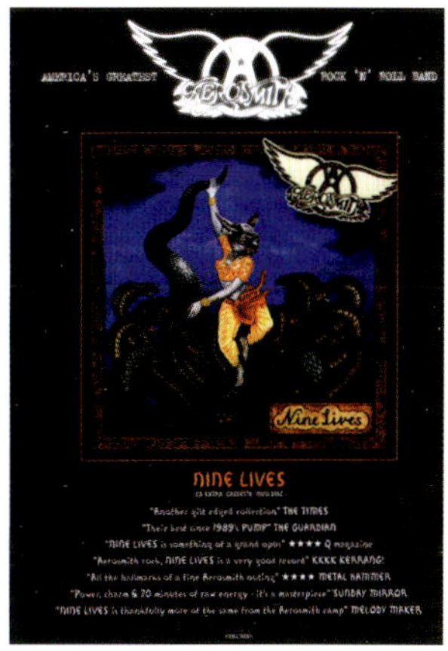

Ads for *Done with Mirrors* (1985), *Classics Live II* (1987), and *Nine Lives* (1997)

Ads for the 1993 remaster program along with a Japanese notice for *Just Push Play*

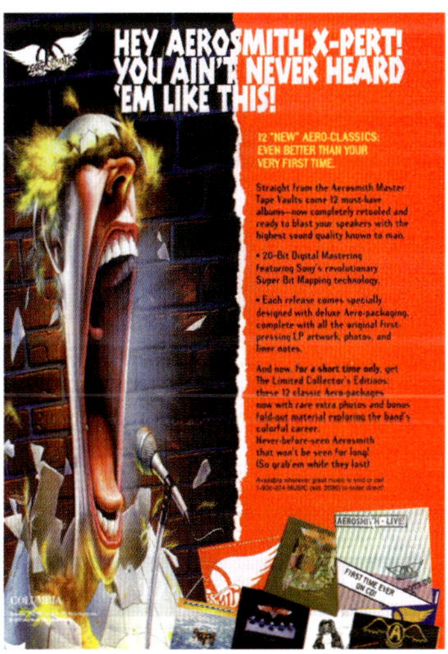

Aerosmith "now," although now is already fifteen years ago! Air Canada Centre, Toronto, Ontario, November 27, 2012. © *Bill Baran*

can be put off by him if you have the wrong attitude; Ted is honest and from the heart. He's a little too macho and chauvinistic for my taste, but he's a good guy."

Reflects David, back on the subject of the rock 'n' roll regions of America, "Well, if you go back to the late '60s, early '70s, you find that on the East Coast of America, or the northeast coast, the biggest bands in terms of record and ticket sales there were basically from England. Aerosmith, besides Boston being their home, so that they really had a deep audience build-up there, really broke out of the Midwest. The further you got from the East Coast, the more kids were into American rock. Plus, it doesn't hurt that Steven Tyler is probably the best front man to come out of America. But our initial interest came from the fact that they were already selling out big places in Boston even before they had a record out. The UK bands, I think they were spending most of their time on the East and maybe the West Coast and skipping over the middle. And Aerosmith were so good, that you would go into . . . you see, radio was totally different then. You could go into a city, create a charismatic reaction, and radio would go on your record the next day. You can't do that anymore. A lot of the ground rules have changed. I think that's a testament to how good Aerosmith was, that they are still around and still headlining. I mean, that's pretty good—we're talking thirty years later."

But there were growing problems, explains David. "For every group, you have one set of problems as you're building and there's another set of problems when you get to the top floor and try to maintain yourself on the top floor. My experience looking at Aerosmith, Nugent, Scorpions, AC/DC . . . not AC/DC as much. I think they were very lucky to get bigger replacing with Brian Johnson after Bon Scott died. But Ted Nugent's history is that he basically stopped growing when he got divorced, and Aerosmith's career was lost for five or six years because of heroin, and Scorpions' career was dramatically hurt by the takeover of the band by the business manager and the bass player.

"So it's one thing to build, and everybody is sort of working as a team, and then everybody gets to the top and they say, 'Oh, okay, I know what to do.' There's a major difference . . . if you're a manager who was on the road with your band, you are basically the next member of the band. We did not design a management company to ever do that. We wanted great tour managers, and we would stay in New York and then go out to important dates. Like if Aerosmith was ever on a stadium date, I was there. But if they were playing Dayton, Ohio, in an arena, probably not. I didn't personally ever want to do that. I also felt, by the way, looking back, if you are a manager who did that, then you ran a big risk of familiarity breeding contempt. You are too close. And from the minute we represented Aerosmith, they had their own accountant in Boston and their own lawyer in Boston, to protect them. And I was not a business manager. If you had an accountant that the attorney thought was good, I thought you were in good hands. I never said to them, 'Let me see your tax returns.'"

And it was still working, somewhat, at this point. "Aerosmith as a band were five fingers on one hand, in a sense. And sort of claws of a fist because they were fighting to be #1. All these bands were competing for the same position. I think we respected Steven Tyler for that, and we tried to, as often as possible, meet his demands, because he was a perfectionist and it was happening."

And that went for radio as well as ticket sales. "Yes, remember, if you're a radio station, you want to be promoting the coolest band in town. So ultimately, radio became a fan of Aerosmith. It was a market-by-market kind of conquest. And in the end, Aerosmith had conquered the whole country. They were like the Marines, conquering beachhead after beachhead, based on great live shows and then word of mouth, which spread to radio."

The major headline of the Aerosmith Express Tour would come from an encounter with explosives the band would have in Philadelphia. Writes Lisa Robinson in *Hit Parader*, "Aerosmith cancelled some scheduled October concerts when a giant firecracker tossed onstage at the first of two Philadelphia Spectrum shows injured Joe Perry's hand and Steven Tyler's eye. A vein was cut in Perry's left hand (his playing hand) and he was rushed to a hospital where he received several stitches. Fragments of the firecracker went into Tyler's eye and singed his cornea. After receiving medical attention, he donned an eye patch.

"Larry Magid—who promotes the rock shows at the Spectrum—admitted that there are definite problems with firecrackers in major arenas with certain bands. 'Aerosmith tends to bring out that element,' he said. 'That's not to say that they're not nice kids or a good group. I like them, but let's face it, this stuff happens.' Magid said that a firecracker had been thrown from the third tier behind the stage and hit part of the set behind the band, causing it to explode and then hit Perry's hand. (Another recent episode in Philadelphia resulted in a shooting outside the Spectrum following a Funkadelic show.) 'Look,' he emphasized, 'it's a problem in America today. We live in a violent society with a high crime rate. If you have 20,000 kids at a concert and one kid throws a firecracker, what are you going to do? Cancel all shows? It's not really a problem of the arenas and the bands—it's a society problem.'"

On September 18, 1978, each of the four members of Kiss issued solo albums. "Yeah, I did play on it," remarks Joe, asked by *Metal Forces*' Dave Reynolds about the Gene Simmons installment, "if you can distinguish my work on it. It was just like a who's who in the music business at the time. I was on a track that also had Rick Nielsen of Cheap Trick and Richie Ranno of Starz . . . and Lassie! It was ridiculous. It was the time when he was going out with Cher, and he was living in Hollywood and sending air tickets to everybody he knew to fly in and work on his record. It was Gene's who's who party."

Joe plays on "Radioactive" and "Tunnel of Love." And speaking of Cheap Trick, it would be Jack Douglas producing the band's visceral, aggressive 1977 debut album, after which Tom Werman would take over the reins on subsequent releases.

Next up for Aerosmith was a long-awaited and entirely warranted double live album. *Live! Bootleg* hit the shops on October 27, 1978, following in the footsteps of a number of successful projects like this. In the early '70s the formula worked just fine for the Allman Brothers, Humble Pie, Uriah Heep, and Deep Purple. More recently, they were joined by Peter Frampton, Led Zeppelin, Foghat, Rainbow, Ted Nugent, Thin Lizzy, and Kiss, who now had two well-regarded concert albums under their belts with the recent release of *Alive II*. Also, the previous month, close competitors Blue Öyster Cult had just issued a second live album, titled *Some Enchanted Evening*. Joining the fray soon would be Pat Travers, UFO, and Judas Priest.

"Well, my theory was that after a few albums, you needed you to have a rest whereby you could maybe take two years to write the next album instead of one year," explains David Krebs. "And by doing that, I bridged the gap with a live album. We thought it was a good idea. You're a live band, you're attracting one million people, what better souvenir than to have a live album from your show? And the label thought that was excellent, and it wasn't expensive, and beyond that, I'm not sure what the answer is. But I do know that with Aerosmith, we wanted them not to have the pressure of another studio album at that time."

"Everything is up there on the stage," answers Jack, on why a hard rock band like Aerosmith is the perfect band to be making a live record. "Would you buy a Jay Z live record? There really isn't much of an alternative. I don't know, Britney Spears live?! I don't know. I don't get it. It's gotta go in the studio and get fixed up. Hard rock is just the music that translates most. For me, at a rap show, the audience is more spectacular than the show.

"But look, Kiss *Alive!* wasn't a live album," continues Douglas. "It was done in the studio. When I did *Bootleg*, that was a real live album. It sounds like hell, and the band plays all those songs too fast. A lot of people love that album. I happen to like it a lot. It sounds like the band live, you know? With their pants down, with all the flaws. And we didn't do very much to fix that up. And the same with *Budokan*, Cheap Trick. Well, I had to do a lot, but only technically to get the thing back . . . to get some presence in it. We didn't fix very much. Those are live albums.

"Now *Frampton Comes Alive!* and the Kiss album just sold a gazillion albums. So they came to us in the show, 'So are you going to do a live album like *Frampton Comes Alive!* and Kiss?' And you know, my big question was 'Well, I thought you said a live album.' Live to me was live. So I went out on the road for six months and recorded Aerosmith live. And I put it together and gave Columbia a live album. A real live album.

"And when they got it, they came to the studio and said, 'You have to be kidding. This is terrible. It doesn't sound like *Frampton Comes Alive!*' And I said, 'Well, of course not, because this is really a live album.' So they said, 'Well, we're rejecting it. We'll give you a week to fix it up and then send it back to us.' So we booked a week of mix time at Record Plant, and we would go to the studio in the morning and then leave. And come back late in the afternoon and check out of the studio. I mean no one . . . we sent the engineers, 'Everybody, go home.' And then a week later we turned in the same record, and they approved it [laughs]."

I asked David the same thing, about why these hard rock live albums did well, and he said, "Because for the most part, those kind of bands are really arena sounds that you want to re-create as a souvenir. I mean, I have never heard one of these albums that you could buy as you leave the show—maybe you have—do they really sound good? I don't know. But Aerosmith *Live! Bootleg* was specifically meant to be kept raw. That wasn't an innocent . . . that didn't happen by accident."

If the idea was to have *Live! Bootleg* sound like a bootleg, that sentiment carried over to the packaging as well, which was a hot mess. Even the track listing is a bit botched, with "Draw the Line" not listed but sort of tucked in as a hidden track. Jack talks about how during the recording of *Draw the Line*, the band was doing a number of live radio concert broadcasts, and some high-quality bootlegs emerged from the situation. So the point was that this would look like one of those, as well as slot right in playing- and productionwise. Ergo, the front cover had text that looked like it was stamped on, and the back cover included a couple of coffee stains. Inside it looked like a real live album; for a gatefold we got forty-eight little live shots with the band looking heroic, especially Steven, mostly in resplendent white.

Says Tom, "He was determined to differentiate himself, and so he wore clothing that we used to kid him a lot about, the stuff that he wore. But then we would notice that people were being very entertained by it. And Steven was very much into learning how to adjust every aspect of his personality and his appearance to create something special for the audience. I was kind of a jeans-and-T-shirt guy, but I had to quickly learn that, okay, walking onstage for me is not just about jeans and a T-shirt. Try to look like some of those English bands [laughs]."

The inner sleeves, albeit gloss, looked like brown kraft paper, with all the crediting rendered in courier font as if from a typewriter, and with a tired ribbon at that. Also included was a four-panel live-shot poster.

"I think that was the band's idea," reflects David. "And I believe it was an attempt . . . remember at that time, there was a huge number of bootlegs out there, so we were probably doing this as some sort of joke on that, calling it *Live! Bootleg*. And I think its production is pretty raw, if I'm not mistaken. But I haven't listened to it in a while. I think it definitely represented what Aerosmith's strength was, which was live."

As Joe explained to me, the studio canon forms the legacy, but playing live is where it's at. "I've always felt that the albums, because of the era we grew up in, that kind of sets the precedent for what I think is valuable. And I've always felt that what you record in the studio is definitely the soundtrack for the live show. And it's funny; sometimes when everything is working perfectly, just the way it's supposed to work, you have great sounds, the audience is with you, everything's perfect—and you still have a lousy night. You can't put your finger on why. And then there's other nights where everything should go wrong. You know, everything does go wrong, the power goes out, twice, you're breaking strings left and right, but it could be one of the best shows you've done in months. So that's the magic to me. That's the unaccountable thing that I like, that intrigues me about rock 'n' roll, that excites me about rock 'n' roll."

"I like to think of us as, sometimes, the best band on the planet," continues Perry. "There are a lot of times when it could be some band in a club, and they're having one of those bad nights. Some magic in there gets lost, but they are the best band in the world that night. You know, I've seen the Stones, and they sucked. I've seen them when just nothing worked. You know what I mean? Nothing locked in. They were just kind of walking through it. Then I've seen them other times when there's no doubt in the world that they're the best band in the world—I mean, hands down. That's what I think of it as, that magic between the live performance and the fans. And in the end, locking up, I have to say, I want to be remembered for some of those nights."

That's a great way to frame this *Live! Bootleg* album. Sometimes it works gloriously, explosively, and sometimes the guys are floundering. But it all sounds heroic, warts and all, the band laying it all out and then resisting the urge to go into the studio and rerecord bits and pieces, which is so often the case. Okay, there was a bit of that, a bit of tinkering back at the Wherehouse, mostly for flagrant technical glitches, but "Last Child" sounds next to falling apart, and "Walk This Way" amusingly speeds up at the end. "Sick as a Dog," with its shaky intro, sounds almost shocking here, next to the sumptuousness of the assembled performance of the song on *Rocks*.

Articulating the buzz of playing live, in conversation with Steve Newton, Tyler says, "When I get up there onstage, I make more sense in my songs than I do in real life. When I'm singin' a song, I call on places that lie dormant in me. Maybe it's unsettled stuff, but why should

I go blow it on a therapist when I can scream into a microphone and get paid for it? And not only do I get off, but people in the audience get off, and I watch them getting off on me getting off on them, and it creates this thing that's just amazing. It gives me goose pimples.

"You're looking at an Italian kid who grew up in the Bronx, that played in the Strangeurs and the Maniyaks and the Kingbees, and all these bands before Aerosmith, and made it as big as the peers I wanted to be like! The Beatles aren't around anymore, but I always wanted to be like the Rolling Stones—I wanted to be Mick Jagger—and Donovan, and the Animals. I wanted to be like those bands, and here I am, still puttin' out good music—thanks to Joe Perry. Who would have thought? So as to how many lives I've got, I honestly, at times—and these are my honest, scary, crying thoughts—I look up and I go, 'Wow, something's goin' on.'"

"They both have their moments," says Brad (who of course takes a credit on "Last Child"), answering the same question as I asked Tom—the records or live? "I do take a lot of pride in performance. We feel good about it, and that takes practice. You really have to be ready to do it. We work at it. You have to stand up and be committed to it. But we do move between them. They are two very different venues. Playing in front of people, you just cannot top that." Contrasting himself with Joe in a live setting, Brad figures, "Joe is much more physical than I am. I'll get out and move around the stage, but he's so much fun to watch. I don't know, I'm definitely more reserved. I guess I'm just concerned with getting it right [laughs], just laying the foundation down."

Live! Bootleg opens with "Back in the Saddle," and there's almost a guitar flub. It's played fast, with energy, and one pleasant surprise is hearing Joey Kramer get busy, with some fancy yet obviously instinctive fills. Steven's vocals drift in and out, just like you'd get on a bootleg. It's from one of those dates with Nazareth opening, July 4, 1977, at Market Square Arena in Indianapolis.

"Sweet Emotion" couldn't possibly sound as posh as on *Toys in the Attic*, and it definitely doesn't. But again, it's a joy to listen to, if mainly for how Kramer goes nuts on the heavy metal outro jam. And that's him adding relentless rhythmic accenting to "Lord of the Thighs" as well, which in this format offers, arguably, more entertainment value over the behaved *Get Your Wings* version. These two performances were taken from a smaller show at the Aragon Ballroom, executed as a radio broadcast performance but then heavily bootlegged.

"I know of about four or five—no, maybe more—bootleg albums that people have of ours," Joe told *Hit Parader* at the time. "Tapes from radio broadcasts, concerts; it really makes us mad. There's nothing 'funny' on this album. No overdubbing. No cheating. It really is all live. We didn't want to just put out a bunch of tapes from our tour. This made it a little different. It was worth it to put out a live album if we could do it this way."

As he said in his book, "I didn't want to do a live album at the time because there were so many perfect live albums coming out, all doctored and fixed and overdubbed. Big deal. Double live album—'standard of the industry.' I felt like we had to avoid that and do a real live album like *Live at Leeds* or *Get Yer Ya Ya's Out* or that old Kinks album."

Side 1 closes with a jarringly thinner, more punk rock performance and recording of "Toys in the Attic." This take hails from an intimate hometown show at the Music Hall in Boston in front of 4,225 fans on March 28, 1978.

On to side 2 of the original vinyl, we get a deconstructed "Last Child." This was from an even smaller club show, executed for use on the live album. Billed as Dr. J. Jones and the Interns, the band played the Paradise Club, also in Boston, to a thousand fans on August 9, 1978. Next is a cover of the Beatles' "Come Together," recorded back at their space, the Wherehouse. Not fakin' it (as Nazareth would say), it ends with a handful of watchers-on clapping, and then a cross-fade into the sound of a bigger crowd. This song is here because Aerosmith had signed on to be part of the *Sgt. Pepper's Lonely Hearts Club Band* movie and double album, which included their rendition. The project, featuring Peter Frampton and the Bee Gees, was considered something of a debacle, with Aerosmith's limited involvement serving as something of a bright spot.

Next is "Walk This Way," here with lots of talk box. It's a raucous, casual version, very jammy, played funkier and with longer fills by Joey, and then, as mentioned earlier, faster at the conclusion. This performance took place at the 4,600-capacity Masonic Hall in Detroit. Closing side 2 is the aforementioned "Sick as a Dog," now merely mortal, from the same show as our "Back in the Saddle" album opener.

Side 3 opens with "Dream On," recorded at the Freedom Hall in Louisville, Kentucky, on July 3, 1977. Next, it's "Chip Away the Stone," written by band associate Richie Supa. It turned out to be the foremost song of value from the album, sounding like a Stonesy Aerosmith-penned classic. It was so well regarded, it was picked to be the only single from the album, issued with both live and studio versions of the song.

Of note, Aerosmith is part of the *California Jam 2* live album, featured there with three tracks, one of which is "Chip Away the Stone," and, oddly, the same version of the song that is on *Live! Bootleg*. On this one you can hear at least a little bit of supporting keyboardist Mark Radice, who is usually not much more of an afterthought elsewhere on the album. Says David, "Well, Richie Supa is a great songwriter, and he is still one of Steven Tyler's best friends, even though Steven lives in Maui, where he's been for a couple years now, and Supa lives in Miami. Supa is in the rehab business, using music as therapy."

Remarks Tom on "Chip Away the Stone," "It's a Richie Supa song that we always thought was going to be a single. It's sort of a pet song, but the public never seemed to like it quite as much as we did." A comparison with the version of the song heard on bootlegs of the Santa Monica Civic Auditorium show casts doubts that the album version comes from that April 8, 1978, performance, as suggested in the credits. In fact, there are discrepancies elsewhere as well, but it's laudable that they've provided as much information on the inner sleeves as they have, including a short quip from the band for each song.

Explained David on the big festival gig known as California Jam 2: "I was a very big proponent of stadium tours, so I really spent a lot of time putting together Cal Jam 2, which was Aerosmith and Nugent coheadlining for 300,000. And after that, because of the expense of converting an open field for a rock festival with a low ticket price at that time, the break-even split figure was, I think, 207,000 tickets. So I said, after that, this is totally stupid. Why don't we try to get into some stadiums? So the next one we did was at the Cotton Bowl, which was an 80,000-seater. I always thought this: If you're my fan and I can get you to see me perform outdoors in a stadium at night and follow my show with fireworks, I have then put forth an indelible impression on your psyche, okay? So, in 1979 we did maybe five or six big festivals. Each one we did something. We did one in Toronto, the Canaddian

World Music Festival, and we gave Canada two d's; that was our trademark. We did it with Michael Cohl, I'm sure. Texxas Jam had two x's. Aerosmith, Ted Nugent, Van Halen . . . those are the few kinds of bands that can do those kinds of dates on a consistent basis. Maybe not anymore. Also the Springsteens and Dave Matthews; they have the same draw in terms of their audience."

Speaking with Sam Dunn, David provides a bit more background on Cal Jam 2, which took place amid many of the dates sampled for *Live! Bootleg*, although the Aerosmith album steers clear of that event in particular.

"It was on March 18, 1978, and it was in a wide-open field that had to have fencing and latrines, and all sorts of amenities put into it. It drew about 300,000 people, and it was coheadlined by Aerosmith and Nugent, but I think it also had Heart and Foreigner. I always believed in long shows. I never heard a kid come up and say, 'You know, there was way too much music.' That's not the way it works [laughs]. Just like three-act packages were very valuable. Now, Bon Jovi tours by themselves. Well, that cuts off the chance of anybody being introduced. So you're in essence slowing down the progression and development of new artists.

"Cal Jam 2 established Aerosmith as an amazing gigantic draw," continues Krebs. "Strategically, we're at a point where I'm beginning to see cracks in both Aerosmith and Nugent, and part of my thinking was to try to do these giant events to build sort of a canopy over them while they recovered [laughs]. I know that because it was not fun, by then."

Recalls the promoter of Cal Jam 2, Don Branker, "Each one of these acts, remember, they're looking at a crowd that is a mile long. You can picture that. It's 350,000 people. You can't see them all from the stage. I do all the announcing, so I had to see it all the time. But it's like the earth curves before you see the end of the crowd, you know what I mean? [laughs]. And of course, Ted Nugent was real hot and had been hot with *Cat Scratch Fever*. He'd always been a good hard rock band, but he actually had a hit record at that time there. So he was very, very hot at the time. Aerosmith, this was actually right before their demise, to be honest with you. It was the *Draw the Line* album that had just come out then, and so they were hot with that there. They did a great show.

"But honest-to-God true story," continues Branker. "I got only one more act to play, and that's Aerosmith. I get a call on the walkie-talkies saying, 'Donnie, can you get to Aerosmith's trailer? We've got a problem.' Those are not words you want to hear. The problem was that my caterer, within the contract, which is one page of how much I'm going to pay them, and the rest is forty-nine pages, which is the lighting and the sound and all the technical requirements and of course the catering requirements . . . in there was a requirement of 2 pounds of jelly beans and no black jelly beans. My caterer had missed it and left the black jelly beans in it.

"So they called me in to tell me that they weren't going to play, which of course to me would have been a full-scale riot. I don't know how many people would be dead, how many of them would been hurt, but I know it would have been horrible. Because in order to gain access onto the inside of a 2 1/2-mile oval Indianapolis 500–type track, there were only two tunnels in. You've got to go underneath the tracks. So nobody could leave it in a very fast way if, God forbid, there was a riot.

"But nevertheless, I told them, 'Well, you are going to have exactly the amount of time it takes for me to get from this dressing room to the stage. I will make the announcement that you don't want to play because somebody forgot to take out the black jelly beans, and I'll pack my wife in my car and watch the riot at home on TV. That's how long you've got.' By the time I hit the stage, they were running behind me. I went up onstage and said, 'Ladies and gentlemen, let's give a warm Cal Jam welcome to Aerosmith!' Of course they did a great show.

"Now, I did not know at that time they were on hard drugs. That was unbeknownst to me. Of course I wouldn't have known that, so now I understand a little bit. But I don't forgive them. I probably won't watch *American Idol* because of it. I'm still upset with Steven."

So Don figures that Tyler was the fly in the ointment. "Yes, it was Steven. I had never met Steven before. Their managers were Leber and Krebs. They were the ones . . . east dressing room had a little room into it, and then there were big trailers. So I had a little room, like a little office into it, and then the dressing room was the bigger part of it. I just went into the office part, and Leber and Krebs told me, and then this guy walks out. I had never seen him before, and to be honest with you, I had been up for four days. Even a one-day festival is four days' worth of work, you know. You are building a city, and I'm responsible for everyone out there. So all I see is this guy walk out with a bunch of . . .

you know, a big mouth, the biggest mouth I ever saw in my life besides Stevie Nicks, and a bunch of silk handkerchiefs. You know what I mean? And he's telling me he's not going to play because somebody forgot to take his black jelly beans out. I know that if that shit happens, my show is not complete, and I would have to refund the show, because they were the headliners. Not forgetting the riots and all that other stuff. I mean, it's a whole quadrant of nightmare for me. It was all Steven."

Besides Don's successful tactics, the other reason that Cal Jam came off was because some of the significant acts were from the Leber Krebs stable.

"Well, Leber and Krebs at that time were managing both Aerosmith and Nugent, and they were at the show," explains Don. "So it was pretty easy, and both acts were with the same agency. So it was a package deal. Plus, Columbia was the number one record company in America at that time. They took these bands, and they would invest money into them."

There was also Frank Marino & Mahogany Rush, both with Leber Krebs and Columbia. "It's interesting that you brought him up," responds Branker. "He was phenomenal, by the way—phenomenal. I'm an old Hendrix fan, and he did Hendrix probably better than Hendrix could have done in groups at that time, if he'd still been alive. But there was another act on that people don't know about, called Rubicon. They came on after Aerosmith, and that was to keep the people there so they would do an orderly egress, you know, little by little, little by little."

This was a two-record band that would soon cough up Jack Blades and Brad Gillis (and right at the end, Kelly Keagy) to Night Ranger. "Right. It was a ploy that we tried to do because if we had 350,000 people leave simultaneously, that would have been another nightmare. Again, remember, they have to walk through two tunnels together. So we thought some people would wait and see. They were a bunch of old horn guys from Frisco, and not a bad band. But they emptied the place out within their forty-five-minute set, which is what we really wanted them to do. I'll be honest with you; once Aerosmith played, I really had completed my work to a certain extent. I really didn't pay much attention to Rubicon. To me it was just watching the people leave and making sure there weren't any problems leaving there. To me, it's just get out there, go on on time, do your best set, make the kids feel good, and stop on time. You know, do a good show and I'll provide everything else for you perfectly."

As for the *California Jam 2* album, "It didn't do very well at all. Not at all. Don't know why—it just didn't. The TV shows did well, but I think the record sold less than 100,000 units. As for Aerosmith, you know, they were on their way out. Basically, right after Cal Jam, they tried to do their own festival in Texas, and it did not fare very well. Then the band just imploded from heroin, unfortunately, until Run D.M.C. But yeah, if everybody just follows the yellow brick road, there really is no reason for problems. I've already dealt with all the problems beforehand. There would be a minimal amount of changeover, and we're ready for you to go. You know, I'm going to give you everything you wanted. But somebody did miss the black jelly beans. Sorry about that. My God, the world won't come to an end."

Back to the *Live! Bootleg* album, "Sight for Sore Eyes" was a capture from the same Boston Music Hall show as "Toys in the Attic" earlier. It has some snap to it and surprisingly represents our first selection from *Draw the Line*. In fact, at this juncture, Columbia hadn't been too happy with sales from *Draw the Line* and hadn't been on board with the live album idea, especially given the rough 'n' ready "bootleg" concept. There was supposed to be an attendant EP, featuring a nine-minute version of Fleetwood Mac's "Rattlesnake Shake," but it was deemed too extravagant, especially given the reluctant release of *Live! Bootleg*.

Side 3 closes with two selections from Indianapolis on July 4, 1977. Both "Mama Kin" and "S.O.S. (Too Bad)" take care of business, anchoring the album, both played briskly and with muscle, once again, Joey playing way more than he does on the originals.

Opening our final side is an archival set, featuring "I Ain't Got You" and "Mother Popcorn," recorded at Paul's Mall in Boston on March 20, 1973 (inner sleeve erroneously cites April 23), and originally used as a WBCN radio broadcast. I remember as a kid thinking it's kind of weird hearing this old cover song, "I Ain't Got You," on both Blue Öyster Cult's 1975 live album and now here again in 1978. "Mother Popcorn" is vintage James Brown, and on it, Steven plays a solid enough James Brown. On both songs, he's using the lower, more grown-up but semifake voice we hear on the *Aerosmith* album. For window dressing, the first one has harmonica from Steven and the second one has horns, with Steven, gracious, in his best James Brown emcee incarnation, announcing David Woodward.

"I thought they worked, don't you?" asks David. "That was another Steven Tyler idea, not mine. And closing with 'Train Kept a Rollin'' made sense because it was a trademark song before they had their first hit."

"The tracks 'Ain't Got You' and 'Mother Popcorn' on the album are legitimate bootleg tapes," explained Joe, speaking with *Hit Parader*. "They're from a live radio broadcast we did about five years ago. Someone taped it off the air and made a cassette. We did a stereo mix for the album—that's why it sounds like that. We wanted to put it on because that's what we sounded like long before anyone knew who we were. There were about a hundred people in the club that night, which was a big crowd for us then. I still like a lot of things about those tracks."

Attached to the end of "Mother Popcorn" is a bracing version of the band's latest anthem and clarion call, "Draw the Line," captured at the Tower Theater, Upper Darby, Pennsylvania, on March 26, 1978, attendance 3,132, in this famous venue frequented by all the greats at the time. The album closes with a headbanging version of "Train Kept a Rollin'" from the same Detroit show that brought us "Walk This Way." Inside it, there's a bit of damp squib "Strangers in the Night" on solo guitar, but soon that's dispensed with for the expected violent, raucous windup, firecrackers crackin' as we're sent off into the night.

By this juncture, as we were getting the band's first double live album, Aerosmith had managed to move on from a hundred fans at Paul's Mall to Cal Jam 2 in just five short years.

"Yeah, that Cal Jam, I think there were 350,000 people there," laughs Tom, in conversation with Sam Dunn. "And oh my God, it was so decadent; we were starting to make money, and we were starting to buy these little packets of stuff, and we would buy bags of them, and it was terrible, because it led to our destruction. But boy, were we having a fun time at that point. We were staying at the Beverly Hills Hotel, and every half an hour somebody was coming and saying, 'My God, there's 175,000 people; no, there's 250,000, there's 300,000,' until there were 350,000 people there. And it was the first time I became aware of what you call delay towers, which are secondary sound systems way out in the crowd. Because otherwise, the people are so far away, they're not going to hear it. So, you have the secondary sound system way out there that is calibrated somehow so that the sound can be coordinated. And from the stage we could see, you know, not that many more people than you could see in a big stadium show. But the thought that way out of the darkness, people were just going all the way to this invisible horizon, that was really cool. It was really overwhelming.

"But you know, one of the sad things about our history, things like that are really inspiring and exciting. But it also brings out a lot of intensity that somehow got the better of us, where at a gig like that, little things become big things. A little thing goes wrong, and it's something to really freak out about. And really experience a lot of pain about. So that was something that went along with the flavor of, oh my God, this is awesome; what we're doing here is awesome.

"And in fact, that night there was a huge screaming match. I can't remember the details of it too much, because it used to happen a lot. I just continued to have a good time, but there was some technical problem. I don't remember anything being to the point of affecting our performance, but there was a lot of screaming and yelling after the show."

6

Night in the Ruts and *Aerosmith's Greatest Hits*

"Talk about monkeys with guns."

Come time to follow up *Live! Bootleg*, it was the same old song and dance. With tensions building in the band and no end in sight for the guys' spiraling drug use, very much like *Draw the Line*, it became a pain getting any work done, especially when it came to getting lyrics out of Steven. A record was indeed started, in the spring of 1979, and Jack Douglas was even there. Soon he'd fall away from the project, replaced by Gary Lyons—Jack was divorcing his wife, and, as it turned out, the guys in the band liked his wife more than Jack!

Then they'd lose Joe. As Perry relates in his book, "I thought we cut some of the best tracks we'd ever done. The guitar interplay between me and Brad broke new ground. Everyone was at the top of their game. When it came time for lyrics, though, Steven began to drift away. Slowly, progress ground to a halt. I started to get annoyed, then aggravated, and then out-and-out pissed. We'd made untold millions. Where did all of it go? We went to work every day, spending a fortune on hotel bills and studio time with nothing to show for it. The whole operation had become a nightmare. I was tired of the bullshit. I just wanted to get in a van and go play rock 'n' roll. I was willing to play clubs—any clubs. I was told that when Steven finally did show up to do his vocals, he was smoking crack."

At the tail end of the process, picking up the slack would be Brad, along with guitar tech Neil Thompson, Richie Supa, and Jimmy Crespo, who would be an official member of the band for the next album. But before he left, Joe was involved with "No Surprize," "Chiquita," "Cheese Cake," "Reefer Head Woman," "Three Mile Smile," and "Bone to Bone (Coney Island White Fish Boy)," and yes, he and Brad are doing some of the best ensemble playing of their career. His last recording sessions for the album would be on May 30, although he was still continuing to play live after that, quitting while on tour after a July 28 show in Cleveland, after which Crespo joined for live performances.

Says David, "Remember, after *Draw the Line*, the two albums that followed were really like pulling teeth because of the drug problems, and they had very few great songs. Not that they are devoid of great songs, but instead of having a ballad and some really great stuff, and nothing mediocre, there's a lot of mediocrity on those records. And when they come to Geffen later, they are in a different position, because, in my opinion, if you look at Aerosmith post-Columbia . . . what is the right word? The main price Aerosmith paid for the early '80s drug addiction is that Tyler, I think, lost his ability to write in the elliptical double-entendre sensibility that he formerly had. And in order to move into a world of several hit singles, I'm pretty sure that if we looked at the writing credits of the Geffen albums, they are filled with cowriters who gave them pop credibility."

For their part, the guys in the band thought that Leber Krebs wasn't paying them enough attention anymore. To be sure, at this point they were starting to manage AC/DC, Scorpions, and Def Leppard as well, but as David has made clear to me on many occasions, he was losing his ability to keep Steven off drugs.

"It was really tough keeping it together," Joe told me, framed as one of the points he wanted to make with his book. "And I want people to see that. And also, I wanted people to see that the problems that we face aren't much different than the problems almost everybody faces, with their families, with their brothers, or brothers and sisters. I mean, I haven't talked to my brother in ten years. Well, you don't have that option when you're in a band. You know, you learn how to work with them. There's that dream and that magic that happens, that you've got a band that works, and you do anything to keep it together. There are bands that don't talk to each other when they're offstage, but they know the value of what they've achieved, and then they figure out a way to make it work. And, you know, it's hard work. It's emotional. It's like, you can get down, but you don't want people to see that.

"I have to say, for sure, *Night in the Ruts* didn't get the notice that I thought it should, because in spite of all the drugs and the partying at the end of that decade, I thought we played some of the best stuff we played in the studio yet. I mean, we were still recording the way that we recorded in the beginning, which is everybody gets in the room and plays, and then you kind of pick the best performance and maybe fix this or fix that. You know, the way that real players record. And I think that some of the playing on that record is great, right down to some of the solos that were being taken while the basics were being done. I think it was one of those records that just never saw the light of day, because I left the band halfway through. I mean, when all my guitar parts were done, and we were waiting for Steven to finish the lyrics, that's when I left the band. And so the band never really toured behind those songs. I feel like some of those babies, some of those songs, just never got to see the light of day."

But a record got issued, and of course still on Columbia, so it was widely distributed as well as promoted well enough, in terms of advertising. Written and rehearsed at the Wherehouse, then recorded at Media Sound and Record Plant, it wouldn't be called *Off Your Rocker*, which Tom has said was a possible name for it. Instead, *Night in the Ruts* hit the racks on November 16, 1979. The "spoonerism" title is one the band had kicking around for a while, but here it was applied to a dirty and depressing shot of the guys dressed as shabby coal miners. It's a stark image, and an amusing concept (cooked up by Tyler), but there's no Aerosmith logo and it's black and white. Against the bright, high-quality music enclosed (credit to the band—despite major turmoil), it really ruined the mood.

For the photo session, Steven first rolled himself in the coal, getting himself good and dirty, then he daubed coal all over the rest of the guys' faces. As he says in his book, "It was a dark and gloomy cover, but we were in a bleak and doomy state."

As Steven told Mary Campbell, "We looked up 1921 shots of old-fashioned mining people. We got the clothes and hats and picks and shovels, and we went into this mine in Los Angeles. It's up in the hills. It's a shaft that goes right through a mountain and branches off. It's in a park now. You pay a fee and do a movie or whatever. The original *Buck Rogers* was done there and *Star Trek* and *The Lone Ranger*."

On the back is another image from the shoot, this time outside, with Steven barely recognizable due to his hair being tucked up under his hat. Along the top are the song titles, annoyingly out of order and rendered in the same sort of roughly painted look as the text on the front. One side of the inner sleeve has individual portraits from the shoot, with each guy looking even sadder than on the front cover. The other side shows an order form for merch plus a summary discography.

Actually, Steven's first idea was to shoot the guys standing in the contents of "twenty or thirty big burlap bags of nuts," inspired by the fact that the band was nuts, but also inspired by the cover of *The Who Sell Out*, where Roger Daltrey is pictured in a bathtub full of baked beans.

"I think it was a reinforcement of how depressed the band was," remarks David, on the album cover. "That's where the band was at emotionally at the time."

Into the album, the first thing we hear is "No Surprize," and somehow, despite switching producers, what's obvious is that this is a great-sounding record, better than the cramped, almost-mono vibe of *Draw the Line*, although not as resplendent as *Rocks*. The guitars are dirty and sitting nicely in the mix, but the best part is Joey's snare, although his high hats and crash cymbals sizzle nicely as well. Tom can also be heard clearly, with Steven maybe a touch low.

Gary Lyons had been around for years, but my favorite projects of his would be this record, along with the first Foreigner, UFO's *Mechanix*, and *Gamma 2*. Asked if there's a Gary Lyons sound (I know the answer already—there isn't), he laughs, "I don't know; I can't answer that. I just recorded it as I hear it. I tend to go into each album with how I want the thing to end up. But you always start with a blank canvas. I could come up with a bunch more clichés. That's pretty much it. You go in, and you work with what you've got. It's very much, each band has their own sound and style, and you just try to enhance it."

Lyons was a musician himself, which helped on the job. "Back then, I played a lot of things. I haven't picked anything up in quite a while, but keyboards, guitar, bass. It was enough to sit down and show somebody what to play. Or to write sections of songs and place them.

"Let's say producer first," answers Gary, when asked if he's more of a producer than an engineer, having engineered so much throughout the 1970s. He also has the engineering credit on *Night in the Ruts*, with Rod O'Brien and Peter Thea assisting. He cites Foreigner as his career highlight, "because that was the biggest hit. I enjoyed working with the Grateful Dead; that was a good challenge. I guess as a producer I would have to say that, and actually, well, Aerosmith."

Which almost turned into a very different project.

"Yes, well, Joe Perry was in and out. Let's see, he started out and then I think he left in . . . actually, I've got a good story for you, if you want. I was always known as a bit of a prankster. When I was bored, I'd always try out some practical jokes. And when Perry was out of the band, David Krebs's office wanted Michael Schenker to replace him. And so, someone came in the control room and asked if it was okay for Schenker to come into the session. And I said, 'Yeah, fine.' And it's always embarrassing when you walk into a recording studio and things are going on. I always feel self-conscious.

"So he walked in, and I just stopped the tape and said, 'Who are you?' 'I'm Michael Schenker.' And he's standing there in black leather, blond hair. And I just told him to fuck off. I called him some Nazi or something, and I just told him to get out. And then he left [laughs]. And I carried on with the session. And who's the guy who used to work with Krebs who went on to manage AC/DC? The guy with a limp. Anyway, so he came back in, very embarrassed, because I had already told him it was okay for him to come in. And he said, 'You know, Michael's . . . you insulted him or something.' And I said, 'Well, send him back in; I'll apologize.' So he came back in the second time, and I said, 'I'm sorry for calling you a Nazi bastard.' And then said, 'Actually, I'm not sorry.

Get the fuck out of here.' So, I kicked him out a second time. That's why he never joined the band."

Crazy as that story is, it was probably for the best. Michael would have lasted five minutes in Aerosmith. His mental state at the time getting added to the Steven situation would have resulted in complete madness. Plus, Michael had no blues in him. He was European to the core, even if, famously, he listened to very little outside music and had almost no influences.

Next, working at S.I.R. Studios, the band auditioned Danny Johnson, from Derringer and Axis. But he'd just gotten a haircut, and Steven thought his hair was too short; otherwise, he'd have gotten the gig, remembers Brad. It was a little more than that; Danny was very much straight and sober, and mutually, both parties looked at each other and didn't see a match, this despite Brad having jammed with Danny in pursuit of a side project together.

They eventually settled on Jimmy Crespo, but why did they need someone so quick to begin with? Surely, they could have finished the album with Joe's contributions and then just done the rest with Brad. Well, it's because label and management had them out touring because record sales were down and they had been spending like drunken pirates. Toys and restaurant bills, dealer payments, and demands from equally high-living wives had caught up with the organization. As David told me over lunch in New York one day, their solution to covering Joe's room service bills was to go get an advance from the label for a solo record, and that's how we got the first Joe Perry Project album.

And incidentally, that thing is a near masterpiece. If Joe had thrown some of those songs into the Aerosmith pot a few months earlier—and I got to choose what went on the album, hah!—*Night in the Ruts* would have been beyond glorious. Credit to this band, though; they were proving themselves incapable of making a bad record anyway, even as they had been further discombobulated by being forced to tour when recording it. With respect to the studio, Aerosmith had been given the usual amount of time, but due to Steven's insane coke hoovering, it wasn't enough, and the organization needed revenue. So now they had to work while working, get a second job, as it were.

"Michael Schenker was one candidate," confirms Krebs. "But there's a woman named Marge Raymond, and Marge Raymond is a great rock 'n' roll singer, very, very powerful, who never quite made it for whatever number of reasons. But Jimmy Crespo was her guitar player. And what I don't know is if I met Marge before I met Jimmy or after; I'm not sure. But that's where Jimmy Crespo was from. And I never got involved. If the band was happy with Jimmy Crespo and Jack was happy with Jimmy Crespo, I was happy with Jimmy Crespo."

As Joey said in his book, "*Night in the Ruts* was still not ready, but we went back on tour again. At the World Series of Rock, fans camped out all around Cleveland Stadium the night before. There were several robberies and shootings, and one guy was killed. Backstage, Elyssa threw a glass of milk at Tom's wife, Terry, which started a fight that proved to be the last straw for all of us. Joe walked out in August. We canceled a world tour. We had been living in a bubble called rich and famous. Nobody could tell us anything, which meant that we had completely lost touch with reality. But now reality was going to come back and bite us in the ass."

"That album was tough," continues Lyons, "because they were distracted. And the task was to put an album together, just trying to extract an album out of them, from that time." Lyons was no saint either, which I've gathered from his stories about working with UFO. When I asked him if he was on the drugs and drink at the time, he says, "Probably. I was working with them and the Grateful Dead at the same time, so I guess you can draw your own conclusions."

"We did some interesting things with Gary," says Brad, vaguely. "All these producers are different. Gary, he didn't work like how we worked with Jack Douglas. Or Bruce Fairbairn. Bruce was much more concentrating on preproduction and songwriting and more detail oriented, I guess, than probably Gary was. Yeah, Gary was probably not as detail oriented all the time [laughs]."

"No Surprize" fits comfortably—and confidently—inside the band's narrative as Rolling Stones with more ideas and talent, or at least conventional talent. It's a core Aerosmith song, again, traditional and boogie rock based, but with a head turn toward heavy rock, at the chorus and at the elevated, modulated part, not to mention the tempo and the hair on the guitars. Joe is there on guitar (and backing vocals), and so is Richie "Chip Away the Stone" Supa.

"This was one of the real good ones from *Night in the Ruts*," says Joe in the *Pandora's Box* notes. "If we'd been more together, that might have been the album where we took what we'd done on *Rocks*, but we were too fucked up to really pull it all together, and to support it."

Adds Steven, "It's ironic that most of the songs that we did that tell the true story of the band end up on some back burner album, so people didn't really hear 'em. This is one where I just spell it all out—and it's also a pretty damn good song."

"We loved the lyrics because they were all true," said Tom in *Walk This Way*. "Even the line about getting pot from the police came from an incident in Charleston, West Virginia, where the cops gave the band some pot they'd confiscated." To be sure, that's in there, but the best part is the opening sequence about getting signed, as well as the always-remembered line "Vaccinate your ass with your phonograph needle!" Staying at the St. Regis Hotel, Steven was so pleased with himself that he had experienced a breakthrough lyrically after two months of writer's block that he called Tom down to his room to hear what he'd come up with.

Next is "Chiquita," which starts with a novel, chattery guitar pattern. Soon Tom and Joe fire up the engine room, before a four-man horn section makes the song sound expensive. Once Steven starts singing (scant words, and not his best), the music is full-on, heroic, heavy metal Aerosmith. The chorus is like that too, only augmented with horns. It's a bit of a "Lick and a Promise" vibe at the chorus, sun-dappled stadium rockin'. There's an interesting, nonobvious break section where they just vibe on that obscure opening riff for a bit. All told, it's a world-beating Aerosmith classic, and the second fine song in a row—both Tyler/Perry—to kick off the album.

Then we're on to Shangri-Las cover "Remember (Walking in the Sand)," written by Shadow Morton, who produced a back-alley Aerosmith record by the New York Dolls called *Too Much Too Soon*. Says Steven in *Walk This Way*, "Ever since I saw Mary Weiss in the bathroom in Cleveland when I was in the Chain Reaction, I had this fantasy about the Shangri-Las and so I cut this song. I harassed the singers—Beth Sussman and someone else—to whisper 'Remember' with the little gasp at the end the way the Shangri-Las had done it. It took two hours to get that little gasp." The backing singers can also be heard in the girl-group washes throughout, adding the weight of history to the song, very much like the horns on the previous track.

It's an exquisite version, sung all thespian by Steven and performed tightly by the band, and it's an ingenious song, a waltz-time power ballad at the verses and a halting four/four for the chorus, finger snaps included. It's arguably the most joyful—and most useful—cover ever on an Aerosmith album, and it's not even one of the handful of rockers. The track was issued as the only single off *Night in the Ruts*, backed with "Bone to Bone (Coney Island Whitefish Boy)," reaching a fairly pointless #67 on the *Billboard* charts. Nonetheless, it's played fairly regularly on classic-rock radio.

"Cheese Cake" is a lascivious but also humorous Steven Tyler sex song, but it's also another strident, high-quality rocker, featuring a pile of signature slide guitar from Joe Perry. Says Joe, "I think probably the only white guy [laughs] that's influenced me as heavily as anybody is Johnny Winter. He's probably one of the best of that style, that kind of Delta blues style, slide guitar players, that ever lived. He's just one in one million. Because he just kinda sucked up like a sponge all of those guys before, and he made rock. As opposed to a guy like Ry Cooder, who's got much more of a defined, I don't want to say delicate . . . I don't know what the right word is, but he's just more of a technical player.

"And he's another genius," continues Joe, on Cooder. "He's inspired me in that I would love to be able to play like that, but I just wasn't born with the kind of ear he has. So sometimes you get influenced by what you can play, and other times by what you can't play. If I try to sit down and try to study some of Ry Cooder's riffs, I'll never get it to sound like Ry, and it won't sound like Ry; it'll sound more like me. On the other hand, I could try to sit down with the other style, more of that Delta, free, sloppy kind of John Lee Hooker thing, which I really love. I mean, that's where I kind of live. That's where my style ends up going."

"Cheese Cake" is a sort of heavy, Zeppelinesque blues song at the verse, but then it ticks over into double time for the chorus and sometimes decides to stay there for the verse structure riff as well, coming out the other end as a slamming hard rocker with a lot of thought put into it, both lyrically and musically.

On the *Pandora's Box* compilation, there's a germination-stage version of the song that they are calling "Let It Slide," recorded in March at Media Sound. Says Steven, "This shows what a song is like in the beginning, and what it can become. And that's a big part of being a band—building something up from a riff." Adds Joe, on the final product, "The song was done in one take with no overdubs. When I played that track, I went from a regular six-string to a lap steel and back, live in the studio. Even though the band was falling apart in every other way, it was a testament to how we were playing."

Side 2 opens with "Three Mile Smile," an absolutely joyous track, due to the parts outside the verse, which is sort of medium-fare Aerosmith hard funk, like "Last Child," "Sight for Sore Eyes," and, even more so, "Discount Dogs" from the Joe Perry Project's forthcoming debut. But it's up tempo and smartly assembled, featuring a sublime break section at the two-minute mark that is the highlight of the album, in large part due to Joey's percussive accentuation.

Then comes the solo section, with Brad remarking that "both Jimmy and I recorded solos for this song. Steven liked Jimmy's solo better, and his is the one that you hear on the record, and I'm still a little pissed about it." Then we get that sweet little "flared" riff again, followed by more soloing and then an outro where the band does the heavy circular riff section at double time. All told, there's a lot going on, and the song deserves its choice placement as side 2 opener. Of note, *Pandora's Box* includes a one-minute piece of music they called "I Live in Connecticut," which is an early run at this song's central riff; toward the end, there's a bonus maneuver that didn't get used in the final product.

Explained Steven in *Walk This Way*, "'Three Mile Smile' comes from the whole era of No Nukes and atomic energy paranoia. Three Mile Island had nearly melted down (March 1979) and everyone was freaked that year. That summer, I was at the famous MUSE (Musicians United for Safe Energy) concert at Madison Square Garden, a complete blackout. I'm hanging backstage with David Crosby, Carly, Springsteen. I'm stoned. Supposed to sing the encore with Carly and all them. Rewritten lyrics to some famous song. Had lyrics written all over my arm. I'm out there singing away, two or three choruses; the place is standing up. I turn around and everybody's gone. I'm so high that I'm still out there at the mic, just me and the drummer. People are leaving the hall."

Typical of the lyrics on this album, there are flashes of brilliance, and of humor, and of brilliant humor, but Steven is brief, belying just how hard it was to squeeze these words of winsome wisdom out of Tyler.

Next is a cover of "Reefer Head Woman," by Joe Bennett, Jazz Gillum, and Lester Melrose (it's complicated; the song evolved over the years, most significantly 1938 and 1945). Remarked Steven in his book, "'Reefer Head Woman' was a 1940s blues record. I had the lyrics in a notebook that got stolen, and I had to call Dr. Demento from the Record Plant, where we finished the album, and the Doctor read the lyrics to me over the phone." Conspicuously, there are three covers out of nine songs on *Night in the Ruts*, with the whole record clocking in at just under thirty-six minutes. Two of them get over the hump, but not this one. It's the sort of pointless, rote, slow blues that a band plays live when they have to fill minutes. And if you ever try to talk about this one, you'll likely say it wrong—it's not "Reefer-Headed Woman," despite Steven saying it like that, repeatedly, through this dull slog of a song. Given the math, is *Night in the Ruts* Aerosmith's *Diver Down*? Not quite, but a good thing we can say about both of these albums: They come out the other end as charmers, despite the shared casual relationship with songwriting.

Regarding the next, sharp, angular original rocker, Steven says, "A Coney Island white fish is a scumbag. When you lived by the Hudson River like I did, you always saw these things floating by on their way to sea. They were rubbers. Guys would tie them up and they'd just keep floating. And that, boys and girls, is a Coney Island white fish."

At the music end, this is an interesting one, with both Tom and Joe noticing its "danceable" quality. "Bone to Bone (Coney Island White Fish Boy)" is a couple of things: It sits at the harder end of the Aerosmith funk metal songs, and it's straightened out to the point where it hints at disco. This is underscored by the guitars and bass playing in unison, as well as Steven's halting, rappy vocal, which also locks in with the riff. Even the similarly "heavy metal" connective riff has pronounced pedigree back to a standard blues scale. There's some slide guitar, which messes with the melody, and there's even a proper modulation. Out the other end, what we have is yet another song that demonstrates that despite booze, cocaine, crack, and heroin driving the car, somehow everybody found pockets of concentration and seriousness enough to make a professional record.

Feeding us a second cover in a row, next is a heavy metal version of "Think About It," B side to the Yardbirds' last single, "Goodnight Sweet Josephine," issued in April 1968. The conundrum is that as a song from the '60s, it's not up to Aerosmith's level of sophistication, and so despite the band heavying it up, it still sounds lackluster, like, in fact, an Aerosmith B side or reject. In other words, "Think About It" sounds like a song that if it was an original, the guys would tear it apart and overhaul it, adding bits, cognizant enough to know that it needs more to hold attention. And in keeping with a growing narrative across the album, there aren't a lot of lyrics. Plus, what there are cannot compete with the bon mots of Tyler upon his originals. It's a trap that bands fall into, thinking that the songs they grew up with as kids are good enough for their own fans, who are a rock 'n' roll generation younger, moved on, accustomed to more-complicated songs. It happened with Rush on *Feedback*, Deep Purple on *Turning to Crime*, and UFO on *The Salentino Cuts*, and it's kind of the case here, even if, thank God, "Think About It" isn't "Shapes of Things."

Night in the Ruts closes with "Mia," and it's not quite up to par either. The last album had no ballad, but before that there was "Home Tonight," "You See Me Crying," "Seasons of Wither," and "Dream On."

Steven explains in *Walk This Way* that it's "an Aerosmith ballad with Richie Supa and guitar tech, Neil Thompson, playing guitars. It was a lullaby I wrote on the piano for my daughter, but the tolling bell notes at the end of the song and the end of the album sounded more like the death knell of Aerosmith for people who knew what was going on." In his own book, he says, "I wrote about my daughter because I missed her and I was missing in action most of the time."

The tolling bells are more like low piano notes, but to be sure, it's an ominous ending, especially to a song written for his daughter, with the implication being that Daddy's likely going to be dead soon. Underscoring the effect is an ornate, stuffy, classical guitar solo with harmonies, on a song that sounds like melancholy Elton John, or, later, "November Rain" from the baby Aerosmith, Guns N' Roses.

Summing up in conversation with Mary Brown, Steven remarked that "my idea of a great album is one that spreads you out, that goes in different directions. On the new one, we've got 'Remember (Walking in the Sand)' from the 1960s. 'Reefer Head Woman,' that was recorded in 1921. 'Three Mile Smile' is about the nukes—how up to date can you get? Some people think 'Mia' is about my daughter. It's about the Indians. It makes me feel good that I was able to strike that vein where different interpretations are possible. I used to ask my friends in art school what something meant. They hesitated to tell me. Art is what you think it is afterwards.

"Doing the songs live from a new album is such a rush," continued Steven. "It is just the greatest. I see the kids singing the words, and I don't even know them yet. I used to write my arms full of words, and then I'd sweat so much. I have sheets all over the floor now with the words to four or five songs. All bands have that, though, especially when they're doing a new album. It gets confusing."

Night in the Ruts would reach a respectable #14 on the *Billboard* chart and certify gold soon enough, on March 13, 1980, followed by its current status at platinum, which was firmed up in 1994. Reviews were mostly negative, but then again, this was the era of new wave, most notably the Knack and the Cars. Punk had fizzled by 1979, and new wave was the result, a version of punk palatable for radio. It was also a recessionary year for the music business, saved by *The Long Run* from the Eagles, *The Wall* from Pink Floyd, and *In Through the Out Door* from Led Zeppelin. Now it was time for the American hard rock bands to fumble the football. If Aerosmith was disappointing the market, so were Ted Nugent with *State of Shock*, Blue Öyster Cult with *Mirrors*, Heart with *Bebe Le Strange*, Styx with *Cornerstone*, and Kiss with *Dynasty*. Even industry bright spot Van Halen was a bit of a letdown with *II*, which wasn't half the album *Van Halen* was. Boston was not going to make another record until 1986, and gone were Aerosmith-like baby band hopefuls such as Rex, Moxy, Starz, and Derringer.

To be sure, Aerosmith's managers were very happy. But it was because of *Highway to Hell*, *Back in Black*, *Lovedrive*, *Animal Magnetism*, and *On Through the Night*, not original stable enablers Aerosmith and Ted Nugent, who were now off the boil.

Notes David, "*Night in the Ruts* is obviously not a great album. There are three covers amongst a total of nine songs. But the album sounds great because Gary Lyons was an excellent producer. He's not of a stature of a Jack Douglas, but the album sounds better than *Draw the Line* because Jack was in as bad shape as the band was during the making of that record."

An evidently young Burr McCutcheon, writing in the Teen Voice section of the *Duluth Herald*, took to reviewing *Night in the Ruts*, stating that "if you're a lover of no-holds-barred rock, Aerosmith should definitely be in your record collection. As you may have guessed, Aerosmith is one of my very favorite bands. This is one group that can bring the music up to the brink of wildness without it falling off the edge. They hold right there with a heavy metal crunch that just about no one can equal. *Night in the Ruts* has all of the crunch of Aerosmith's earlier albums. After five top-notch studio albums and last year's complete killer live album, Aerosmith would still be flying high, except for one big detail, which will force them down for repairs. Joe Perry decided to try the solo route and left to form his own band right after they finished this album. This means that a new guitarist and, more importantly, a songwriter, must be found. I hope they succeed."

Equally amusing but harder to agree with is George Bounacos, who seems to have it in for Steven. "The first cut on the album is 'No Surprize,' which shows you how much most hard rockers care about spelling. It is a fast hard rocker with excellent guitars and drums. The one problem with the song is Steven Tyler's voice. I can understand any rock 'n' roller's lyrics—except Steven Tyler's. The words are completely unintelligible. 'Chiquita,' the next song, was written by Tyler and Perry. This song can overwhelm you, but it tends to become monotonous. Joey Kramer's drum work is sharp, and Tyler's voice here sounds like it's on the road to recovery. On side 2, 'Three Mile Smile' and 'Reefer Head Woman' are basically prototypes of one another. I assume these two songs are about girls, but it's hard to tell with Tyler's voice. One thing is certain though; Tyler can screech better than anyone in rock music.

"'Think About It' has a nice beat," continues Bounacos, "but again, this tune starts to get monotonous. Only Perry's guitar seems to save it from being a total bore. The only other complaint I have about this song is that somebody should tell Tyler not to sing in a falsetto pitch anymore. It just doesn't become him. Finally, we get to 'Mia,' the album's last song. Two things show this song is out of place. One is a piano and the other is understandable lyrics. It is a legitimate ballad, and definitely the best cut on the album. If Aerosmith doesn't release the song as a single, they are nuts. That's how good it is. As noted, Aerosmith is going to have to do some heavy innovations to reach their once spectacular height. The album is great, and if some of the vocals could be blocked out, I'd nominate it for heavy metal album of the year. While Aerosmith will never win any awards for clarity in vocals, they have one of the best bands around. I'd recommend this album to just about everyone, but pop fans should not expect a new quieter Aerosmith because this is their first studio album in a couple years. They still know how to rock."

"What would have happened if The New York Dolls had been The Boston Dolls?" asked James Spina, in his review of the album for *Hit Parader*. "Then what would have happened if those Dolls had been into The Yardbirds instead of the Stones? And what if those Dolls had been successful in translating their club scene energy into a larger scale of concert movements? You get the picture. This band is almost ten years old, and they still knock me out. Covering The Shangri-Las and old Yardbirds on one disc is pure pleasure. Perry is the perfect rock fan turned guitar hero. And Tyler is his perfect foil. It's hard to determine which is more powerfully abrasive, the former's guitar sound or the latter's vocals. I sometimes feel that their success robbed them of the credit they deserved for forefronting the street punk wail that often gets traced back directly and solely to The New York Dolls. In any case, *Night in the Ruts* is a right-in-the-guts masterpiece of '70s-style rock that can easily slip into this new decade."

It really was a good album, and in fact Steven Tyler himself has been known to call it his favorite of the catalog.

"That's one record that stands out," agrees Joe. "It's really overlooked. The band was playing great, and like I say, most of that stuff was done live in the studio. And when I left the band before the record came out, it didn't really get the kind of tour behind it that it should have gotten, that year, year and a half of playing it live. It kind of fell by the wayside. But just as a rock record, I think that was one of our best."

"*Night in the Ruts*, that's when everything really went to shit," reflects Tom. "And we were playing stadiums. And it's just, talk about monkeys with guns—you give these guys a situation where they're playing in front of 50, 60,000 people, and what are they doing? They get burnt out and fucked up on dope."

"I don't consider it much of a record myself," laughs Brad. "There's some cool stuff on it, but it just doesn't hold a candle for me, to like *Rocks* and *Toys in the Attic*, when the band was in its most creative period. Yeah, we started to lose some of the cohesiveness of the songwriting, I think. We had a lot of things going on that kind of led to drifting away from the music. That was a bad period with Joe, with the drug abuse and the alcohol, and with people starting to think they were too big for Aerosmith or whatever. It was everything going slowly out of control, and of course the music suffered."

And then, just like that, Brad was part of Whitford St. Holmes, who managed to get a record out in 1981, on Columbia. The St. Holmes part of the equation stood for Derek St. Holmes, coguitarist and co-lead singer in Ted Nugent's band. "Well, that was right after Joe. He had left the band. I was still working with Aerosmith, although we weren't really working. We had the period where we ended up getting Jimmy Crespo, and we did some live shows."

Brad hung on through that period, as part of an idling Aerosmith and this album with Derek not getting off the ground. "Yeah, we were trying. We were supposed to start working on that record [meaning the next one, *Rock in a Hard Place*], and we were having a terrible time getting anything to happen at that period. We actually recorded the first Whitford St. Holmes record; we recorded and finished it in about four weeks, in the springtime, and that's when I was still in Aerosmith. Nothing was happening, so I was working on that. And actually, we had that album completed, and I went back to work with Aerosmith, and we were just trying to come up with some ideas for the new record, and we came up with zilch [laughs]. And then that summer I decided to walk away from Aerosmith for a couple years. It was just too . . . it was just not happening [laughs]." As for *Rock in a Hard Place*, "I worked on some of that. I worked on a little bit of it. I don't even know if the little bit that we recorded, if that was kept [laughs]."

Asked by Dave Reynolds about Whitford St. Holmes, Joe Perry said, "I don't think it did too well, but it was a great album. There were some good tunes on it. I don't know what Derek is doing at the moment. One of the biggest mistakes he made was leaving Ted. You see, anytime you fuck with a winning combination, then you're in trouble. Aerosmith took so much for granted. It's like Steven said, 'Fuck you, Joe. I don't need you.' And I said the same kind of thing. And I would play small halls and be happy. I didn't mind playing the small halls, but I missed the camaraderie and the talent of Aerosmith. Nobody can imagine what these five pairs of eyes have seen in the business."

Brad would get back into the fold first by playing live with the Joe Perry Project in 1983. Up into 2016, he'd get back together again with Derek for a second Whitford St. Holmes album, called *Reunion*.

"Anybody who tells you that rock 'n' roll isn't a business," he says, before he leaves us for an album, "must be just so well off that it just doesn't matter. Believe me, not everybody is that well off. But we just have such a passion for doing what we do. We just love to play. And we have a vehicle called Aerosmith to do this, and you just can't say no to it. It's like a beautiful mistress."

Explains David on Brad's side project: "When Joe Perry left Aerosmith, we got him a record deal with Columbia. When Brad Whitford left Aerosmith, I had always been a big fan of Derek's, so I put Derek and Brad together and also got them a deal with Columbia. Previous to that, we had done St. Paradise, which was a similar situation, in 1979. The problem was, I don't think Whitford St. Holmes had a phenomenal song. I think that's what was lacking. Brad was always very easy to get along with. Something that is very surprising, by the way, I've gone back and looked at every Aerosmith album to see who really wrote the stuff and Brad actually cowrote a lot of the key songs, as did Tom. People always think of Aerosmith as the product of this Tyler/Perry writing team, but that is selling those other two guys short. 'Sweet Emotion' is Tom Hamilton. Brad was a very laid-back guy. He had no ego of any consequence, just like Tom Hamilton had no ego. As an observation, I thought Aerosmith was the quintessential American band. Two Protestants, two Catholics, and one Jew."

Asked who's who, David says, "Joey Kramer is Jewish, Tyler is Protestant, I think Tom Hamilton is Protestant, which would leave the other two to be Catholic. But I'm not positive. I know Tyler is Protestant and I know Kramer is Jewish. But I thought that was an interesting dynamic. But yes, that album, there wasn't that one song of high caliber. Well, let's go back. It may be that Brad Whitford had hits, and maybe Derek didn't write at the same level as Steven Tyler, because all of the songs Brad wrote were cowritten with Steven Tyler. Derek was a good writer, but I'm not so sure he was a great writer. Tom Allom was producing, and he was a great guy. He did the best he could, I guess, with the material. But Derek St. Holmes, great singer, great rock 'n' roll artist. I have to think about this. One could build a rock supergroup around Whitford and St. Holmes again. There must be a great drummer out there somewhere, with big rock credentials. That might be a good idea in the amphitheater world. If they could get a special guest slot as part of a three-act package, that could be a very viable thing. Because you're not going to see Aerosmith live anymore. Anyway, back to the '80s, by 1984 both Brad and Joe were back in Aerosmith, so that was the end of both bands. We only did one album. I guess Columbia didn't pick up the option."

And back to Aerosmith proper, "Like I say, man, if three or four choice cuts of Grade A beef from Joe's solo album got worked up for *Night in the Ruts* instead of, say, 'Reefer Head Woman.' 'Think About It' or 'Mia'—mama mia!"

Let the Music Do the Talking saw issue in March 1980, a mere four months past the Aerosmith record. Like Brad and Derek, Joe was signed to Columbia. Producing was Jack Douglas. Joe split the vocals on the record with Ralph Morman. Rounding out the lineup was David Hull on bass and Ronnie Stewart on drums. They were all pretty much unknowns, although Hull was in two-record Boston band Dirty Angels. As for which songs I would have loved to have heard on the Aerosmith record, well, that would be "Conflict of Interest," "Shooting Star," "The Mist Is Rising," and the opening title track, which got reworked (and made vastly inferior) for Aerosmith's *Done with Mirrors* album from 1985.

Joe would follow up with *I've Got the Rock 'n' Rolls Again* in 1981, followed by a new label deal with MCA for the final album, *Once a Rocker, Always a Rocker*, in 1983. It was a case of diminishing returns.

"I kind of worked with different people on each one," says Joe. "And the energy behind it, for the first one I had some riffs that hadn't been used for Aerosmith, so I kind of had a body of work for that solo record. The second one, I worked with a pretty successful local artist here, Charlie Farren, and he had a bunch of cool songs and ideas we collaborated on. We kind of fleshed out each other's ideas, so it bears a little more of his style in there, because we worked together on that."

I've Got the Rock 'n' Rolls Again is more chaotic, more garage rocking than the debut, not as structured and well written. Nonetheless, the title track is a bodice ripper, as is opener "East Coast, West Coast." Joe agrees on my assessment of the wild second record. "Yeah, well, sure, as opposed to the kind of more guitar-riff-oriented stuff that the first one was. Then the third one was, again, I was on the road constantly and we just needed a record out there, so we kind of banged that one together on the fly. It certainly didn't have the thought or care put into it that the first one did."

"It was great therapy," Joe told Dave Reynolds, in 1987. "I think I wrote some really good music on 'em, and I worked with some good people, even though I had to fire the original singer, Ralph Morman, in the middle of my first tour, because he was living the lifestyle too much. The last album I did, *Once a Rocker, Always a Rocker*, was too rough, and I can't listen to it because it was a really painful time for me. But it was good to be involved in that, and, fortunately, no one hates me for it."

David Krebs had the following to say about Joe Perry's solo situation.

"At the end of a tour, there's a report I get from my own accounting department. So when Aerosmith came back from the last tour, and we checked what everybody had spent on room service, everybody was in and around $14,000, and Joe Perry and his wife, Elyssa, were at $84,000. I don't remember if I talked to Joe before I brought this up at the meeting. I wish I could remember that. But at the meeting, I brought up the fact, hey guys, you guys, we're writing off the $14,000 for each guy as a business expense, but Joe Perry spent an extra $70,000. I'm the manager. It seems to me it's my obligation to point that out.

"It's very possible at that time—and I don't know the exact chronology—but there's a confluence and/or separation of this meeting with the band and Joe Perry's $84,000, with the Cleveland date in 1979, where the famous story is that Joe Perry's wife throws milk at Terry Hamilton, Tom Hamilton's wife. There's a big to-do at the date. I'm at that date, because I think that show had Aerosmith, Nugent, Scorpions, and AC/DC, if I'm not mistaken. So, it must've been a big day.

"But at that point in time, the ravages of heroin were rather significant, especially for Steven Tyler and Joe Perry. And I have had, since at least '76, tremendous difficulties in trying to figure out how to educate them away from heroin. And at that moment in time, with that fight and what was happening between Tyler and Perry, when Perry leaves, I make the decision that in order to have any success in terms of how significant their heroin problem is, that it will be better if they're separate and not together. That was a definite decision made at that time.

"At the same time, we had the ability to put Joe Perry into a deal with Columbia. And to give him the opportunity to get out from under Steven. Because it was becoming very difficult to get songs finished by Steven Tyler. There was a tremendous amount of pent-up frustration in someone like Joe Perry, who is writing songs, and nothing was happening. So, Joe Perry leaves Aerosmith, we're still the manager, we get him the record deal. I hear what he's doing, but I tell him I didn't think Ralph Morman was the right singer. I didn't think he could go all the way with Ralph Morman. I told him that.

"In any event, myself and Steve Leber sat down and decided that with this room service situation, you know what? To pay this back, he should do a solo album. So that's why the Joe Perry Project happened. Also, again, Joe was being driven crazy by how slow Steven was at coming up with lyrics, and he just wanted to work. My theory for why he used Ralph Morman as a singer is that he wanted to be the leader of a band where a guitarist usually isn't. Steven was the leader of Aerosmith. Steven is an eleven, Derek St. Holmes is an eleven, Charlie Huhn and Ralph Morman are both sevens. He wanted a weaker singer so he could be the leader.

"But I have to stress, I told Joe Perry that I didn't think he would make it with Ralph Morman as his singer; I made that point to him. I didn't press him beyond saying it maybe once. But I also realized and agreed that after dealing with such a superego perfectionist as Steven Tyler—and I mean superego in a nice way, in many ways, by the way—that Joe Perry needed a rest from a stronger performer than himself. So if one had to measure Ralph Morman against Steven Tyler, Joe Perry probably needed an emotional rest, once he split. He was willing to put up with somebody who was not up to par."

I asked David if he was aware that Ralph Morman had a drinking problem.

"Of course. But more so, he just didn't have it. He didn't have the whole picture. It's very hard to follow an artist like Steven Tyler who is so brilliant. I believe he had discovered Ralph because he was popular up in the Boston area; I'm not sure. So whatever touring they do, I don't think that they cut through. I don't think Ralph Morman is a strong enough singer to accomplish, but if one looks back, to conjecture, it's very, very possible that Joe Perry at that point did not want to contend with another singer as strong as Steven Tyler."

Asked about the band name and the first album cover, David says, "I was fine with the band name. I thought the cover went great with the album title, *Let the Music Do the Talking*; I thought it was perfect. And I thought that the title track was the best song on the album. I thought it could've been marketed better by Columbia."

With Jack Douglas producing the album, David figures, "Keep in mind that there were various stages in his career that Jack was out of control, like at the Cenacle, making *Draw the Line*. But it was almost universal that everybody was doing cocaine. At least in New York. And we were all very good friends. Steven Tyler was married, living in New York on the Upper East Side. Richie Supa was living on the Upper East Side around the corner from me. So as much as we tried to fix the issue . . . and one of the other things in terms of dealing with people who are addicted, which was never advice given, surprisingly—like I said earlier—is that hey, if they're with a girlfriend and they're both addicted, there's no point sending him away and not sending her away. Because he's going to come back and get addicted again."

Surprised to hear that Steven had a place in New York, apropos of nothing, I asked David how he kept the place.

"He had a big place up in New Hampshire, and his apartment in New York was very nice, probably a two-bedroom at 85th and Madison, I think. His wife, Cyrinda, was very classy. I'll remind you of the story; remember, we managed the Dolls. Cyrinda Foxe is married to David Johansen, but she's also friendly with Joe Perry's wife. And Joe Perry's wife invites Cyrinda out on an Aerosmith date, and a romance develops between Steven Tyler and Cyrinda, and she leaves David Johansen for Steven Tyler. And we're the managers of both bands. Very interesting situation. Cyrinda had some film experience. I think she may have been one of the Warhol girls. I'm not sure anymore. But they had a nice place, kept it nice. They lived at a top-level doorman building, and they had a daughter, Mia. It was upscale, with very classy furniture. Look, if you live in New York and you can afford it, you want to live in a doorman building."

Back to the Joe Perry Project, I asked Krebs about David Hull and Ronnie Stewart. "All I remember is that they were very good. And look, Ralph Morman was a good singer. It's just that on a one to ten, Steven Tyler is an eleven. And if you're a seven or eight or even a nine, there is a difference. On the album, Joe Perry is writing most of the stuff, music and lyrics. If the entire album had been at the level of the title track, I think it would've done a lot better. But at the same time, historically, labels, when they dealt with someone of consequence leaving a band to go solo, in the back of their mind I'm sure it's half-hearted help that is offered in terms of breaking that breakaway artist.

Because the feeling was always that the artist should come back to the band. I saw that with Joe Perry, and I saw that also when I managed Richie Sambora for a short time. They were much more interested in him coming back to Bon Jovi than being a star with a solo career."

And that song of which David speaks, as mentioned earlier, later wound up on an Aerosmith album, *Done with Mirrors*.

"Yeah, look, that's an Aerosmith song," points out Krebs. "I don't think the other songs are as good as the average Aerosmith song. And Ralph Morman as a singer did not have the excitement to cut through live. So you end up with that album not selling so well. I don't think we're managing Joe any more by the time of the second album, *I've Got the Rock 'n' Rolls Again*, and for sure by the third album, the MCA one, *Once a Rocker, Always a Rocker*, where he's with Tim Collins out of Boston.

"Let's see; hold on a second," corrects Krebs. "If I'm not mistaken, when we split with Steven Tyler in March 1984, our papers on management still ran into 1985. That's my recollection. I would think that Joe Perry's papers might've expired in 1982. Wait, here's what happens. MCA drops Joe Perry because Irving Azoff comes in to run MCA. It's fortunate for Aerosmith, because they're all signed to us. But Steven Tyler is involved in a deed of moral turpitude at such a level that I call Steve Leber and say I have no more answers. We'll have to let them go. So it's a fortunate happenstance for Aerosmith. The failure of the MCA album in '83 for Joe clears the way for a reunion to happen in early '84. So, Tyler goes back to Boston and Aerosmith gets back together again. So we're dealing with the fact that the Joe Perry Project has no more places to go. It becomes a very opportune time for them to come back."

Putting a brave face on the new Aerosmith lineup, Steven told *Hit Parader*, "It was difficult that the person who started the band with me—the person who helped to create Aerosmith and had so much to do with the writing and all—chose to take a step in the other direction. But I think it's a good thing, in a way. Aerosmith's music was going forward, but my writing with him was slowed down because he had so many songs of his own, he wanted to do. Joe was really getting fed up with our music, and our new guitarist, Jimmy Crespo, is brand new and really happy about being in the band as opposed to sticking out like a sore thumb. Down through the ages of this band, there was a prevailing factor that was getting in the way of me and Joe. I never denied that I couldn't be who I was without him. Let's just say that there are no bad feelings anymore; he just went his way and we went ours."

On the subject of rumors about the band, Steven says, "I hear rumors all the time, that I've separated from Cyrinda, that I have throat cancer, and the thing is that none of it is true, so it doesn't bother me. All anybody has to do is see that 19,000 people per city are coming to see the band. That's all that counts." Furthermore, he calls *Night in the Ruts* "the band's best album to date, except for the next one. The band now, it's incredible. When Jimmy Crespo gets up to play, the whole place knows it. He has his own style, and he certainly puts his two cents in. Everything's going wonderfully—it's incredible."

"I'm not anything like Joe as a player or anything," mused Jimmy Crespo, speaking with Deane Zimmerman. "I just look at it like I'm joining a band that's already established and I'm just a new member. I don't see it like I'm taking someone else's place, because you can't do that. You just become another part of the group, and whatever you contribute is what you do. If looked at in any other way, it would be catastrophic. Everyone in the group was great. They gave me all the freedom that I needed, and it just worked out fine. There was none of the stuff that could have gone down, which I'm really thankful for.

"I was happy when they asked me to join," continues Crespo, who got the gig after a couple of auditions. "It would be stupid of me not to admit it. But I go into everything I do with the attitude that I'm going to do my best, even in audition, and if anything comes of it, great. If nothing, well, at least I did my best. I felt good when I auditioned, so I wasn't super surprised, but I was happy. I don't feel like it's something I don't deserve or something out of the ordinary. It's great and I'm very thankful for it. But I really worked my ass off for it, so I don't feel like it's any kind of dream. I don't feel stunned. It's just like anybody else doing some kind of work—you get what you put in. I have a pretty large background in music, being that I've been spread out so much, but rock 'n' roll is really my mainstay as far as a diet is concerned, and the rock music we're doing with Aerosmith, that's really like home. But being that I have all the other stuff, I think that I can contribute other things to the group, add different colors. Not change, because you can't change Aerosmith—I think it's great; why change it? But I would like to add something to it."

As for touring, Jimmy says, "I've never done a tour at this pace before, and it's exhausting. But I still love it. The faster the better; it keeps me really going. Sometimes I could use a little more rest, but I think it's great. I'm in it for the music. I love to get up there and play. The applause is part of it. It's nice to be appreciated; it's nice when somebody says they like you and they get into what you're doing."

Championing the new guy, in February 1980 Tom told the *Miami News*, "You know, it's almost eerie the way our fans took to Jimmy Crespo. We thought there'd be all these signs in the audience saying, 'Where's Joe?' But they accepted Jimmy immediately. We really expected a lot more trouble than what we got. With Jimmy, the sound of the band is now totally under control, which it wasn't before. He's also a good backup singer. With Jimmy, this is simply the way that Aerosmith should have always sounded. Hey, we're still nasty, still tough, but there's a lot more polish there now, the polish that was always missing."

Continues Tom, "Last night, again we played to a pretty rowdy crowd, and I tell you, after Philadelphia, I looked straight up and out into the audience all night, so I'd be ready when somebody threw something. I got hit in the head with a quarter last year. Man, kids don't understand that a quarter, by the time it reaches the stage, is like a bullet. Lately, it's been getting better with the crowds, but it's still not that safe."

On November 11, 1980, Columbia issued *Aerosmith's Greatest Hits*, celebrating "Dream On," "Sweet Emotion," "Walk This Way," and a bunch of other songs that did okay out there in the world. Many are in accursed edited form. The album's astounding current RIAA-certified diamond status, with over twelve million copies sold in the United States, is testimony to the strength of the band's catalog. What *Greatest Hits* doesn't celebrate is *Night in the Ruts*, which is represented with but a single track, "Remember (Walking in the Sand)," which, of course, the band didn't write. By the way, speaking of who didn't write what on *Night in the Ruts*, note that Brad, Tom, and Joey don't have a single credit between them on that album.

Complained Steven, speaking with Carol Brown, "It was supposed to have been *A Decade of Greatest Hits*. After all, most bands putting out a greatest-hits album are either folding or about to, which is far from true with us. I tried to explain this but got nowhere, and that's something the boys and I are going to do something about. We're going to split up in packs of three and go out into different markets, take over for a couple hours, and do DJ spots. I think that would be very apropos for this particular album. So the kids get to know that, because it is a greatest-hits LP, the band's not going down the drain."

To prove that the band wasn't comatose, Tyler reported to Brown that "we've been doing some club gigs and really enjoyed getting close to the kids again. Unfortunately, we can't play to all of them, but we did a nonpolitical rally in November, which went out over the airwaves, and a ten-year anniversary gig in Boston, which was broadcast to thirty or forty million people. And we've been writing; I've been getting closer to Jimmy Crespo, the new member who took Joe's place. I did the No Nukes thing, the Paul Simon movie. I produced some new groups and, well, I've done a whole bunch of things.

"We have heard lately that people in the Midwest and L.A. are beginning to ask, 'Where are you?' That there are signs written on the highway overpasses in black spray paint which say 'Aerosmith, where are you when we need you most?' It won't be long now before we're back out there. But I wouldn't want to put a date on it, except to say early spring, because I wouldn't want to disappoint anyone."

On the topic of getting songs out, you can read between the lines, with Steven telling Carol, "You don't think of it as a 'Can you top this?' situation. In fact, if you think about it too much, things get out of shape, especially in rock 'n' roll. I find that in being creative, if you give things too much thought, they get well, sterile, as opposed to spur [of] the moment. So for me to tell you that there's another plateau I want to go to higher than where we've been already, which has been to the top, would be misleading. But there's always where the kids take us, and how we get ourselves off by writing and creating, coming up with new songs and new ideas. If you don't give it too much thought, you'd be amazed at the stuff which comes out."

In closing, he says, "A true art form is to write something and have it mean something different to a lot of different people. If I were to write a poem right now, and you were to ask me what I was writing about, I wouldn't tell you. I'd rather let you think whatever you will about it. And that's the pleasure—that's the fun of it all."

7
Rock in a Hard Place

"We'd be trying to keep Steven as straight as possible."

"Keep in mind the following," says David Krebs, on the unraveling that is to end our story.

"The first album was followed by *Get Your Wings* about twelve months later. *Get Your Wings* was followed by *Toys* about twelve months later. *Rocks* was following from *Toys* thirteen months later. *Draw the Line* took seventeen months, and *Night in the Ruts* took twenty-three months. *Rock in a Hard Place* took thirty-three months. So you get the picture, don't you? So, at the same time, what happens is this—it's very interesting: A band whose track record was that they never missed a date became a band that you can never be sure if they would make the date. So, my recollection is this: In those thirty-three months, remember, Aerosmith was signed to Columbia Records through a production deal with Steve Leber and myself. My recollection is that in the thirty-three months it took them to do *Rock in a Hard Place*, we spent $2 million. And that was a lot of money in the 1980s. And we realized, Steve Leber and I, that there was a downside of having a production deal [laughs].

"And I think that you would find that Jack Douglas became as addicted as anybody else," continues Krebs. "Or matching the worst. So if you have a drug-addicted producer with the band, where the top two guys are also drug-addicted, you're not going to wind up with a brilliant album. So based on how long it took, based on the fact that you started to see the sales curve go down, you're dealing with . . . *Toys* aside, *Rocks* is probably a four-million-seller as we speak, and I would bet *Draw the Line* is two million and then the next one is one million and then the next one is gold, and that's it."

Asked about these harrowing times, promoter and David Krebs associate Nick Caris says, "I represented the Joe Perry Project, and then quite quickly after that I represented the—what I call the—Joe Perry–less Aerosmith. And this was a time when the drugs were still extremely prevalent. I mean, it got to be really rough. It was tough. It was hard enough to get Aerosmith to do two days in a row, and three days were like impossible. So it got really crazy. And then Joe showed up at the end. There was the hatred, the love/hate thing, between them. But they were joined at the hip, really, and creatively they were definitely one and one equaling five, you know?

"So, Joe showed up at one date up in Boston, and somehow he got back in the dressing room. Because he wasn't supposed to. Joe Perry was not supposed to be allowed into any Aerosmith show. But he got past Joe Baptista, the tour manager, who was great. And Steven couldn't even finish the show. He got back in there, and they did whatever they did, and that was it. So it got to the point where without them straightening out, you couldn't even keep them out there anymore. So despite security guys and whatever, we'd play a show with Aerosmith, and we'd be trying to keep Steven as straight as possible, which at that time was impossible. It was just enough to get 'em to the show, have them play, and try to keep people away from them.

"I remember one time with him, we were at Alpine Valley, which is outside Milwaukee, and they had the Alpine Lodge, which was a classic—like you think of—lodge called the Alpine Lodge. You know, three stories, spread out all over the place. So what happened is, we had to go from Milwaukee after we played that date, to Detroit at Pine Knob the next day, and we put Joe into bed, and we put a security guy . . . we had two security guys that we carried with us, just basically to watch over them.

"We put a guy on the front door, and the next morning we went down to get Steven, and he wasn't responding. So we finally got in, and he was out cold. What we saw on the table near the window, what he had done was, he had taken the thread that comes in the sewing kit you get when you check into the hotel. He had taken the thread, tied it together. The fans used to kind of roam through the lodge area, and some of them would be staying there, of course. And I guess they were below his window, and he was talking to them, waving to them, and he put the string down with a bottle and they gave him some kind of pills, probably 714s or some heavy shit or whatever. And there were still some of them on the table, and he was out cold.

"So I looked over at Joe Baptista and said, 'What are we gonna do?' 'Cause we had to leave from Milwaukee and go to the airport and fly to Detroit. Well, we had a green canvas, and we basically rolled up Steven in it and carried him over our shoulder, onto the airplane. This was before the heavy security. Imagine that today. And we put him in a first-class seat. He never responded, he was still breathing, got to Detroit, pulled out the green canvas bag again, over the back of our shoulders; we're taking turns carrying him. We get to Pine Knob and he's totally out—no response, just out. But he's breathing.

"We're back in the dressing room, and we had about ten more minutes before we would have to cancel the show. Because you had a heavy curfew; it was $10,000 a minute for every minute you went over. And it was getting to the point where if we didn't call the show, we were screwed.

"And just as we were waiting for a couple of the other people involved to come back to the backstage area to discuss what we were gonna do, and look at the calendar, and could we possibly reschedule this under the guise of somebody being sick, all of a sudden—boom! Who walks into the dressing room? Steven. 'Hey, what's happening?' It was just the funny look on his face, because, you know, even when those guys are ripped, Steven is just an extremely intelligent guy and he was fun to be around, even when he was ripped. Joe was a little bit different. Joe could get more ornery. He could be walking up and down the halls at four in the morning, banging on rooms looking for drugs. Steven was much cooler, and he was fun.

"But, I mean, it got out of hand. Finally, they came in and they started working with Tim Collins, who was managing the Joe Perry Project at the end. And he got 'em back and he talked to all of them and set the rules down, which were very heavy. And he got them sober."

I asked Nick what he thought of the rest of the guys in the band. "I really like those guys; they were great. I love Joey. I used to talk to Tom all the time. I didn't spend a lot of time with Brad. Not for any reason; it just seemed like I always ended up with Tommy and Joey Kramer. Probably out of the whole band, Tom Hamilton seemed to be the one that was the most like a businessperson, that would ask the kinds of questions that would get him and I talking about the theories behind things and stuff like that. But yeah, I remember that one place they were recording at. David and I drove up there and we said, 'What's happenin'?,' and Joe was on the second floor of this house, and he had a gun up there. He'd been up there two or three days, shooting this gun off; I mean, it's in the Aerosmith book too. I said, 'I'm not going in there.' So it was nuts. But I mean, when you think about the amount of drugs that we all did in those days, and you think that those guys are still together now and alive—and that we're all alive—it's crazy. But they're all really good people, really good people."

The central narrative of the *Rock in a Hard Place* album cycle is the shocking detachment of both guitarists, Joe Perry and Brad Whitford, from the band, to be replaced by Jimmy Crespo and Rick Dufay. Concerning the former, the guys liked Jimmy's confidence and leadership skills. Speaking with Tim Sommer from *Sounds* at the time, Tom said, "Well, they pretty much had to be like that to fill Joe Perry's shoes. And the amazing thing about Jimmy is that his ideas are . . . it's the shinier side of the coin. A lot of people don't know that we've already toured with Jim—did a twenty-date tour. I remember noticing from the first gig that I didn't get any vibe or feelings from the audience or the people around me of 'Where's Joe?' or anything like that, because Jimmy's a commanding guitar player. Makes our old stuff sound really good, just like the new stuff." Adds Steven, "His ideas are just what I've always really wanted as far as a guitar player goes."

"Jimmy is a little more calculated and polished," surmised Tom, speaking with Steve Newton. "One of the things that was great about Joe and not so good about him was that he would just go for it, for whatever came into his head. And if the idea to stop playing was in his head, he would do that too. But Jimmy is real conscious of dynamics and coming down to low volume when the verses call for it. Jimmy Crespo used to play in a band called Flame, and when that band folded, he was doing a lot of studio work. We were introduced to him through a mutual friend, Richie Supa, the person who wrote 'Lightning Strikes.' Richie said, 'Why don't you try this guy out?,' and so he was one of about six or seven guitarists that we auditioned. He was the third player we saw, and we knew that he was the right one right off. So we let the other guys have their shot, but it was pretty much Jimmy all the way."

When Tim Sommer notes correctly that *Rock in a Hard Place* sounds very much like a solid, traditional Aerosmith album, Tom says, "That's because of Jimmy's style. He was into the same kind of music and into writing the same kind of music that we've always done. And I guess part of it was just plain old luck that we got a guy who fitted so perfectly that we could still put out a record that sounded like an Aerosmith record. People hear the record, and I've heard a lot of people say, 'Yeah, that sounds like Aerosmith.' And that's really gratifying, because we could have come out sounding like a different band. We didn't want that. We didn't want a guy to copy the old ways, but we also didn't want to change the whole format of the band. Jimmy worked in really good."

As for Rick Dufay, Tom told Sommer, "He's from New York and had done a solo album with Jack Douglas. So we were rehearsing, finishing up one of the last tracks, and Jack suggested we check him out. So we brought him over to rehearsal. And so began the task of evaluating Rick Dufay [laughs]. Things are working out pretty good. He came into the band, actually, at the end of the album; 99.9 percent of the guitar work is all Jim. Rick came in and did a couple of vocal parts, backup parts, and played guitar on 'Rock in a Hard Place' and I think one other tune. Jimmy, when he writes a song, is very particular about how everything guitarwise goes down. He took over completely and was calling the shots guitarwise. Hopefully with the next album, Rick will get the chance to show his creativity a little bit."

Added Steven, "Rick, he didn't get a chance to do very much on the album. Not only that, but we liked the idea of going into the studio with one guitar player, seeing as how Jimmy wrote a lot of the music. He put the rhythm down, and also the leads, so there wouldn't be so much mush."

As Tom told Steve Newton, "Rick did an album, produced by Jack Douglas, called *Tender Loving Abuse*. Jack sort of snuck him into our practice one day. Brad was a rock—I'll say that. Brad would never make a mistake, and you'd never hear anything coming out of his amp that he hadn't meant to come out. Rick is also really solid, but sometimes he'll come out with something that you're not expecting."

"We hadn't really thought of it as far as the album went," agrees Tom, on making the album with one guitarist. "But we knew we needed another guitar player for touring and eventually as another band member, because we are a two-guitar band."

Both Tom and Steven seemed enthusiastic about Aerosmith's odds in 1982. "That shouldn't really be a problem at all," avows Tyler. "We did it before and we could do it again. I don't think it's going to hurt at all getting back out there and doing what we did before. I know they're hungry for it. I know they want it. All the fucking kids out there want to hear some rock 'n' roll. We were always a people's band. Being off the road sort of starts getting you down after a while. Not only that, but I toured myself, getting so used to it, ten, twelve years solid, touring, and when you finally get home, it can be quite boring."

Adds Tom, "You see over those years that we've been semi off the road. I say 'semi' because we did some club dates when we were doing the album. People have still been buying our records. We've sold a million and a half records in this time that we've been supposedly broken up or whatever. So we knew that there were people waiting for the album out there. Plus, we've been getting good airplay over the last few years, so we know they're out there. And as far as exactly how the market is going to affect our record, it's too early to tell right now, but right now it's doing really good. We've got no reason to expect anything but going all the way with it. We feel that we've proven that we can still do it with our album, and we're going to go out and show them what we can do on the road."

Back to Crespo, Steven told *Hit Parader*, "Jimmy's been just incredible. When Joe left, we really never missed a beat. One day I was up at my manager's office, and I see this guy hangin' around. So, naturally, I check out who he is, and I find out he's a guitarist. He just had an interesting look about him. When I found out who he was, I invited him down to jam with us. From the first moment we started rehearsing, the chemistry was right. You could just feel it when we started to play. Jimmy fit in like a glove. He could play this real delicate piece and then just take off on this incredibly raunchy thing that was just great. Now that Rick Dufay's in the band, he's started working with Jimmy, and they seem to play off each other real well. Jimmy handles most of the leads and Rick does the fills, and they both seem very happy with what they're doing—which, I may add, is a nice change from the two characters we had before."

The subject of Joe and Brad bolting—Whitford informed them on the phone—inevitably came up in interviews for *Rock in a Hard Place*. Asked about Joe, Steven told Philip Bashe from *Circus*, "It's a strange thing he's searching for, something that I still don't understand. I look at what he's doing now, playing clubs as part of the Joe Perry Project, and I scratch my head and wonder what he was really looking for. I guess I don't know the guy. We went all this time busting our humps to make it. We really had a firm ground, and suddenly he's off and running. It makes me want to get out and kick ass all over again. It just makes me better in the long run."

Says Tom, "It was never difficult to maintain that enthusiasm. After Brad left, we just redoubled our efforts. We're really confident. Compared to what I've been seeing on the charts lately, our album is really going to stand out. We're not ready to accept anything but at least what we had before."

"Joe and Brad started talking about going off on their own," said Steven, to *Hit Parader*. "They were getting a little itchy about not touring, so they got involved in some outside projects. They started to get more interested in those things than in the band. I said to Joe, 'Hey, man, what about the band?' He just gave me his standard 'Yeah, I know' answer, and a month later I found out that he'd split. Joe Perry and I had been pretty close for a long time, but I just said, 'Good luck, man,' and that was that. Joe and I were like brothers. We worked together long enough for me to respect the man for as long as I live. More important, I can't even remember the last time I spoke to him—it's been months! I'm not saying that if he had wanted to play with us again, we wouldn't have been able to work things out. But the fact is that there was absolutely no contact between us over the new album. I don't know if he could have found time for us. He seems so wrapped up in his group right now that the only person he has time to get in touch with is himself. That's the way he wants it. There are a lot of people out there who don't think Aerosmith is Aerosmith without Joe, and I understand that. But I'm just knocked out by the way this band looks and sounds right now."

But there were roadblocks. Explains Steven, "The thing that slowed us down the most was my injury. I got that riding my motorcycle a couple of years ago. I was really tearing along, and I tried to downshift. I was wearing moccasins at the time, and the bike just kept going. The force tore my shoe apart and literally ripped the heel off my foot. They rushed me to the hospital and had to sew it back on. I was in a cast for months after that. Obviously, that put a hell of a dent on what we wanted to do. With my foot like that, we couldn't tour."

And as he described the accident to Tim Sommer, "I took my heel off in a motorcycle accident, and that was a good seven or eight months. It was pretty bad. I was in a cast for seven months, and I was in the hospital for four just laying [*sic*] there. I really took a tumble, so I couldn't do much. But the boys were rehearsing. We spent a good year lurking about in studios. We came up with enough songs and we got enough riffs and licks to last us for the next ten years out of all this. So it was a good thing. Besides, there was nothing wrong with taking a break. I think it gets stale after a while, if you keep on going back to the same Santa Monica Civic Center for the fourth time. Between '75 and '80, we played there four times, and it just gets old. It's good to take a break. So we took a break, looked back, saw what we did, and jumped into the '80s. Nothing wrong with that."

First herding the cats would be producer Tony Bongiovi, cousin of Jon Bon Jovi, entering the fray here after having worked with Gloria Gaynor, Talking Heads, the Ramones, Tuff Darts, and the Rezillos.

Recalling the sessions, Tony first says, "Oh, Jimmy Crespo. That didn't work very well [laughs]. He was okay. You know, Joe Perry was the writer and guitar player, so that made a big difference. But Jimmy was okay. But he was a player, a musician, that somebody found to put in the band. He's an excellent player, okay? But he's not a writer, like that. But he was in there. But the primary Aerosmith group, it didn't matter who played guitar, okay? You have to have somebody play guitar, but the songs were the songs. Steven's the singer, and there's the bass and drums. They worked together as a unit, so the guitar would be mostly to fill. Because that band is all about Steven—that's Aerosmith. Joe wrote the hits, guitar player / songwriter; there's a difference. He wrote the hits, and Steven wrote the hits with him. So the guitar playing was different. With Joe, because the style of the guitar playing fit the writing, there's a difference when you're a songwriting/player than just a player. And that's true with all kinds of music. And Rick Dufay, I don't know him. I don't think he worked on the sessions I worked on.

"I'll tell you how that worked out," explains Bongiovi. "I gave the album back to CBS. I left three-quarters of the way through. Because I told Tony Martell, I can't do this anymore. I went through $600,000. And Jack Douglas came in and finished it. So I worked with Jimmy. It's possible Rick could've finished the album, and maybe even gone back and overdubbed the stuff that was on the sessions that I did. But I wouldn't know that. So whoever they put on the album cover is what they put on the album cover. I don't have any knowledge of him working on it."

Jimmy Crespo indeed is writing most of the material with Steven here.

"I didn't know that either. By the time they got to me, all that stuff was worked out. So my job is 'Okay, what song are we doing?' 'This one is called this.' And as a producer, sometimes you have to make suggestions. And sometimes you have to just sit there and wait. But a lot of the things that happened with the band happened before I got them."

As for how so much money got spent, Tony laughs and says, "A lot of it was when Steven was in his phase there; most of it was that. And that's what ran the bills up. Not showing up for six, seven hours, three days in a row. Columbia is paying the bill, and that's what I couldn't handle. I couldn't do it anymore. It was too much for me to handle. I wanted to do other things with my life. And I basically went to CBS, and Tony Martell, and I gave it back. And then he picked up Ozzy

Osbourne, who was a pleasure to work with. That was really fun. But Steven . . . Aerosmith was a whole mess because of those things."

Asked if Joey and Tom gave him any problems, Tony says, "Well, Joey, in fact, Joey later used my studios here. He and Tommy, they're just great musicians, and they're really good for that band. They played great. But were they upset with that at the time? Yeah, wouldn't you be?! [laughs]. We would sit there and talk about cars and this and that, and they just got out there and they just wanted to play. And they were so good. The band was one of the best bands ever. They would get it on the first take. And I'd make some changes, and they would adapt the changes and make it their own; they took suggestions. But yeah, they were good—those guys could play."

"We were paying through the nose for every hour we sat there dicking around in that recording studio," wrote Kramer in his book. "The Power Station was brilliant in its day, and our producer, Tony Bongiovi, who owned the place, was pulling what little hair he had left out of his head. Tony was the consummate professional, and he just couldn't deal with the nonsense that was going on among us. After a while, he gave up, and they brought Jack Douglas in, because he was just as much into the drugs as we were. Jack got it finished and mixed, and the record is what it is, after we'd dropped $1.5 million on studio time. *Rock in a Hard Place* hit #32 on the charts. We also did a pretty primitive-looking video of 'Lightning Strikes' to promote it. The record doesn't suck. There's some really good stuff on it, but it's not a real Aerosmith record, because it's just me, Steven, and Tom, with a fill-in guitar player. Brad played rhythm on 'Lightning Strikes,' the single. Otherwise, it's Jimmy doing all the guitar work."

Explained Tom in *Walk This Way*, "For two years the album we were working on, *Rock in a Hard Place*, was always two months away. It was hard times. We sold our house and moved to a condo, and everyone else cut back too. Joey and I were determined to hang in there with Steven, but Brad couldn't handle it. The truth is, we were raging. There were a lot of drugs around. This was when freebasing cocaine was in vogue, the precrack era. So you can imagine how nuts it was. By this time, Jack Douglas was back on the project. The original producer, Tony Bongiovi, either got fired or left. Things were insane, and Jack came back to help us."

Added Joey, "We ended up erasing the stuff that Brad did, and me, Tom, and Jimmy Crespo did all the tracks. I actually got to express myself a little, which hadn't happened before. I was writing songs, doing production work. Hey, it was almost like it was my own band. I did what I had to do to get the record out."

"Steven and Jimmy wrote some good things together," remembers Jack. "'Jailbait,' 'Bitch's Brew,' 'Bolivian Ragamuffin,' 'Jig Is Up.' They had a couple of unfinished things—'Joanie's Butterfly,' 'Rock in a Hard Place'—that I was able to help them with. We worked in the winter and spring of 1982 in New York and at Criteria Studios in Miami. At this time, there was talk of them going on tour that fall to support the album, and they needed a guitar player to replace Brad. So I brought in Rick Dufay, a true character, a kindred spirit. I thought he would mesh well with the band, so we flew him to Florida, and he joined Aerosmith. I think he played on one track on the album, 'Lightning Strikes,' which Richie wrote. There were some interesting things on that album. We were doing stuff with vocoders that hadn't been done before."

A record eventually emerged, with *Rock in a Hard Place* hitting store shelves on August 27, 1982. Amusingly, it's a title that would have also made sense for the last album—and vice versa. For cover art, the guys went with a shot of Stonehenge, suggested by David Krebs—it goes with the title. On the back, the guys were brave about presenting to us the new band, although, amusingly, Jimmy looks like Joe and Rick looks like Brad. On the inner sleeve we got credits, a reminder of the illustrious discography, plus the mystical lyrics of "Prelude to Joanie," a nice touch, and a harkening back to Zeppelin and others, this highlighting of an important and choice lyric from the album, which this certainly is.

The album opens in blistering fashion with "Jailbait," which finds Steven instantly singing along to headbanging guitar and bass. Joey quickly crashes in (along with some well-placed vibraslap), and we're off to the races like "Toys in the Attic" or, much later, "Young Lust" from *Pump*. Soon we get bass from Tom weaving with Jimmy's guitar in creation of the first bit of riff beyond the nihilistic, punky intro sequence, with Joey bashing away on his crashes.

Then everything stops and Steven sings in unison with a new riff. This serves as a verse structure, but soon there are more surprises. A verse 2, of sorts, features entirely new music, with Joey doing a military march, single-stroke roll beat, akin to Golden Earring's "Radar Love" and Mötley Crüe's "Kickstart My Heart." Again, Steven is following the high, descending riff cooked up by Jimmy—this is one of four tracks credited to just Tyler and Crespo. There's some added percussion, likely a tambourine track, within this highly rhythm-based segment. Then we're into an even heavier section that serves as the chorus, but executed like an inspired jam. Helping create this blustery atmosphere is all kinds of huffing and hissy at the vocal end, with Steven showing no signs of his degraded state, so bad, in fact, that Jimmy became Steven's nurse, telling Mick Burgess, "He was pretty sick, and I just took care of him and even had to wipe his ass for him!"

Later, amid the relentless mayhem of the song, there's new music for a break section, with Joey switching to the bell of his ride cymbal. Next, we get another couple of verses, and then we're off racing into more of the jamming, with roaring guitars and a reverse volume effect accompanied by more vocal acrobatics from Steven.

At the lyric end, "Jailbait" isn't much, but it's obviously about sex with an underage girl, even if the sparseness and fragmentation of the words, perhaps mirroring Steven's drug-addled state of mind, don't reveal much. All told, "Jailbait" is an explosive opener, speedy, fresh with ideas, performed with verve. It holds up a licked finger to the winds of change happening with the industry, blowing across the Atlantic from the New Wave of British Heavy Metal, and soon to create a healthy environment for all forms of heavy music in America for a decade to come.

Remarked Tom in the *Pandora's Box* notes, "This is a Jimmy Crespo riff. The song really made us feel like we had one in the pocket. It seemed impossible to hear it without getting blown away." Adds Joe Perry, "Even though I wasn't around for that song, I think it's pretty hot. I would have done it a little differently, but if anything, I'm a little jealous that I didn't play on it."

Next comes "Lightning Strikes," which emerged from a song called "When the Lightning Strikes" by Richie Supa. This was recorded early on, so there's some Brad Whitford rhythm guitar on it. It's considered to be the only single from the album, although there's no 7-inch for it. It charted, but only on the *Billboard* subchart called Mainstream Rock

Tracks, reaching #21. A creepy, druggy, darkly shot production video was made for the song, directed by Arnold Levine, who did a number of important early-days videos but was soon out of the game. The guys dress up like a greaseball '50s street gang and head out into the alley, threatening the camera with weapons. But it's the opening footage in the studio that captures the malevolent and squalid state of the band at this time. Notable is Rick Dufay, who by all accounts was a whirlwind of terror in the band, inflicting psychological and sometimes physical damage upon Steven as some sort of drug-fueled goading mechanism.

The lyrics are all about fighting too, placed upon a second absolutely swell Aerosmith track that beats the odds while the guys fight for survival. It's also a second song that could be called heavy metal, again preparing the band for the rockin' marketplace exploding left, right, and center around them but destined to leave them out. As an aside, our bar band in the '80s, Torque, played this song, pretty much to blank stares. In fact, in the performing of it (me on drums), I remember it eventually dawning on me that despite its swagger and sturdy riff, there really isn't much to it (certainly at the drum end), and it's not much of a single, set in an oddly reclining place as far as beats per minute and lacking hook.

"Bitch's Brew" keeps the high-volume party going, as well as the nonobvious song construction we got with our opener. Also like "Jailbait," there's vibraslap and tambourine as part of the percussive arrangement. But most impressive is the sequencing of the parts. First there's a mellow intro, with Steven sounding like an old bluesman. Next is a prechorus, followed by the chorus, and then we're into a sort of melodically floating verse structure. Halfway through, there's a modulation to a break, along with some whistling and trashy, splashy drumming from Joey. This dissolves for a secondary break, a quiet one, where Jimmy does an amusing cameo vocal, sounding like Bob Dylan. The guys jam it out in fine, groovy, arena rock fashion, with Steven once again providing all sorts of vocalized percussive appointments.

"Bolivian Ragamuffin" starts fast and riffy, strafed by slide, but then collapses into half time, becoming, arguably, the band's finest hard-funk song. At the verses, it's an easy-drinking four-four, but there are extra beats thrown in around it, with Kramer necessarily cooking up a bizarre, complicated beat to compensate. Rising to the challenge, Steven comes up with some zesty, near-nonsensical wordplay that is a laugh riot. The speedy intro motif returns around the two-minute mark, again, Joey driving the song with inspiration and the bell of his ride cymbal heard loud and clear. After some soloing over a descending chord sequence, we're into an even heavier break section, which rises in intensity once again before an extended, percussive windup with Steven scatting over top. What emerges out the other end is a bona fide Aerosmith classic, and the fourth very strong song in a row to start the album.

"That was Steven's idea," Tom told Steve Newton, asked about side 1 closer "Cry Me a River." "He was in a record store down in the Village in New York, and he happened to see an old Julie London album. He picked it up and brought it up to the studio, and we listened to that one song and started figuring it out, changing the horn and string parts into guitar parts. It went pretty good, so we stuck with it." Steven tells a slightly different story, about hearing the song on "an old honky-tonk station" while out on tour in Texas somewhere, maybe Beaumont.

Muses Tony Bongiovi, "'Cry Me a River' [he sings a bit of it], well, you see, now, Steven could sing that. Because he was a singer's singer. That's the difference. Those guys are a real rock band. The Ramones are kind of a signature band, whereas Aerosmith could play—they could do Gershwin sets, okay? Steven is phenomenal. That's the best rock singer I've ever worked with. But like I say, I go into the studio with them, and at that time, Steven had a little problem, okay? And I had to sift through a nightmare of 'Where are you, Steven? Why aren't you here? You know, you can't come to the studio in that condition.'

"But on the other hand, 'Cry Me a River,' I used to run a 7½ tape before I'd run the multitracks [note: This is a tape speed that is a little quicker, to save on tape]. And I'd record everything that we're doing. This way we have it, as a point of reference. The version that made it to the album is that 7½. That's how little . . . It's first take—that was it. And that's the mix that made it. We never got it after that. I mean, they're so talented as a band, probably one of the most talented rock bands that I've ever worked with. And they've got, without a doubt, the best rock singer of all time. And very personable."

In the end, despite the speed with which they captured this song, Tony told me that they had an entire transport truck full of tape outside, which is a big part of why the record cost $2 million to make.

"Cry Me a River" is essentially an old, bluesy pop song, written by Arthur Hamilton in 1953 and made popular by Julie London in 1955. It fits the Aerosmith narrative, somewhat close to the vibes of "Remember (Walking in the Sand)" and "Reefer Head Woman," but it paints a different part of the canvas, sort of torch-song-like. And it definitely breaks rank with the shiny rockers that precede it on this album. In that respect, it's jarring like "Big Ten Inch Record."

Side 2 of the original vinyl opens with "Prelude to Joanie," which is a minute and a half of the aforementioned vocoder vocal placed on a bed of angelic voices. It's unintelligible, and so it's helpful that we get the printing of the lyrics on the inner sleeve. It's awkwardly titled, because it's really the prelude to "Joanie's Butterfly," the resplendent first actual song on the side.

"Joanie's Butterfly" begins with exquisitely recorded acoustic guitars, with Steven singing up top, harmonizing and doing backing vocals with himself. Tyler says that the music originated with a riff he'd heard Jimmy playing in a hotel room. Which is perfect, because there's a certain golden-era Rolling Stones quality to the chord shifts, and then a descent into uneasiness that takes us back to "Prelude to Joanie." Accompanying is a sort of bongo drum percussion track and warm waves of bass, which is also Stonesy, like something from *Beggars Banquet* or *Exile*. After almost two minutes of this, it comes to a close and actually goes silent for a moment. Then the band kicks in, and it's still sounding like the Rolling Stones offering good tidings. Then we're off on a psychedelic excursion, with the band playing along to the dark motif found in the intro. More magic comes with the "No, no, no, took off in flight" segment, yet again evoking the Stones, Faces, and the Dolls, but recorded to exacting, high-fidelity standards. All told, it's a masterpiece of a track, ambitious, ultimately egregiously overlooked, and actually—surprising to me—often denigrated by ardent Aerosmith fans. And part to part, it all makes sense; it all flows, even when the lyrics are super obscure.

Recalls Steven in his autobiography, first with some background: "I was stoned out of my mind on drugs all the time. I moved out of my house in Sunapee and into Jack Douglas' apartment in New York in the winter of 1982; then I got an apartment in New York and started to work on the next album. Our cocaine was written into the budget as

24-track reels of tape. Even if you were out on a yacht or an island somewhere, recording on a mobile unit, they'd fly drugs out to you in sea planes.

"I wrote the songs on *Rock in a Hard Place* with Rick Dufay and Jimmy Crespo. Two of these songs, 'Prelude to Joanie' and 'Joanie's Butterfly,' are about a hallucinatory horse with wings and feathers. I bought some opium from a dealer named Reinhart, a tongue of opium, black and thick, about three inches long, half an inch wide and half an inch thick. I didn't smoke it. I rolled it into little balls and swallowed it. I'd eat it. And it was like, *fuck!* The best high on the planet is opium.

"I remember being so high one night, one of those nights when you can't sleep, you're in this wakeless, sleepless place, and a story came over me. I was in a barn, in a stall, and there was a lot of hay, and this horse gave birth with the waters of life pouring out of her. It was a beautiful white horse, and its baby was this kick-ass rocking horse. That's what I called it. It had wings and feathers. I couldn't figure it out. How would a horse have feathers? But that was the fantasy. I wrote two songs around this opium vision. 'Prelude to Joanie' told the story. The second song was 'Joanie's Butterfly,' which I named for a vibrator in the shape of a butterfly. Women strap it on and it stays right here, and it goes 'Zzzzz!' But for whatever reason, that's what I called the song, and took the dream poem into a hallucinatory journey.

"We put some freaky effects on *Rock in a Hard Place*," continues Steven. "I used a vocoder, essentially a frequency phaser or oscillator that had been used by Pink Floyd and Wendy Carlos. I was talking to one of the recording engineers, and he said, 'I can create this interesting audio hallucination, if you're interested.' 'Oh yeah?' I said. 'Let's do it.' He explained that it was a bizarre effect you can create using two stereo speakers in which a third sound appears to be coming from behind you. And I thought, wow, that is so cool. So on 'Prelude to Joanie,' I hit an African drum with my elbow, and it made this 'ooouuum' sound. You can hear it in the song really loud. If you put your speakers in two corners of the room facing you, suddenly you'll hear a sound. It appears to be coming from somewhere behind your head. People listening to the track would get up from the record in the middle of the song when they heard the drumbeat and go to the door behind them to see who knocked. We could really fuck with people with this device. I got sold on it and bought it, but little did I know that it doesn't work unless there's music playing as well. That's what throws the knockout of phase."

Seconds Jack, "We mixed the album so well that when it was released, we started to get letters from kids. 'We were smoking a joint and listening to "Joanie's Butterfly," and we thought we heard something behind our heads. How did you do that?'"

In reality, this passage can be heard in the quiet respite late in "Joanie's Butterfly." Steven describes the sound accurately, and it's the kind of sound that you tend to get out of a darbouka or doumbek drum, or some other kind of Moroccan or otherwise African percussion instrument. Both Steven and Jack are credited with percussion on the album, so presumably they are both participating here, given how much is going on. Credited with "Guitar O.D." on the song is John Lievano, and credited with violins—which can be heard ornately at the end—is Reinhard Straub, likely not the gentleman of whom Steven speaks above!

Tyler's also said that the song has an Indian/Ethiopian flavor to it, and that the vocoder effect is similar to something that Hitler used to do when sending secret messages. He also appreciates the fact that the song starts fairly happy sounding and then goes dark, which is a vibe he regularly likes to put into Aerosmith ballads.

Steven credits Jack with bringing the track across the finish line, telling Tim Sommer from *Sounds*, "We missed him a hell of a lot. We had worked with Gary Lyons, who was really good, but for this album in particular, there were some songs that really needed a different application—like 'Joanie's Butterfly,' and Jack's really good at that. He sussed the flavor of that song out right away. He's really adaptable to our style. And also, I wanted to get in there a little more than I'd been in the past, as far as the way I think things should sound, coproduce it with him, get my hands wet. I guess it *was* an important move. But more of us, mentally—we've tired of shopping around. We were kind of like, where we were, our nest."

"Rock in a Hard Place (Cheshire Cat)" is a tough shuffle, sort of "Same Old Song and Dance" slightly faster and feistier, or "One Way Street" newly paved. It arrives on a reverse fade and becomes something that classic-era Whitesnake might do, but arranged and recorded more muscular, up into the John Sykes era. It has so much tradition; it sounds like a cover but it's not. This is underscored by the pervasive, bass-guitar-adjacent sax licks from John Turi. The chorus features bluesy vocal phrasing from Steven, and in total there aren't many parts. Toward the end, signaled by a cat snarl, the band gets blustery, executing some almost doomy chord changes. And as Joey has alluded to before, he's very much part of the fray, playing with energy and looseness, doing some cool combinations while the song unravels toward the end. Meanwhile, at the literary end, like "Bolivian Ragamuffin," Steven plays an exaggerated version of a hillbilly sitting on his porch and muttering colorful nonsense, yukking it up and remembering some gal, much to the delight of his moonshine-sipping audience.

Strength to strength and continuing the foundational anchoring of the project, "Jig Is Up" is a heavy metal-funk song, joining the collection of like-minded compositions that Aerosmith has built across all previous albums. The central intro and connective lick are almost underachieving, kept modest by Joey playing a four-on-the-floor beat. But like any good band, Aerosmith know that they then have to raise the stakes for the verse, which they do, turning the song almost arena rocking and certainly somehow Zeppelinesque. Then there's a break that's even more heroically heavy metal, evoking developments in "Black Dog" later on in that track.

Lyrically, the theme continues, with Steven stringing together imagistic phrases and fragments that sound like they come from obscure but outsider and profane blues songs from the 1930s. Underscoring the old jazz and R&B vibe of what's coming out of Steven's mouth is an effect on the "chicken scratch" funk guitar that makes it sound like a trumpet with a wah-wah-creating bell mute on it. "Jig is up" is never said, just like "rock in a hard place" isn't part of the previous song's ramblings. Near the end, the first half of Jimmy's solo is elegant and lyrical (before it gets standard), reminding one of Andy McCoy from Hanoi Rocks, who seems to have learned from the best anyway; namely, Joe Perry.

Rock in a Hard Place closes with "Push Comes to Shove," which further solidifies this theme of tradition, triggering a debate on whether the album we've just heard is maybe too blues based for the rock marketplace of 1982. The song very much squares off the album, ending side 2 the way that side 1 ended, with something of a ballad. But this is an up-tempo enough song, a sort of lazily swinging shuffle, and like "Cry Me a River," it's something that might fit in the pop idiom of the

'30s, '40s, or '50s. Steven sounds even more like that old cracker on the porch, practically playing a role. Plus, he's doing the same thing he's doing on the songs that have already rolled on down the tracks; namely, reminiscing about some roll in the hay years ago.

In the end, *Rock in a Hard Place* closes this run of seven Columbia albums much the way it began, with Aerosmith delivering their adapted, hybrid, evolved version of the American Songbook. I think the theme has to be, as Joey put it, "The record doesn't suck." But it's more than that, and history has borne this out: *Rock in a Hard Place* sits among Aerosmith's very best albums, especially when it comes to ardent followers of the band. In that respect, it's Aerosmith's version of *Drama* from Yes, not commercially successful (although *Rock in a Hard Place* did certify gold, in 1989), but beloved by fans, who now seem pretty reconciled with the compromised lineup.

More on the business results, the album got to #32 on the *Billboard* charts, hanging around for eighteen weeks, which is similar to how it fared on *Cash Box*. And I can tell you, having lived through that period, for an album that certified gold, albeit much later, there was very little excitement about Aerosmith in 1982 and into 1983.

As Tim Sommer wrote, "Fact is, Aerosmith have turned out to be one of America's great rock bands. With their new LP, *Rock in a Hard Place*, they have firmly asserted their claim to true greatness. After disappearing for a while, Aerosmith reappeared in the '80s, seemingly the decade they weren't supposed to belong in because certainly contemporaries like Blue Öyster Cult and Ted Nugent were just plain out of their element in the '80s. Those bands had made their definitive or necessary statements in the '70s (and don't they seem like period pieces now!) and today are just riding out their dwindling momentum from the excesses of the earlier decade.

"But in 1982, Aerosmith made a new album, a great album, very much 1982 and very much Aerosmith. They had made it into their second decade as a relevant band. They need not remain a frozen image of 1976 glory. *Rock in a Hard Place* could be definitive Aerosmith. At least it's a good place to start. It showcases their skills as hard rock naturals scraping solid and fiery riffs plus good humor over ten well-paced songs. It's nothing short of classic, reminiscent of the easygoing, yet hard and tough literate sleaziness of Mott the Hoople or the Small Faces."

Writes Roman Cooley from the *Calgary Herald*, "A song dubbed 'Bolivian Ragamuffin' convinced me that Aerosmith has not, despite considerable evidence to the contrary, started to take themselves too seriously. There's a little more gray hair, sure, but Aerosmith is still able to match utterly juvenile sloppiness with ferocious intent, a volatile combination. For every piece of flatulent filler on this album—and there's plenty of it—there's a snide, egocentric gem of clever rock spurred by lead singer Steven Tyler's tortured vocals. While not on the scale of *Toys in the Attic* or *Rocks*, Aerosmith's latest beats the drudgery of *Night in the Ruts*, an earlier comeback attempt. Sure, Aerosmith take themselves seriously once in a while, but as long as no one else does, we're safe."

Even *Rolling Stone* was kind, with J. D. Considine writing, "As the title of this album makes clear, Aerosmith is caught between a rock and a hard place. In the three years since the group's last studio album, *Night in the Ruts*, a minor revolution has taken place in heavy rock, and its insistence on hard, fast power chords has made Aerosmith's bluesy boogie almost obsolete. Worse, Joe Perry, the fleet-fingered guitarist who plays Keith Richards to Steven Tyler's Mick Jagger, left the fold for a solo career. As a result, Tyler and company were forced to choose between the old sound with new faces or a complete change in approach. They went for the former, and on first hearing, it almost seems to work. Perry lookalike Jimmy Crespo is no slouch at turning out hard-edged guitar hooks that make up in drive what they lack in swing, and both 'Jailbait' and 'Lightning Strikes' throb with the sort of nasty glee that's always been an Aerosmith trademark. But despite an occasional burst of primal energy, much of the LP rocks by rote. In all fairness, it's a good formula, and even the weakest examples here hold up well enough under repeated listenings. Not so the ballads, though: Steven Tyler is unable to energize the slow numbers, and they drag interminably, undercutting the album's pacing in their wake. Maybe next time Aerosmith will stick to the rock; for now, however, they're really stuck in a hard place."

It's a fair cop. Alluded to there at the beginning is the reality that there's been a rapid evolution in heavy metal, slingshot by the New Wave of British Heavy Metal. Put up against *Blackout, High 'n' Dry, Diary of a Madman, Mob Rules, Screaming for Vengeance, Denim and Leather, Ace of Spades*, and *The Number of the Beast*, well, *Rock in a*

Hard Place sounds like a swell album from 1977, maybe even the follow-up that *Draw the Line* should have been. The rest of Considine's review strikes an appropriate tone as well. Bottom line, he finds the album pleasant enough, and for a *Rolling Stone* review of a band and album like this, in 1982, we'll take it.

Writes Roy Trakin in *Hit Parader*, "And you wondered why the music business is in trouble? Hard to believe this decimated band took over three years to record this, but then Tyler Rico must have some pretty time-consuming hobbies. With guitarist Joe Perry and Brad Whitford gone, what's left is singer Steve Tyler's brainchild (no cracks now)—for better and worse. Festooned in Keith Richards scarves and Jagger-esque smirk, Tyler's lost in some kind of time warp. *Rock in a Hard Place* roars off the starting line like it was 1975 again, with the typically leering misogyny of 'Jailbait,' 'Lightning Strikes,' 'Bitch's Brew' and 'Bolivian Ragamuffin.' The aimless riffing is so indistinguished and amelodic that, if you didn't know better, you might mistake the thrashing for hardcore punk.

"Still, despite the band's plodding, some of Steverino's more outrageous conceits enter the 'so bad it's amazing' category. He obliterates the cocktail-lounge chestnut, 'Cry Me a River' with a wacky, hard rock croon. He scores points by harking back to *Satanic Majesties* Stones for a timely, psychedelic medley which includes vocoder, acoustic guitars and butterflies. There's even a drooling, barroom blooze that's likably sloppy, if not earthshattering ('Push Comes to Shove'). But this band's stock-in-trade is pull-back-the-throttle rock, and, while they deliver in the title track, for the most part Aerosmith lacks a simple, but basic, ingredient: solid tunes. Without them, there's really nothing to separate this once-proud outfit from any number of similar ones who have passed Aerosmith by. Of course, I could be wrong. One can never underestimate the incredible loyalty of those heavy metallers."

It's an interesting take. Ironically, starting right about now, *Hit Parader* is going to become the most heavy metal of the big American music magazines right through to the end of the decade, even if *Circus* will hoe the same row. And yet, one senses a certain impatience from Roy with Aerosmith continuing to be heavy, when maybe the average rock fan has moved on. Or does he think that if Aerosmith is going to commit, then *Rock in a Hard Place* is not heavy metal enough?

Again, Steven seemed quite pleased with the final results, telling *Hit Parader*, "I look at this album as a cross between *Toys in the Attic* and *Rocks*. We recorded it in bits and pieces over the last couple of years, and in fact we have enough material for almost another complete album already in the can. It's not like we've been sitting on our ass watching the world go by. We've been working damn hard. I coproduced this album with Jack Douglas, who worked with us in the very beginning, and I think it's vintage Aerosmith—if there is such a thing. Now all I'm waiting for is the chance to get back on stage and show everyone who thought we were dead that we're back and better than ever."

He's right about it being vintage Aerosmith, in that half these songs, crumpled up, could have fit on the debut. And he's actually not that far off with that first bit, although given his state and his status as a jaded rock star, it was probably by accident. It has the visceral excitement of *Rocks*, along with the clean, powerful recording, and then it has "Cry Me a River" and "Push Comes to Shove," creating a melange that reflects the eclecticism of *Toys in the Attic*.

"We've got a lot to prove to a lot of people," stated Steven. "I don't mean the critics—I mean the fans. They're the only ones I give a damn about. They're the ones who supported us in the beginning and stood by us over the years. We owe everything—and we know it! We really want to do a mutha of a tour this time. We want to pull out all the stops. We want the people to leave the hall saying to themselves, 'That's one fuckin'-A rock 'n' roll band!'

"When you've been in this business for as long as I have, you've got to learn to take care of yourself," continued Steven, perhaps telegraphing a reckoning. "I'll never deny that I've had a fine ol' time for myself over the years, and I don't think that's gonna change. But we all mature and grow and I'm no exception. It's been a long haul with this band, but I wouldn't change a second of it."

"*Night in the Ruts*, I think, is a record that was almost good, and *Rock in a Hard Place* should've been really good," Tom told me. "I mean, that's the record that we did with Jimmy Crespo, and he did a lot of fantastic guitar playing and writing on that album. But I think that the writing partner . . . Steven was pining away for Joe, and I don't think he responded creatively with Jimmy the way he wanted to see. He wanted to get back with Joe. But some of us realized that this wasn't the time of them being able to work together. It was not there yet. So, you know, we did that *Rock in a Hard Place* album, and it came out really good. I think it's a very interesting, fun to listen to album, but I can understand why some of the ideas might be too weird and abstract for some of our fans. I mean, it's a good record.

"But those two bring some negativity," continues Hamilton. "I'm proud of those albums, but that's when the band was really going through hell, and it's hard to remember that music without the other stuff going along with it. Obviously, I get more objective as time goes on, but it wasn't the best era of the band. We didn't know what was going on with the band. We managed to keep putting out records, and all those records have cool stuff on them. There are a lot of nuggets on *Draw the Line* and even *Rock in a Hard Place.* It's valid music, but that was a tough time—the band was splitting apart. A band is a complex set of relationships that evolves over time. It ebbs and flows. You have moments like we had when we made *Get Your Wings*, *Toys*, and *Rocks*, and then we kind of like trashed ourselves."

EPILOGUE
"Were we still relevant?"

"I mean, the Aerosmith story is this," surveys David Krebs, exasperated. "We had them signed for many years and albums, when in 1984, I had heard some stuff whereby I knew that I was never going to be successful in curing Tyler of heroin. I mean, at the end, I had a psychiatrist friend of mine, Lloyd Moglen, on tour with them, but he came back with the verdict that this was unfixable. I told Steve Leber that night. I said, 'We've got to let him go.' So they went. They were still signed to us, and we knew they had to come back to us to get out, and that's what happened. If you'd asked me back in 1979 if I thought they were still going to be big forty years later, I would have said you're crazy. But that's what happened: These guys got so deeply into heroin that I couldn't do it anymore."

But you gotta hand it to these guys in Aerosmith—they were tough under pressure. It showed in that there are no unprofessional, casual albums, with *Draw the Line* coming closest but still fooling most of us. And then despite Steven being a wreck, the guys pulled off a lot of shows in support of *Rock in a Hard Place*, playing for much of November and December 1982 (with Nazareth, Pat Travers, and Rose Tattoo) and then admirable enough chunks of shows clear through to October 1983. This followed upon nearly two months of pretour rehearsal work put in at the Capitol Theatre in Concord, New Hampshire, so at least the guys had a fighting chance.

As Tom admitted to Steve Newton, there was keyboard support. "There's a much-better onstage mix, and there's much more in the way of dynamics, so the audience hears every instrument with better separation and tone. Plus, we've got a guy with us on keyboards named Bob Mayo, who used to play with Foreigner and Peter Frampton, and he's also doing some backup vocals. So, between him, Jimmy, and Steven, we've got plenty of harmony now, whereas it used to be that the only one in the band that could really sing was Steven. I don't like to call it a comeback—I don't feel that we've really been that far away. But I suppose that's the way we have to look at it, considering that most people figure we had faded into the distance."

Despite late in the sequence trying to launch "Bitch's Brew" to radio, the album's life cycle was over, and ticket sales slowed. They'd now played much of the beginning of 1983 with Pat Travers supporting, and later Anvil, Zebra, Kix, Johnny Van Zandt, and a hot new band called Dio. The set list shortened, with only "Lightning Strikes" from the new album surviving the cull. Steven was still on the hard stuff, and then he got arrested in Arizona. Joey got pneumonia and had to be replaced by Bobby Rondinelli from Rainbow. Joey had recovered sufficiently enough to come back for a February 8 show at the Agora in West Hartford, Connecticut (capacity 1,500), with the *Rock in a Hard Place* lineup playing their last show on the seventeenth of that month, 1984, in Providence, Rhode Island.

"I wanted to continue with Aerosmith," Steven told Dave Reynolds in 1987. "My ego didn't want to say Aerosmith was over just because Joe left. What the fuck does he know, anyway? Fuck him. I'll show him who needs him anyway. That's what I said at the time, and that wore thin real fast. How many bands can make it without the real lineup and expect fans to believe it is? Would you go and see the Stones without Mick Jagger or Keith Richards? I wouldn't. Like Kiss! Ace isn't in the band anymore. It's not really the original thing now, is it?"

"Depending on the day, hate has usually been based on resentment," reflected Tom, speaking with Paul Gargano. "Resentment is something that builds up over time, if you don't deal with it. One thing that we have now that's really good for us is we have a way of dealing with resentment. Resentments still build up. But instead of going to all our separate mansions on the hill and getting obliterated and keeping our resentments intact until the next time, we actually get together and we talk about stuff; we actually fight about it. I had a lot of resentment about stuff that Joe and Steven did back in the early days, but I don't know, I've always been this really reserved kind of person. I don't just come out and say what's in my mind and 'Hey, fuck you.' I'm more that way now than I used to be, but back then, I wished everybody could be nicer to each other. Now when shit comes up, we deal with it."

In large part due to the work that manager Tim Collins did toward getting the band clean, Aerosmith was to experience what is perhaps the greatest second-act story in all of rock 'n' roll.

But it didn't start off so great. Past the focus of our story—namely, the Columbia years—Aerosmith signed with David Geffen and Geffen Records, marshaled by A&R guru John Kalodner. The first record under the new collaboration would be *Done with Mirrors*, issued on November 4, 1985. Universally met with blank stares, despite its basic, raw, and rocking nature, it managed to certify gold, but that's it.

As Joe Perry told me, "That's the one where the band dropped the ball," noting also that it's liked by very few, "except for the hardcore fans," with Joe adding that "I have a hard time even listening to that record. I know what a struggle it was for us to do that. It was great to be back and playing with the band, but we were still pretty screwed up and running on the vapors of the '70s, and it just wasn't working right. You know that one most important change hadn't occurred yet. So it's kind of hard for me to hear that, and yet it was important for us to do that. You just can't go back and say, well, if we hadn't done that, how would we have learned that we needed to change things? I have a hard time having any regrets about anything, but that record is tough to listen to."

"Yeah, well, the '80s was a dark time," adds Brad. "A lot of stuff was going away, and a lot of stuff is coming in to fill the slot. The hair metal bands, if you recall, and also dance bands, were getting huge, and we were wondering how we fit in, *where* we fit in, and were we still relevant? It was a matter of questioning who we were. But we didn't really need to. We started to reestablish ourselves, and I guess get a little more faith in what we were doing.

"*Done with Mirrors* was a difficult album to make," continues Brad, "and I don't really feel like it got the best of our efforts. We were still finding out again who we were, and we were still regrouping and getting back together. Like I say, I felt that for some of it, we weren't really giving it our best efforts. Maybe we weren't ready. We were still in our party period, where it was just still one long Friday night."

"It's the only cold streak I ever had in my career," John Kalodner told me. "Usually I had hits, one hit a year. I did *Vision Quest*, I think, in 1985. Aerosmith had a flop record with *Done with Mirrors*, and I had signed Cher against David Geffen's wishes. So I was worrying about Aerosmith's record and was getting ready for Cher. So I was not in big favor at the time. And Mo Ostin told Geffen he should get rid of me."

Things would turn around, however, dramatically, precipitously. Next would be *Permanent Vacation*, produced by Bruce Fairbairn, recorded at Little Mountain Sound in Vancouver and issued on August 18, 1987. It would go on to certify at five-times platinum, establishing

Aerosmith as one of the most successful bands of the late '80s, participating in the hair metal sweepstakes at the front of the pack but retaining their reputation as a '70s-anchored band with substance.

"I remember being at the rehearsals for *Permanent Vacation*," explains Kalodner, "after Tim Collins cleaned them up off drugs in Boston in the fall of '86, winter of '87, and how they behaved and how I behaved. It had been so extreme. Everything with these bands, especially with Aerosmith and all that greatness, there are so many extreme things that happened. Anyway, I finally got Bruce Fairbairn, finally told Aerosmith either they were gonna use Bruce Fairbairn or it wasn't going to work. But there are two albums where I learned so much: the Whitesnake '87 record and *Permanent Vacation*. And then I really honed it down, with Aerosmith, when they did *Get a Grip*. I got five commercial songs out of them, and that record was one of the biggest-selling rock records ever. And I made them go back and do *Get a Grip* again. The entire record, I threw out. But yeah, I went into the '90s having learned from the Whitesnake experience. You know, when I made the huge Aerosmith record, it was having known that I fucked up the follow-up Whitesnake record. And then with *Get a Grip*, in the rock era, I think only Bon Jovi and maybe Metallica have outsold that record. Because it had five hit singles on it."

And beginning with *Permanent Vacation*, Aerosmith became huge MTV video stars. "Yes, a big part of it are the Marty Callner videos," says John. "Which I paid a fortune for. I mean, that was another gigantic contentious issue within the record company—how much I spent on those videos."

"Well, I'm grateful for John," says Tom Hamilton. "Doing those ballads on those few albums scared the shit out of me. You know, I thought this is beyond what this band should be doing. But grunge was happening, and a lot of the radio stations across the country that used to advertise that they played Aerosmith were now advertising that they didn't play Aerosmith. We were really stuck with a dilemma, and we were determined to make sure that we were on a comeback. And we were determined that that comeback succeed.

"We had a period of frustration with the creative process in the band, and we really wanted to try to open it up to collaborating with other writers and seeing what it would be like to go through an Aerosmith album with just a different vibe, less of a pressure vibe. And it wound up expanding everyone's musical knowledge and making our records really good. So, John, he was right at the forefront of that and sitting us down and talking to us about things. He had a super awareness of the fan base out there, and what people were wanting to hear at that point and listen to, and he wanted to make sure that we knew that.

"I mean, we still wanted to make Aerosmith albums," continues Hamilton, "but he helped us see that it wouldn't be bad to have a song that went up on the charts. It wouldn't be bad to have a Top 40 hit. You know, feel like our feet were really on the ground. Plus, when we first put the band back together in 1984, we did *Done with Mirrors*, and it was a crappy record. So we really worked hard to arrive at that point where we were ready to consider opening up the creative process and bringing in outside people. That was a very difficult decision, but it was the right one for the band as far as longevity goes."

"John was a tremendously huge force," seconds Brad. "We signed a new record deal with Geffen Records, and John convinced us to expand our horizons, and he felt that our formula of how we were operating and how we were writing was tired. It was. We had sort of just emptied that glass out [laughs], and he said to Steven and Joe, you should try writing with some of these people I know, some of these songwriters that I like.

"And this didn't fit well—or didn't sit too well—with the band at first. I mean, we don't like that shit. It was a little hard to take. But we did end up exploring that, and we did end up with some great songs, some great material, that allowed us to carry on. And John was the driving force behind all that. He was in the process all the way. He would come in, and if he didn't like something, he would say, 'I don't like it!' [laughs]. And if he liked something, he'd say so. So he kept pushing us to expand our writing horizons and to try to do better, and to be better musicians. He had a huge effect—huge."

Talking another time with Tom, he framed the second wind for the band this way.

"Even our earlier albums had a lot of little studio creative things going on. So, I don't know, maybe we should restrain ourselves, find a happy medium thing.

"We said, look, let's jump-start the creativity in here. Let's do something to shake it up, instead of just sitting there in the studio, you know, wishing for it, for something from the past to come back. So, we said, to hell with it, we'll probably get trashed, but let's work with other people outside the band, and it got the engine going, and we put out the *Permanent Vacation* album.

"But, you know, these are Aerosmith albums," he says, defending. "These guys . . . none of these people ever came in and said, 'Here's a song—play it.' I mean, there are a couple of exceptions. 'I Don't Want to Miss a Thing' is maybe one of, say, two or three. But the vast majority of the material that we've come up with with outside writers is Aerosmith music. It gets cowritten primarily with Steven and Joe, and then the whole band puts their take on it, and we make it an Aerosmith song. There's been a lot of stuff along the way that we didn't use because somebody came along and said, 'Well, this can be a hit.' And we'd say, wait a minute, we're not doing it just for that. It's great to have hit songs. Every band has to have hits at some point if they want to continue what they're doing. And that could also mean deep-cut obscure hits, because that's what your core fan base wants."

Still, the "song doctor" situation has been a hard sell, with most of the wrath saved for the increasing dominance of outside-sourced power ballads, which aren't so much taking over the albums, but more like the airwaves and headlines, becoming the big hits from each successive smash album.

"Well, I think it's the fans who are going to be the judge of that," dismisses Joe. "You know, we've always been able to . . . we've always made advances by bringing in outside ideas, whether it's using world instruments or orchestras or whatever. And bringing outside writers in really helped make us successful in a commercial sense and really brought in our audience. I mean, if we had just continued playing the same old hard rock in that little mix, yeah, we would have been like that great hard rock band from the '70s. But we never would have had 'Cryin',' 'Crazy,' 'Amazing,' 'I Don't Want to Miss a Thing,' and it's hard to argue with that kind of success. We are basically entertainers wanting to play our music for the most people. And to further that goal, we've used other writers. We have fun writing our own stuff, and we also have fun playing stuff we've written with other people. I'm sure we'll do both as we move along."

"*Permanent Vacation* was a lot of fun to do," recalls Mike Fraser, engineer on the album, offering a little more on Joe's reference to world instruments there. "Just because I guess these guys are fresh out of rehab and sort of rediscovering themselves. I know they kept saying, wow, this is so great to be able to actually do music and to know what you're doing [laughs]. Because before, they'd be in such a haze that people would just tell them, 'Okay, go out there and sing; go out there and play,' and they didn't even know what they ended up with until they heard the record later. So I remember that being really exhilarating. I remember one night, Bob Rock and I, at the beginning of *Permanent Vacation*, I think it was a Saturday night or something, and these guys walk in wearing their long trench coats and stuff, and we thought, 'Wow, how great to have Aerosmith here on a Saturday night,' you know? [laughs]."

But it wasn't all efficient record making. "They'd have plenty of arguments amongst themselves," says Mike. "You know, Steven drove Joey nuts, most of the time. But it was all part of the creative flow. There were never any harsh or bad feelings, as far as I remember. But I guess Steven's a bit of a drummer too, so he's always on his case. What was it? 'Rag Doll,' over and over and over again, and then finally Steven says, 'Well, if you don't get it this next take, we're using a drum machine.' So we ended up using a drum machine [laughs]. But I think at the end of the day, we had Joey go out and play over the top of the drum machine, just to get the more real toms and cymbals and stuff like that in there.

"And yeah, for all the little sound effects, we got this guy named Randy Raine-Reusch. He travels the world and collects all these weird little instruments and learns how to play them, so that was really quite cool. Steven and Bruce went over to his place and, I think, spent a whole day going over all his stuff, and they brought them all back into the studio, and that was actually quite cool. We spent hours with that, but he only put little tidbits between the songs."

This would also become a growing complaint from the old-school fans, this sense that the albums were becoming increasingly overworked or overproduced, with too much ear candy, drum treatment, and multiple guitar tracks. In any event, next came *Pump*, with the band returning to Vancouver, Bruce Fairbairn and Mike Fraser. "Love in an Elevator, "The Other Side," and "Janie's Got a Gun" helped push that album, issued on September 12, 1989, past an astounding seven-times platinum.

"The *Pump* album really felt like the *Rocks* album," figures Tom. "Those albums, I just remember feeling like they had an easy flow. They were both really challenging and really fun records to make. And the *Pump* album, we had already made a record up in Vancouver with Bruce Fairbairn that we were really happy with, so we went and did that one, and that one was the equivalent of when we started with Jack Douglas with *Get Your Wings* and then did *Toys in the Attic*. So we went ahead from *Permanent Vacation* and did *Pump*, and it came out really good. Especially sonically, the production on it is just awesome as well. Yeah, *Permanent Vacation* is, you know, a party album, with a lot of different kind of stuff on it, and *Pump* is more of a hard rock album."

"We worked really hard on that record," recalls Joey. "That was an exceptionally hardworking record. We did preproduction with Bruce Fairbairn, who also did *Get a Grip* and *Permanent Vacation*. And that happens to be one of my favorite Aerosmith records. I love it. I was always happy with the playing on it; I was always happy with the songs on it. The production, for the time that we made the album, was top flight. I still enjoy listening to it now, although it's a little on the wet side [laughs]. But that was a fun record to make; I think it was basically the first record that we all made together when we were finally all sober. So that was kind of a landmark. The playing and the songwriting on that was really us at our best."

Seconds Joe, "*Pump* is probably my favorite record because we were on a roll from *Permanent Vacation*. There was a kind of energy around us. It kind of matched up, because here we were, old dogs, going fifteen, twenty years of being in the business, and I felt we were reaching a creative stride there, after all the trials and tribulations and all the personal bullshit we had been through."

Sometimes great production comes from happy accidents. "I remember getting a bass sound for *Pump*," says Mike, "and we had Tom out there and he's playing away, and we're saying, 'No, try a little more of this.' And he'd be doing his amp, and we went, 'Oh, that's it! Don't touch a thing!' And he said, 'I didn't. I didn't move anything.' 'That sounds great!' And we went out there and the speaker's ripped. So that's the bass sound of *Pump*, and it just sounded great [laughs]. We used that throughout the album. I have to admit, the whole time we were doing 'Love in an Elevator,' I hated that song. I thought, 'Oh, what are they doing this for?!' Now, in retrospect, it's like, oh, okay [laughs]. It's one of their biggest songs. Actually, I like it now. But I don't know what it was about that song that just didn't turn me on, as the big Aerosmith fan that I am."

The textures and treatments seemed to multiply on *Get a Grip*, issued on April 20, 1993, and going on to certify at seven-times platinum. It's also over an hour long, and it's the record that gave us "Cryin'," "Crazy," "Amazing," and epic lead single "Livin' on the Edge." To sell this well—twenty million copies worldwide—when grunge is all the rage, is testament to the strength of Aerosmith's second wind. At this point, it's Ozzy, AC/DC, Metallica, Bon Jovi, Guns N' Roses, and the boys from Boston who are the last titans of the '80s hard rock scene left standing and standing tall.

Inside records such as *Get a Grip*, along with follow-up *Nine Lives*, Joe Perry is building himself a new sound, and maybe a guitar player identity for the first time. It comes from his restless search for fresh, pioneering tones, and then a "guitar-strangling" playing style to go along with it, something you also hear in Slash and, down more of a heavy metal pathway, Zakk Wylde. Ted Nugent had—and has—this as well.

"I think that's a reaction to the heavy metal kinds of sounds that were really prevalent in the '80s and early '90s, and the whole soloing and guitar technique and all that," reflects Joe. "It started to all sound the same, going for that compressed, really overdriven sound, big, fat slabs of power chords. And to feel like that's the be all and end all, that's a short dead-end street to me. I think being able to use those kinds of guitar sounds, thinner, say, country kind of clean guitar sounds, to me, I feel like I can be more expressive in those spaces. It's easier to make the guitar speak in a mix, and in a band situation and in an ensemble. I mean, some of those big, heavy, ripping sounds are really good when you're on your own, but I think when you're starting to play with a really driving rock band, some of that stuff can get lost. Anyway, it's just kind of a broader look on how you can use guitar. I remember hearing some guitar player from the '80s—I don't even remember his name—but he was with a big metal band, and I was talking to some producer, and he says that the only thing he uses is the Gibson and the Marshall, and that's it; there's no variation. It's always set the same way because that's his favorite tone, and that's it. It's like, everything else has to work around that. And to me that's boring; I come from the opposite end of the thing."

But then peak Aerosmith was over. Next came *Nine Lives*, issued on March 18, 1997. Now off Geffen and back onto Columbia, the band could get the album only to double platinum, a definite fail, considering the

$30 million the label paid to claw Aerosmith back. This was followed by the experimental and poppy *Just Push Play* album, issued on March 5, 2001. It's pretty much the worst-reviewed album in the band's career. "It's a funny thing," Tom told me. "When the *Just Push Play* album came out, it, like, went into a void. And I was kind of surprised. There are all kinds of different reasons why people love or don't love an Aerosmith album, but I thought songwise, it was a really good album." Now the guys were down to single platinum, with the follow-up from 2004, *Honkin' on Bobo*, an album of blues covers, certifying at gold and no higher.

Plus, there were relapses. Says Tom, after one of these had come and gone, "Steven has been quite spectacular; he definitely gets the most-improved award. You might remember a few years ago, it got to the point where it was the band versus Steven, and him saying, 'I'm gonna go out and do a solo album and to hell with you guys!' We were saying, 'Well, we're going to find somebody else to sing, and we're going to go out on the road.' And you know, we really pursued that. I don't think it would've been something we called Aerosmith, but if we would've had an opportunity to put something together that fans would like to hear, and we could go out on the road and tour, we would've done it, for sure.

"But Steven was going through a tough time. And this is all stuff Steven talked about. I'm not squealing on him or anything. But he was in bad shape. And the closer we got to pulling the trigger on trying to put something else together, you know, the closer we got to that, the closer he got to going into rehab. And he did, and he did it just in the nick of time. And he came out of there and just couldn't wait to get back in the band. And it was a joy. He was relaunched as a person. It was great, a good experience, an incredibly positive experience.

"And you know, he went off and did the *American Idol* thing, and if you read the press, you might get the idea that we were all pissed off about it. I was kind of rooting for him. I wasn't happy about how we were told about it or how it came about, but I really thought, wow, nice going. He worked for something—you tried for something, and you got it. He got to do it, and he became a success at it. And it was great for a couple of years, but then I think while the rest of the band was really chomping at the bit to do a record, and finally the desire got to him, that's when we started to get ready to go and make a record."

The last Aerosmith album to date has been *Music from Another Dimension!*, issued on November 6, 2012. It reviewed not much better than *Just Push Play*, and by all accounts it seems like the experience of making it, its (typically) difficult birthing, plus the reaction to it, has marked the death of the band as a creative entity—fourteen years down the line, there's not been another Aerosmith album.

There were even bad omens in the years leading up to that record, which came fully eleven years after the ridiculed *Just Push Play* project, with Brad telling me in the interim how they tried to make a new album "many times. "Since *Just Push Play*, which is what? Fifteen years ago? And then there's the blues record. But we tried to start this album a couple of times, and it just turned into a disaster. So, there were serious doubts, yes. Every day around here seems to be a roadblock."

And then there's Joe, who, when I asked him if the band will ever do another album, says, "Well, probably the perfect example to that answer is the last record. We went into that record with Jack Douglas, basically trying to, you know, set the same kind of vibe we had for, say, *Toys in the Attic*. You know, everybody gets to throw in an idea or two, and if it makes the cut, it goes on the record.

"And I kinda had this feeling like, I don't know when we're going to cut another record. I don't know, the way the music business is; who knows if there's going to be albums in two years, three years? So I had this feeling like, just put it out there. If Tom has a song, do it. If Brad has a song, do it. And if Steven and I have a song, do it. Just put it out there.

"And I know I got a lot of complaints: 'Oh, there's too many songs on the record.' Well, you know, the business being what it is—and that's what it is—you know, Steven wanted to have these four ballads on the record. And the band, having the reputation of having gotten on the radio with the ballads, mostly, that's what the record company did. They put out the ballads. They came and went. We let Steven have his way. In fact, we used a different producer for those songs. And I think the album kind of speaks for itself, in answer to that question.

"I mean, just looks at the songs that my name is under, and you'll see kind of where I go [laughs]. And then look at the name Steven. Especially the songs that I wrote myself. You know, I wrote a couple of songs that were only put on as like a special added track for Britain, or whatever. There's a song, 'Oasis in the Night,' which is a ballad. I can't believe that I'm actually writing ballads now. Or a song called 'Something,' with Steven playing drums, which went on the album. That's the kind of stuff that comes from me. And that song Brad wrote, 'Street Jesus'; I mean, if that doesn't show the heart and soul of Aerosmith, I don't know what does. But then when you listen to those ballads, you kind of go, oh, okay, the guy's got a great voice, but hey, what's it really do? I mean, is this something we're really gonna play live? And knock it out of the park? I don't know. It's just kind of a drag, that whole ballad thing."

Which is why we celebrate the Columbia albums inside the pages of this book. Scratch any long-suffering Aerosmith fan, and they will swear by any and all the albums up to *Rock in a Hard Place*, to a significant extent anyways. And then it becomes some manner of loyalty test how many records they tack onto the end of their personal "worthy" list.

In the end, it's been a harrowing trip, one of the craziest in all of rock. Of course, documenting that hasn't been the mission of this book—you can get that in the band's own books. Rather, what I've wanted to accomplish here has been a celebration of each of the songs across the first seven Aerosmith albums, and it is hoped that I've added to the written record in that respect.

"Obviously, we've kept it together," says Brad, in closing. "You just don't see that. I don't think there is anything anybody can throw at this band, and we can't beat it and come out the other side. We've gone through everything a band can go through. We've gone to hell and back many times and survived. You just have to get out of the way or get on board [laughs]."

"And that's one more thing," adds Joe. "How the hell did a guy who grew up with no music around him, in a small town, with a whole different vision of my own way that I wanted to go, get kind of sideswiped by this beautiful insane thing called rock 'n' roll? That captured me and has still got me by the throat, and it won't let go."

"There's no such thing as an Aerosmith record that snapped by in a breeze," laughs Joey Kramer. "It just doesn't exist. It's just that we are always believers in making it better; no matter how good we do something, we're always looking to make it better. And however that happens and however that comes about, there always seems to be a lot of heartache and blood, sweat, and tears. But that's what we're all about. That's what makes those records what they are."

Discography

Well, I hope you learned some cool stuff reading this book, and I hope it's gotten you playing the records. Speaking of the records, here's a discography reflecting exactly the way the albums were presented in the book, including the live one and the hits pack, but stopping at *Rock in a Hard Place* (i.e., staying faithful to the stated Columbia years narrative of this book).

Aerosmith

January 5, 1973, Columbia KC 32005

Produced by Adrian Barber

Side 1

1. Make It (Tyler), 3:45
2. Somebody (Tyler, S. Emspack), 3:45
3. Dream On (Tyler), 4:28
4. One Way Street (Tyler), 7:12

Side 2

1. Mama Kin (Tyler), 4:25
2. Write Me a Letter (Tyler), 4:11
3. Movin' Out (Tyler, Perry), 5:03
4. Walkin' the Dog (R. Thomas), 3:12

Get Your Wings

March 15, 1974, Columbia KC 32847

Produced by Jack Douglas and Ray Colcord; executive producer, Bob Ezrin

Side 1

1. Same Old Song and Dance (Tyler, Perry), 3:53
2. Lord of the Thighs (Tyler), 4:15
3. Spaced (Tyler, Perry), 4:21
4. Woman of the World (Tyler, D. Solomon), 5:51

Side 2

1. S.O.S. (Too Bad) (Tyler), 2:50
2. Train Kept a Rollin' (T Bradshaw, L. Mann, H. Kay), 6:05
3. Seasons of Wither (Tyler), 5:07
4. Pandora's Box (Tyler, Kramer), 5:42

Toys in the Attic

April 8, 1975, Columbia PC 33479

Produced by Jack Douglas

Side 1

1. Toys in the Attic (Tyler, Perry), 3:05
2. Uncle Salty (Tyler, Hamilton), 4:08
3. Adam's Apple (Tyler), 4:34
4. Walk This Way (Tyler, Perry), 3:39
5. Big Ten Inch Record (F. Weismantel), 2:10

Side 2

1. Sweet Emotion (Tyler, Hamilton), 4:34
2. No More No More (Tyler, Perry), 4:35
3. Round and Round (Tyler, Whitford), 5:02
4. You See Me Crying (Tyler, D. Solomon), 5:12

Rocks

May 3, 1976, Columbia PC 34165
Produced by Jack Douglas and Aerosmith

Side 1

1. Back in the Saddle (Tyler, Perry), 4:40
2. Last Child (Tyler, Whitford), 3:27
3. Rats in the Cellar (Tyler, Perry), 4:02
4. Combination (Perry), 3:38

Side 2

1. Sick as a Dog (Tyler, Hamilton), 4:25
2. Nobody's Fault (Tyler, Whitford), 4:40
3. Get the Lead Out (Tyler, Perry), 3:42
4. Lick and a Promise (Tyler, Perry), 3:04
5. Home Tonight (Tyler), 3:15

Draw the Line

October 28, 1977, Columbia JC 34856
Produced by Jack Douglas and Aerosmith

Side 1

1. Draw the Line (Tyler, Perry), 3:23
2. I Wanna Know Why (Tyler, Perry), 3:09
3. Critical Mass (Tyler, Hamilton, Douglas), 4:51
4. Get It Up (Tyler, Perry), 4:02
5. Bright Light Fright (Perry), 2:20

Side 2

1. Kings and Queens (Hamilton, Kramer, Tyler, Whitford, Douglas), 4:55
2. The Hand That Feeds (Hamilton, Kramer, Tyler, Whitford, Douglas), 4:22
3. Sight for Sore Eyes (Tyler, Perry, Douglas, D. Johansen), 3:52
4. Milk Cow Blues (K. Arnold), 4:15

Live! Bootleg

October 27, 1978, Columbia CG 35564

Produced by Jack Douglas and Aerosmith

Side 1

1. Back in the Saddle (Tyler, Perry), 4:11
2. Sweet Emotion (Tyler, Hamilton), 4:43
3. Lord of the Thighs (Tyler), 7:13
4. Toys in the Attic (Tyler, Perry), 3:45

Side 2

1. Last Child (Tyler, Whitford), 3:03
2. Come Together (J. Lennon, P. McCartney), 4:51
3. Walk This Way ((Tyler, Perry), 3:35
4. Sick as a Dog (Tyler, Hamilton), 4:35

Side 3

1. Dream On (Tyler), 4:31
2. Chip Away the Stone (R. Supa), 4:00
3. Sight for Sore Eyes (Tyler, Perry), 3:13
4. Mama Kin (Tyler), 3:42
5. S.O.S. (Too Bad) (Tyler), 2:39

Side 4

1. Ain't Got You (C. Carter), 4:00
2. Mother Popcorn (J. Brown, A. Ellis), 6:49
3. Train Kept a Rollin' (T. Bradshaw, L. Mann, H. Kay) / Strangers in the Night (B. Kaempfert, E. Snyder, C. Singleton), 9:49

Night in the Ruts

November 16, 1979, Columbia FC 36050

Produced by Gary Lyons and Aerosmith

Side 1

1. No Surprize (Tyler, Perry), 4:26
2. Chiquita (Tyler, Perry), 4:25
3. Remember (Walking in the Sand) (G. Morton), 4:05
4. Cheese Cake (Tyler, Perry), 4:16

Side 2

1. Three Mile Smile (Tyler, Perry), 3:43
2. Reefer Head Woman (J. Bennett, J. Gillum, L. Melrose), 4:03
3. Bone to Bone (Coney Island White Fish Boy) (Tyler, Perry), 3:00
4. Think About It (K. Relf, J. McCarty, J. Page), 3:35
5. Mia (Tyler), 4:14

Aerosmith's Greatest Hits

November 11, 1980, Columbia AL 36865

Various production credits

Side 1

1. Dream On (Tyler), 4:25
2. Same Old Song and Dance (Tyler, Perry), 3:01
3. Sweet Emotion (Tyler, Hamilton), 3:12
4. Walk This Way (Tyler, Perry), 3:31
5. Last Child (Tyler, Whitford), 3:26

Side 2

1. Back in the Saddle (Tyler, Perry), 4:40
2. Draw the Line (Tyler, Perry), 3:23
3. Kings and Queens (Hamilton, Kramer, Tyler, Whitford, Douglas), 3:46
4. Come Together (J. Lennon, P. McCartney), 3:45
5. Remember (Walking in the Sand) (G. Morton), 4:05

Rock in a Hard Place

August 27, 1982, Columbia FC 38061

Produced by Jack Douglas, Steven Tyler, and Tony Bongiovi

Side 1

1. Jailbait (Tyler, Crespo), 4:39
2. Lightning Strikes (R. Supa), 4:26
3. Bitch's Brew (Tyler, Crespo), 4:13
4. Bolivian Ragamuffin (Tyler, Crespo), 3:33
5. Cry Me a River (A. Hamilton), 4:06

Side 2

1. Prelude to Joanie (Tyler), 1:30
2. Joanie's Butterfly (Tyler, Crespo, Douglas), 5:32
3. Rock in a Hard Place (Cheshire Cat) (Tyler, Crespo, Douglas), 4:41
4. Jig Is Up (Tyler, Crespo), 3:10
5. Push Comes to Shove (Tyler), 4:27

Interviews with the Author

Bongiovi, Tony. March 25, 2015.
Bouchard, Albert. 2009.
Bouchard, Joe. 2009.
Branker, Don. 2009.
Caris, Nick. July 10, 2015.
Cefalu, Ernie. November 2009.
Douglas, Jack. 2009.
Fraser, Mike. May 16, 2005.
Hamilton, Tom. October 28, 2005.
Hamilton, Tom. April 30, 2014.
Hamilton, Tom. April 22, 2015.
Hunter, Steve. June 12, 2013.
Kalodner, John. April 15, 2014.
Kramer, Joey. June 5, 2002.
Krebs, David, 2009.
Krebs, David, 2010.
Krebs, David. November 28, 2012.
Krebs, David. December 8, 2012.
Krebs, David. February 18, 2013.
Krebs, David. April 1, 9, 18, 23, 2013.
Krebs, David. July 3, 2013.
Krebs, David. March 2014.
Lyons, Gary. May 2007.
Perry, Joe. April 30, 2005.
Perry, Joe. October 24, 2014.
Wagner, Dick. November 19, 2002.
Wagner, Dick. 2009.
Wagner, Dick. January 11, 2014.
Whitford, Brad. September 17, 2012.
Whitford, Brad. February 12, 2015.
Whitford, Brad. May 11, 2016.

Additional Citations

Aerosmith with Stephen Davis. *Walk This Way: The Autobiography of Aerosmith.* New York: Avon Books, 1997.

Angel, Johnny. "Kickin' Back with Jack Douglas." KNAC.com, February 28, 2000.

Atkinson, Terry. *Aerosmith* review. *Los Angeles Times*, February 17, 1973.

Bashe, Philip. "Aerosmith Are Back, but Have They Waited Too Long." *Circus*, 1983.

Bell, Max. *Rocks* review. *New Musical Express*, July 3, 1976.

Bensoua, Joseph. *Aerosmith* review. *Daily Breeze* (Hermosa Beach, CA), October 14, 1973.

Bensoua, Joseph. "Aerosmith Interview: They've Come a Long Way Fast." *Daily Breeze*, December 9, 1973.

Bensoua, Joseph. *Toys in the Attic* review. *Daily Breeze* (Hermosa Beach, CA), May 16, 1975.

Bibens, Conrad. *Draw the Line* review. *St. Joseph (MO) News-Press*, December 24, 1977.

Bounacos, George. *Night in the Ruts* review. *Rocky Mount (NC) Telegram*, February 17, 1980.

Brown, Carol. "*Greatest Hits* Won't Stop Aerosmith." *The Day*, December 17, 1980.

Campbell, Mary. "Aerosmith Bounce Back . . . and Band Leader Steve Tyler Is Happy." *Rocky Mount (NC) Telegram*, February 17, 1980.

Canouse, Scott. "Thrilling Performance at BSC as a Night of Music Is Held." *Berwick (PA) Enterprise*, February 5, 1973.

Columbia Records. *Pandora's Box* liner notes. November 19, 1991.

Considine, J. D. *Rock in a Hard Place* review. *Rolling Stone*, October 28, 1982.

Cooney, Roman. *Rock in a Hard Place* review. *Calgary (AB) Herald*, October 9, 1982.

Demorest, Stephen. "Hot 'Rocks': Aerosmith's New Yankee Hanky-Panky." *Circus* 134 (June 17, 1976).

DiPerna, Alan. "Classic Rocks." *Guitar World*, April 1997.

Dunn, Sam. Interviews with Tom Hamilton and David Krebs.

Gaines, Steven. "Aerosmith Maintain Mental Health with 'Toys' in the Attic." *Circus Raves*, 1975.

Gargano, Paul. "Walking the Aerosmith Way." *Metal Edge*, 1997.

Gill, Julian. *Aerosmith: On Tour, 1973–85*. DeJulien, 2021.

Goldstein, Toby. *Draw the Line* review. *Crawdaddy*, 1977.

Hill, Dennis. *Draw the Line* review. *Press of Atlantic City* (NJ), December 25, 1977.

Hogan, Tim. "Aerosmith Is Turning Over." *Circus* 128 (March 2, 1975).

Howard, William. "Aerosmith, Mott the Hoople Dazzle Fans at Orpheum." *Boston Evening Globe*, October 29, 1973.

Jackson, Dana Sue. *Rocks* review. *Detroit Free Press*, June 22, 1976.

JM. *Get Your Wings* review. *Ann Arbor (MI) News*, May 19, 1974.

Kelp, Larry. *Draw the Line* review. *Oakland (CA) Tribune*, December 25, 1977.

Kramer, Joey, with William Patrick and Keith Garde. *Hit Hard: A Story of Hitting Rock Bottom at the Top*. New York: HarperCollins, 2009.

Marlowe, John. "Aerosmith: They've Controlled the Sound, but Not the Audiences." *Miami (FL) News*, February 1, 1980.

McCutcheon, Burr. *Night in the Ruts* review. *Duluth (MN) Herald*, January 21, 1980.

Millburg, Steve. "'Unsubtle' Rock Sells Sellout on Aerosmith." *Omaha (NE) World-Herald*, August 21, 1976.

Newton, Steve. "Aerosmith's Tom Hamilton Says Some Drugs 'Just Go Damn Well with Music.'" *Georgia Straight*, October 20, 1994.

Newton, Steve. "When Aerosmith Broke Up with Bruce Fairbairn and Hit the Musical Skids." *Georgia Straight*, October 16, 1997.

Newton, Steve. "Aerosmith Without Joe Perry: Remembering *Rock in a Hard Place*." GeorgiaStraight.com, January 20, 2013.

Perry, Joe, with David Ritz. *Rocks: My Life In and Out of Aerosmith*. New York: Simon & Schuster, 2014.

Reynolds, Dave. "Who Dares Wins." *Metal Forces* 26 (1987).

Robinson, Lisa. "The Hit Parader Interview: Joe Perry." *Hit Parader* 151 (February 1977).

Robinson, Lisa. "The Hit Parader Interview: Aerosmith." *Hit Parader* 162 (January 1978).

Robinson, Lisa. "Steven Tyler Says 'Everything's Fine.'" *Hit Parader* 192 (July 1980).

Ryan, George H. *Pure Gold from Rock and Roll's Golden Boys.* March 1976.

Sommer, Tim. "Tim Sommer catches Aerosmith on the boil." *Sounds*, January 1, 1983.

Spina, James. *Draw the Line* review. *Hit Parader* 167 (June 1978).

Spina, James. *Night in the Ruts* review. *Hit Parader* 190 (May 1980).

Trakin, Roy. *Rock in a Hard Place* review. *Hit Parader* 221 (February 1983).

Tyler, Steven, with David Dalton. *Does the Noise in My Head Bother You?* New York: Ecco, 2012.

Uncredited. *Aerosmith* review. *Evening Sentinel* (Ansonia, CT), March 3, 1973.

Uncredited. *Get Your Wings* review. *Blade-Tribune* (San Diego, CA), Tempo section, April 14, 1974.

Uncredited. "Aerosmith Bootleg Gold & Platinum." *Hit Parader* 178 (May 1979).

Uncredited. "Aerosmith: Moment of Truth." *Hit Parader*, December 1982.

Welch, Chris. *Get Your Wings* review. *Melody Maker*, December 28, 1974.

Welch, Chris. *Toys in the Attic* review, *Melody Maker*, July 12, 1975.

Welch, Chris. *Rocks* record review. *Melody Maker*, July 10, 1976.

Zimmerman, Deane. "Aerosmith News: Jimmy Crespo Talks About His Place in the New Lineup." *Hit Parader* 193 (August 1980).

Special Thanks

A hearty thanks to Agustin Garcia de Paredes for doing a preliminary copyedit of this thing before I shipped 'er off to Schiffer. He's been there doing that for a pile of my books and, in fact, likely has the only complete collection of them in the world, outside of myself (who might even be missing one or two).

Complete Martin Popoff Bibliography

2026

Punk and New Wave Record Ads
Aerosmith '72–'82: The Columbia Years:
Metallica: Album by Album
Kiss '76

2025

Walking in the Shadow of the Blues: The Whitesnake Story
Taken by Force: Sixty Years of Scorpions
Midnight Mover: Accept '79–'96
Seven Decades of Deep Purple: An Unofficial History
A Million Vacations: The Max Webster Story
The Unholy Scriptures: The Complete Unofficial Chronicle of Ronnie James Dio's Solo Canon
A Dangerous Meeting: In the Shadows with Mercyful Fate
Guns N' Roses at 40
Hallowed by Their Name: The Unofficial Iron Maiden Bible
Blockbuster! The Sweet Story

2024

Judas Priest: Album by Album
Behind the Lines: Genesis on Record; 1978–1997
Entangled: Genesis on Record, 1969–1976
Run with the Wolf: Rainbow on Record
Van Halen at 50
Honesty Is No Excuse: Thin Lizzy on Record
Pictures at Eleven: Robert Plant Album by Album
Perfect Water: The Rebel Imaginos

2023

Kiss at 50
Dominance and Submission: The Blue Öyster Cult Canon
The Who & Quadrophenia

Wild Mood Swings: Disintegrating the Cure Album by Album
AC/DC at 50

2022

Pink Floyd and The Dark Side of the Moon: 50 Years
Killing the Dragon: Dio in the 1990s and 2000s
Feed My Frankenstein: Alice Cooper, the Solo Years
Easy Action: The Original Alice Cooper Band
Lively Arts: The Damned Deconstructed
Yes: A Visual Biography II; 1982–2022
Bowie @ 75
Dream Evil: Dio in the '80s
Judas Priest: A Visual Biography
UFO: A Visual Biography

2021

Hawkwind: A Visual Biography
Loud 'n' Proud: Fifty Years of Nazareth
Yes: A Visual Biography
Uriah Heep: A Visual Biography
Driven: Rush in the '90s and "In the End"
Flaming Telepaths: Imaginos Expanded and Specified
Rebel Rouser: A Sweet User Manual

2020

The Fortune: On the Rocks with Angel
Van Halen: A Visual Biography
Limelight: Rush in the '80s
Thin Lizzy: A Visual Biography
Empire of the Clouds: Iron Maiden in the 2000s
Blue Öyster Cult: A Visual Biography
Anthem: Rush in the '70s
Denim and Leather: Saxon's First Ten Years
Black Funeral: Into the Coven with Mercyful Fate

2019

Satisfaction: 10 Albums That Changed My Life
Holy Smoke: Iron Maiden in the '90s
Sensitive to Light: The Rainbow Story
Where Eagles Dare: Iron Maiden in the '80s
Aces High: The Top 250 Heavy Metal Songs of the '80s
Judas Priest: Turbo 'til Now
Born Again! Black Sabbath in the Eighties and Nineties

2018

Riff Raff: The Top 250 Heavy Metal Songs of the '70s
Lettin' Go: UFO in the '80s and '90s
Queen: Album by Album
Unchained: A Van Halen User Manual
Iron Maiden: Album by Album
Sabotage! Black Sabbath in the Seventies
Welcome to My Nightmare: 50 Years of Alice Cooper
Judas Priest: Decade of Domination
Popoff Archive 6: American Power Metal
Popoff Archive 5: European Power Metal
The Clash: All the Albums, All the Songs

2017

Led Zeppelin: All the Albums, All the Songs
AC/DC: Album by Album
Lights Out: Surviving the '70s with UFO
Tornado of Souls: Thrash's Titanic Clash
Caught in a Mosh: The Golden Era of Thrash
Rush: Album by Album
Beer Drinkers and Hell Raisers: The Rise of Motörhead
Metal Collector: Gathered Tales from Headbangers
Hit the Lights: The Birth of Thrash
Popoff Archive 4: Classic Rock
Popoff Archive 3: Hair Metal

2016

Popoff Archive 2: Progressive Rock
Popoff Archive 1: Doom Metal
Rock the Nation: Montrose
Gamma and Ronnie Redefined
Punk Tees: The Punk Revolution in 125 T-shirts
Metal Heart: Aiming High with Accept
Ramones at 40
Time and a Word: The Yes Story

2015

Kickstart My Heart: A Mötley Crüe Day-by-Day
This Means War: The Sunset Years of the NWOBHM
Wheels of Steel: The Explosive Early Years of the NWOBHM
Swords and Tequila: Riot's Classic First Decade
Who Invented Heavy Metal?
Sail Away: Whitesnake's Fantastic Voyage

2014

Live Magnetic Air: The Unlikely Saga of the Superlative Max Webster
Steal Away the Night: An Ozzy Osbourne Day-by-Day
The Big Book of Hair Metal
Sweating Bullets: The Deth and Rebirth of Megadeth
Smokin' Valves: A Headbanger's Guide to 900 NWOBHM Records

2013

The Art of Metal (coedit with Malcolm Dome)
2 Minutes to Midnight: An Iron Maiden Day-by-Day
Metallica: The Complete Illustrated History
Rush: The Illustrated History
Ye Olde Metal: 1979
Scorpions: Top of the Bill (updated and reissued as *Wind of Change: The Scorpions Story* in 2016)

2012

Epic Ted Nugent

Fade To Black: Hard Rock Cover Art of the Vinyl Age

It's Getting Dangerous: Thin Lizzy, '81–'12

We Will Be Strong: Thin Lizzy, '76–'81

Fighting My Way Back: Thin Lizzy, '69–'76

The Deep Purple Royal Family: Chain of Events, '80–'11

The Deep Purple Royal Family: Chain of Events Through '79 (reissued as *The Deep Purple Family Year by Year* books)

2011

Black Sabbath FAQ

The Collector's Guide to Heavy Metal, Volume 4: The '00s (coauthored with David Perri)

2010

Goldmine Standard Catalog of American Records, 1948–1991, 7th edition

2009

Goldmine Record Album Price Guide, 6th edition

Goldmine 45 RPM Price Guide, 7th edition

A Castle Full of Rascals: Deep Purple, '83–'09

Worlds Away: Voivod and the Art of Michel Langevin

Ye Olde Metal: 1978

2008

Gettin' Tighter: Deep Purple, '68–'76

All Access: The Art of the Backstage Pass

Ye Olde Metal: 1977

Ye Olde Metal: 1976

2007

Judas Priest: Heavy Metal Painkillers

Ye Olde Metal: 1973 to 1975

The Collector's Guide to Heavy Metal, Volume 3: The Nineties

Ye Olde Metal: 1968 to 1972

2006

Run for Cover: The Art of Derek Riggs

Black Sabbath: Doom Let Loose

Dio: Light Beyond the Black

2005

The Collector's Guide to Heavy Metal, Volume 2: The Eighties

Rainbow: English Castle Magic, UFO: Shoot Out the Lights

The New Wave of British Heavy Metal Singles

2004

Blue Öyster Cult: Secrets Revealed! (updated and reissued in 2009 with the same title; updated and reissued as *Agents of Fortune: The Blue Öyster Cult Story* in 2016)

Contents Under Pressure: 30 Years of Rush at Home & Away

The Top 500 Heavy Metal Albums of All Time

2003

The Collector's Guide to Heavy Metal, Volume 1: The Seventies

The Top 500 Heavy Metal Songs of All Time

2001

Southern Rock Review

2000

Heavy Metal: 20th Century Rock and Roll

The Goldmine Price Guide to Heavy Metal Records

1997

The Collector's Guide to Heavy Metal

1993

Riff Kills Man! 25 Years of Recorded Hard Rock & Heavy Metal

See martinpopoff.com for complete details and ordering information.

Index

In terms of methodology, first, we've exempted adding page numbers for the names of Aerosmith band members, due to the fact that they are a constant throughout. However, they have been left in the index, along with the designation "see introductory note."

Second, given that the chapters are both structured and titled primarily by album, names of the Aerosmith albums covered by this book have been given the designation "see Chapter [#]." This at least tells you where the brunt of the action happens with respect to that record. I have, however, indexed Aerosmith album titles for records not covered in detail by this book.

Third, there are a fair number of additional miscellaneous entries that have been given the "see introductory note" designation for the same reason as above, namely that the high number of times that they are mentioned renders the indexing of each instance somewhat meaningless.

Finally, to keep things somewhat concise, I've left out numerous proper names, band names, album titles and song titles that were merely incidental to the story, often because they were used for comparative purposes only. Nor did I include every city in which Aerosmith played a show or all the support acts that might have been mentioned in the text. Still, I endeavoured to dig deep.

The Author

Martin Popoff, at approximately 7,900 (with over 7,000 appearing in his books), has unofficially written more record reviews than anybody in the history of music writing across all genres. Additionally, Martin has penned approximately 140 books on hard rock, heavy metal, classic rock, prog, punk, and record collecting. He was editor in chief of the now-retired *Brave Words & Bloody Knuckles*, Canada's foremost heavy metal publication for fourteen years, and has also contributed to *Revolver, Guitar World, Goldmine, Record Collector*, bravewords.com, lollipop.com, and hardradio.com, with many record label band bios and liner notes to his credit as well.

Additionally, Martin has been a regular contractor to Banger Films, having worked for two years as researcher on the award-winning documentary *Rush: Beyond the Lighted Stage*, and on the writing and research team for the eleven-episode *Metal Evolution* and on the 10-episode *Rock Icons*, both for VH1 Classic. Martin is also the writer of the original metal genre chart used in *Metal: A Headbanger's Journey* and throughout the *Metal Evolution* episodes. Then there's his audio podcast, *History in Five Songs with Martin Popoff*, and the YouTube channel he runs with Marco D'Auria, *The Contrarians*. Martin currently resides in Toronto and can be reached at www.martinpopoff.com.